BASIC COMPUTER SIMULATION

BASIC COMPUTER SIMULATION

BY LAWRENCE L. McNITT

TAB BOOKS Inc.

BLUE RIDGE SUMMIT, PA. 17214

FIRST EDITION

FIRST PRINTING

Library of Congress Cataloging in Publication Data

McNitt, Lawrence L.
BASIC computer simulation.
Includes index.
1. Digital computer simulation.   2. Basic (Computer
program language)   I. Title.   II. Title: B.A.S.I.C.
computer simulation.
QA76.9.C65M4   1983   001.4′34   83-4843
ISBN 0-8306-0185-6
ISBN 0-8306-0585-1 (pbk.)

Cover illustraton by Al Cozzi

Contents

List of Programs

CHAPTER 8—MANAGEMENT GAMES

Introduction

Simulation includes physical, mathematical, and computer models. Although simulation modeling predates the computer, the practice of simulation has greatly increased in importance with the arrival of high-speed digital computers. Computer simulation has become widespread in business, economics, medicine, engineering, and space technology.

The purpose of this book is to bring the models and methods of simulation to students and professionals who are only now gaining ready access to computer resources. Simulation is for the curious. It is for those who want to explore the unknown, solve the unsolvable, search for the unsearchable. Not all problems have neat, easily found answers. Simulation models and methods help in the search for better products, methods, and control. The digital computer and simulation methods open doors that have previously been closed.

This book contains sample programs in the BASIC language that will run on most microcomputers. The programs have been tested on a Radio Shack TRS-80 Model III. They use a universal subset of BASIC so that they can be converted for use on other computers with few changes. In order to make the displays easier to read, you might want to add the screen clearing statements that are appropriate to your microcomputer. To stop the scrolling of the display, you can insert an appropriate input statement such as PRINT "PRESS ENTER TO CONTINUE": INPUT Z in places where a pause is needed.

Why use BASIC for computer simulation? BASIC is easy to learn and simple to use. It is a universal language that is available on the least expensive personal computers as well as on large computer systems. Computing power is no longer a scarce, expensive commodity to be rationed out to the technically elite. Anyone can have undivided, uninterrupted access to powerful computer resources.

The tools and techniques of computer simulation deserve a wider audience than the relatively few who now use this technique on large systems. Computer simulation modeling is practical with microcomputers.

This book does not require extensive technical knowledge of either computer programming or mathematics. Technical topics are approached intuitively for the purpose of understanding rather than for mathematical rigor. This book can be used for self-study and as a text in computer simulation.

Chapter 1
Models

Computer simulation is a powerful technique with a broad range of applications. It is a tool that provides answers in the design and operation of complex systems. Simulation involves models that represent the entity under investigation, but it is more than just the model itself. It is a methodology for evaluating models.

This chapter introduces the concepts of computer simulation and modeling. It reviews systems concepts, identifies types of models, and contrasts methods of analysis.

SYSTEMS AND MODELS

A *system* is a collection of interdependent objects having a defined purpose. There are transportation systems, production systems, military systems, and educational systems. An airline company will consider its pilots, ground crew, and fleet of aircraft as a system. The aircraft manufacturer will consider the aircraft itself as a system during the design and production stages. A subcontractor will consider the engines as yet another system.

The collection of objects in a system are called *components*. These components have attributes and performance patterns. The system operates in an external environment that contains controllable and uncontrollable factors that influence the system and its performance.

Many systems involve control. Control may come from the outside or the system may exhibit self-control. The system may involve man-machine cooperation, or it may be under automatic control.

Systems analysis is the study of systems. The purpose may be to design a new system or to improve an existing system. It may involve direct manipulation of the system itself. Systems analysis usually involves indirect study of the target system through models of all or part of that system. Systems analysis involves a cooperative effort by machines and people. Machines are tools that amplify the capabilities of people. They are also valuable for routine calculation and for storing, retrieving, and summarizing information. People are better at recognizing patterns, especially with the help of visual aids.

1

A *model* is a representation of a system or a component of that system. Models are of many types. Physical models abound. Wind tunnel tests involve scaled-down models that permit reliable measure of windflow patterns. Aircraft simulators provide surprisingly realistic training for pilots.

Mathematical models consist of sets of one or more mathematical equations. The equation

$$v = a * t$$

gives the velocity of an object under constant acceleration at time t.

Graphs and diagrams are models. They aid in visualizing the system and its performance. A computer program is also a model. The purpose may be to maintain a paper record of dollar transactions. It may be to carry out the calculations needed to evaluate a mathematical model. The primary emphasis in this book will be on mathematical models that involve computer programs.

Mathematical models are of many kinds. There are *deterministic* models, which are nonrandom. Given a specific set of inputs to the model the outcomes will always be the same. A *stochastic* or *probabilistic* model involves chance elements. Analysis of a stochastic model involves identifying averages and average trends. The outcome for any one replication is uncertain even though the expected outcomes may be determined.

Models may be *static* or *dynamic*. A static model involves one set of outputs. A dynamic model involves a series of discrete state changes or a continuous flow of changes. A dynamic model usually represents the behavior of the system over time.

There must always be a reason for expending the time, money, and effort to carry out a systems study. The purpose will determine what performance objectives will be measured. The purpose may be to optimize the system performance with respect to one particular performance objective. It may be to provide a good compromise that satisfies several objectives.

To be useful, the model must fairly represent the entity being investigated with regard to the characteristic under investigation. To keep the system study from becoming too costly, the systems analyst must narrow the scope of the study to the intended objectives.

COMPUTER PROGRAMMING

Computer programming is an art. It brings out the best of human creative genius. To some it is fun. For others it is as intellectually stimulating as a chess match. Computer programming is also a science. The rigid language rules of the translator allow no deviation. Writing programs for other people to read requires just as much discipline as writing articles for publication. Style is just as important in programming as it is in writing.

The following programs illustrate programming style. This book contains many computer programs illustrating aspects of computer simulation. Studying these programs is far easier if the programs use a consistent, readable style.

The following programs compute the velocity in feet per second and the distance traveled in feet for each of the first few seconds of an object's movement. Let T represent the time in seconds; A, the acceleration in feet/sec/sec; V, the velocity in feet per second; and D, the distance in feet. The equation

$$V = A * T$$

gives the velocity, and

$$D = .5 * A * T * T$$

gives the distance traveled.

Primitive Programs

Primitive programs are simple programs designed to solve one problem and to be thrown away. The programmer may write a primitive program to demonstrate a particular algorithm (solution method). A primitive program is difficult to read and almost impossible to reuse. There are few large, primitive programs because the programmer drowns in a sea of confusion and despair before it is finished. Large programs must be carefully designed. Program 1-1 illustrates a primitive program. Figure 1-1 shows the results of running the program.

Computer output must be labeled. This is necessary for interpretation. A few lines giving the purpose is also helpful in case the program does not function correctly. A standard message should be used to signal the end of the program. Program 1-2 includes labels. Figure 1-2 shows the results of running the program.

The output from large programs soon becomes a jumbled mess. A simple yet useful technique consists of separating sections of the output with blank lines. The resulting white space improves the readability. Program 1-3 uses white space. Figure 1-3 shows the results of running the program.

Modular Programs with Sequential Organization

Different techniques are needed to improve the readability of the program listing. One method is to use remark statements to draw attention to section names. A list of variables is also mandatory for anyone trying to make sense of a program listing. A sequentially organized program that automatically falls through from one program section (module) to the next can be understood easily. Program 1-4 illustrates this technique. Figure 1-4 shows the results of using the program.

Modular Programs with Hierarchical Organization

Large programs are difficult to read and to understand. One method of trying to bring order out of chaos is to impose a hierarchical structure on the program. The main routine consists of a set of subroutine calls with conditional statements allowing flexibility. As any module grows to unman-

Program 1-1

```
10 REM 1-1
20 FOR T = 1 TO 10
30 LET V = 8 * T
40 LET D = 4 * T * T
50 PRINT T,V,D
60 NEXT T
70 END
```

1	8	4
2	16	16
3	24	36
4	32	64
5	40	100
6	48	144
7	56	196
8	64	256
9	72	324
10	80	400

Fig. 1-1. Sample results from Program 1-1.

ageable proportions, it is subdivided into lower-level subroutines. This programming style is almost mandatory for large programs. For the sake of consistency, the programs in this book use this style illustrated by Program 1-5. The results are shown in Fig. 1-5.

Exercise 1-1

1. Write a program to compute the future value of an investment at the end of each of the first few years. Test the program using an initial investment of $12,500 over a five year period at an interest rate of 13.75 percent compounded quarterly.
2. An ancient artillery piece has a muzzle velocity of 460 feet per second. If wind resistance is not a factor, compute the distance to the point of impact if the angle of elevation of the barrel is 20, 22, 24, . . ., 60 degrees.

ANALYTIC SOLUTIONS

A model represents some characteristic of the system or system component under investigation. Sometimes the behavior of the model is of interest. The model must fairly depict the behavior of the real entity. At other times the model is analyzed for specific answers; for example, what state must the model be in for specific inputs? For what inputs is some measure of performance at an optimum? A model can answer questions such as "If an object is accelerating at a constant rate of eight feet/sec/sec, how long will it take to reach one-quarter mile

Program 1-2

```
10 REM 1-2
20 READ A,N
30 PRINT "COMPUTE THE VELOCITY IN FEET PER"
40 PRINT "SECOND AND DISTANCE TRAVELED IN"
50 PRINT "FEET AT THE END OF EACH OF THE"
60 PRINT "FIRST FEW SECONDS FOR AN OBJECT"
70 PRINT "UNDER CONSTANT ACCELERATION."
80 PRINT "TIME","VELOCITY","DISTANCE"
90 FOR T = 1 TO N
100 LET V = A * T
110 LET D = .5 * A * T * T
120 PRINT T,V,D
130 NEXT T
140 PRINT "END OF PROGRAM"
150 DATA 8,10
160 END
```

```
COMPUTE THE VELOCITY IN FEET PER
SECOND AND DISTANCE TRAVELED IN
FEET AT THE END OF EACH OF THE
FIRST FEW SECONDS FOR AN OBJECT


UNDER CONSTANT ACCELERATION.
TIME            VELOCITY            DISTANCE
 1                 8                  4
 2                16                  16
 3                24                  36
 4                32                  64
 5                40                  100
 6                48                  144
 7                56                  196
 8                64                  256
 9                72                  324
10                80                  400
END OF PROGRAM
```

Fig. 1-2. Sample results from Program 1-2.

Program 1-3

```
10 REM 1-3
20 READ A,N
30 PRINT
40 PRINT "COMPUTE THE VELOCITY IN FEET PER"
50 PRINT "SECOND AND DISTANCE TRAVELED IN"
60 PRINT "FEET AT THE END OF EACH OF THE"
70 PRINT "FIRST FEW SECONDS FOR AN OBJECT"
80 PRINT "UNDER CONSTANT ACCELERATION."
90 PRINT
100 PRINT "ACCELERATION IN FEET/SEC/SEC",A
110 PRINT
120 PRINT "TIME","VELOCITY","DISTANCE"
130 FOR T = 1 TO N
140 LET V = A * T
150 LET D = .5 * A * T * T
160 PRINT T,V,D
170 NEXT T
180 PRINT
190 PRINT "END OF PROGRAM"
200 DATA 8,10
210 END
```

```
COMPUTE THE VELOCITY IN FEET PER
SECOND AND DISTANCE TRAVELED IN
FEET AT THE END OF EACH OF THE
FIRST FEW SECONDS FOR AN OBJECT
UNDER CONSTANT ACCELERATION.

ACCELERATION IN FEET/SEC/SEC         8

TIME                VELOCITY        DISTANCE
  1                    8              4
  2                    16             16
  3                    24             36
  4                    32             64
  5                    40             100
  6                    48             144
  7                    56             196
  8                    64             256
  9                    72             324
 10                    80             400

END OF PROGRAM
```

Fig. 1-3. Sample results from Program 1-3.

Program 1-4

```
100 REM *********************************
102 REM *    1-4                        *
104 REM *********************************
106 REM   AUTHOR
108 REM      COPYRIGHT 1982
110 REM      BY LAWRENCE MCNITT.
112 REM   PURPOSE
114 REM      VELOCITY AND DISTANCE TRAVELED
116 REM      BY AN OBJECT UNDER CONSTANT
118 REM      ACCELERATION.
120 REM   SYSTEM
122 REM      UNIVERSAL SUBSET
124 REM      OF BASIC.
200 REM *********************************
202 REM *    VARIABLES                  *
204 REM *********************************
206 REM    A    ACCELERATION IN FEET/SEC/SEC
208 REM    N    MAXIMUM NUMBER OF SECONDS
210 REM    T    TIME IN SECONDS
212 REM    V    VELOCITY IN FEET PER SECOND
214 REM    D    DISTANCE IN FEET
1000 REM *********************************
1002 REM *    INITIAL MESSAGE            *
1004 REM *********************************
1006 PRINT
1008 PRINT
1010 PRINT
1012 PRINT "PROGRAM 1-4   "
1014 PRINT
1016 PRINT "COMPUTE THE VELOCITY IN FEET"
1018 PRINT "PER SECOND AND DISTANCE TRAVELED"
1020 PRINT "IN FEET AT THE END OF THE FIRST"
1022 PRINT "FEW SECONDS FOR AN OBJECT UNDER"
1024 PRINT "CONSTANT ACCELERATION."
1100 REM *********************************
1102 REM *    GET DATA                   *
1104 REM *********************************
1106 READ A,N
1108 PRINT
1110 PRINT "ACCELERATION IN FEET/SEC/SEC",A
1200 REM *********************************
1202 REM *    PROCESS                    *
1204 REM *********************************
1206 PRINT
```

```
1208 PRINT "TIME","VELOCITY","DISTANCE"
1210 PRINT "SECONDS","FEET/SEC","FEET"
1212 FOR T = 1 TO N
1214    LET V = A * T
1216    LET D = .5 * A * T * T
1218    PRINT T,V,D
1220 NEXT T
1300 REM ********************************
1302 REM *    FINAL MESSAGE             *
1304 REM ********************************
1306 PRINT
1308 PRINT "END OF PROGRAM"
1310 STOP
8000 REM ********************************
8002 REM *    ACCELERATION             *
8004 REM *    MAXIMUM TIME             *
8006 REM ********************************
9000 DATA 8,5
9999 END
```

(1320 feet)?" and "If the function f(q) gives the cost per unit of a certain product at a production quantity q, what is the quantity that minimizes the production cost per unit?"

Systems analysis costs time, money, and effort. Solving models for particular answers constitutes part of that cost. Some models are easy to solve. The model

```
PROGRAM 1-4

COMPUTE THE VELOCITY IN FEET
PER SECOND AND DISTANCE TRAVELED
IN FEET AT THE END OF THE FIRST
FEW SECONDS FOR AN OBJECT UNDER
CONSTANT ACCELERATION.

ACCELERATION IN FEET/SEC/SEC        8

TIME              VELOCITY          DISTANCE
SECONDS           FEET/SEC          FEET
   1                 8                 4
   2                16                16
   3                24                36
   4                32                64
   5                40               100

END OF PROGRAM
```

Fig. 1-4. Sample results from Program 1-4.

Program 1-5

```
100 REM ********************************
102 REM *    1-5                        *
104 REM ********************************
106 REM   AUTHOR
108 REM       COPYRIGHT 1982
110 REM       BY LAWRENCE MCNITT.
112 REM   PURPOSE
114 REM       VELOCITY AND DISTANCE TRAVELED
116 REM       OF AN OBJECT UNDER CONSTANT
118 REM       ACCELERATION.
120 REM   SYSTEM
122 REM       UNIVERSAL SUBSET
124 REM       OF BASIC.
200 REM ********************************
202 REM *    ORGANIZATION              *
204 REM ********************************
206 REM   900   MAIN ROUTINE
208 REM         1000   INITIAL MESSAGE
210 REM         1100   GET DATA
212 REM         1200   PROCESS
214 REM         1300   FINAL MESSAGE
300 REM ********************************
302 REM *    VARIABLES                 *
304 REM ********************************
306 REM    U$   USER RESPONSE
308 REM    A    ACCELERATION
310 REM    N    MAXIMUM NUMBER OF SECONDS
312 REM    T    TIME IN SECONDS
314 REM    V    VELOCITY IN FEET/SECOND
316 REM    D    DISTANCE IN FEET
900 REM ********************************
902 REM *    MAIN ROUTINE              *
904 REM ********************************
906 REM INITIAL MESSAGE
908 GOSUB 1006
910 REM GET DATA
912 GOSUB 1106
914 REM PROCESS
916 GOSUB 1206
918 REM FINAL MESSAGE
920 GOSUB 1306
922 IF U$ = "Y" THEN 912
924 PRINT
926 PRINT "END OF PROGRAM"
```

```
999 END
1000 REM ****************************
1002 REM *    INITIAL MESSAGE        *
1004 REM ****************************
1006 PRINT
1008 PRINT
1010 PRINT
1012 PRINT "PROGRAM 1-5    "
1014 PRINT
1016 PRINT "COMPUTE THE VELOCITY IN FEET"
1018 PRINT "PER SECOND AND DISTANCE IN FEET"
1020 PRINT "AT THE END OF EACH OF THE FIRST"
1022 PRINT "FEW SECONDS FOR AN OBJECT"
1024 PRINT "ACCELERATING AT A CONSTANT RATE."
1099 RETURN
1100 REM ****************************
1102 REM *    GET DATA               *
1104 REM ****************************
1106 PRINT
1108 PRINT "ACCELERATION (FEET/SEC/SEC)";
1110 INPUT A
1112 PRINT "UPPER LIMIT FOR TIME (SEC) ";
1114 INPUT N
1199 RETURN
1200 REM ****************************
1202 REM *    PROCESS                *
1204 REM ****************************
1206 PRINT
1208 PRINT "TIME","VELOCITY","DISTANCE"
1210 PRINT "SEC","FEET/SEC","FEET"
1212 FOR T = 1 TO N
1214    LET V = A * T
1216    LET D = .5 * A * T * T
1218    PRINT T,V,D
1220 NEXT T
1299 RETURN
1300 REM ****************************
1302 REM *    FINAL MESSAGE          *
1304 REM ****************************
1306 PRINT
1308 PRINT "TRY ANOTHER SET OF DATA (Y/N)";
1310 INPUT U$
1312 IF U$ = "Y" THEN 1399
1314 IF U$ = "N" THEN 1399
1316 PRINT
1318 PRINT "INVALID RESPONSE"
```

```
1320 GOTO 1306
1399 RETURN
9999 END
```

$$D = .5 * A * T * T$$

gives the distance, D, as a function of the acceleration, A, and the time, T. How long will it take for the object to go a certain distance? Solving for the time, T, gives

$$T = SQR (2*D/A)$$

as a function of D and A. Although the square root may be positive or negative, only the positive square root is of interest.

Not all problems have easy algebraic solutions. In finding analytic solutions, symbol manipulation is more important than computational skills, although both play a part in the final analysis.

When faced with a problem involving mathematical equations, the first question to ask is whether or not analytic solutions exist. If they do exist, try them. Often, simulation methods are a last resort when analytic methods aren't feasible. Because of this, many feel that analytic solutions are elegant and that simulation methods employ brute force.

An analytic approach is used in the following: An object starts at rest and undergoes constant acceleration A for T seconds. The model

$$D = .5 * A * T * T$$

gives the distance traveled at the end of time T. Solving for T, the formula

$$T = SQR (2 * D / A)$$

gives the time required to attain the distance D.

An automobile at a drag race undergoes constant acceleration for one-quarter mile (1320 feet). How long will it take to finish the race at an acceleration rate of eight feet/sec/sec? at sixteen feet/sec/sec? The solution equation can be placed in a computer program just as well as the definitional equations. Program 1-6 computes the time taken to cover the quarter-mile distance for selected acceleration rates. Figure 1-6 shows the results.

Economic Inventory

One of the simplest models in business analysis is the economic inventory model. Two

```
PROGRAM 1-5             TIME    VELOCITY    DISTANCE
                        SEC     FEET/SEC    FEET
COMPUTE THE VELOCITY IN FEET   1    8        4
PER SECOND AND DISTANCE IN     2    16       16
FEET AT THE END OF EACH OF     3    24       36
THE FIRST FEW SECONDS FOR AN   4    32       64
OBJECT ACCELERATING AT A       5    40       100
CONSTANT RATE.                 6    48       144
                               7    56       196
                               8    64       256
                               9    72       324
ACCELERATION (FEET/SEC/SEC)   10    80       400
? 8

UPPER LIMIT FOR TIME (SEC)     TRY ANOTHER SET OF DATA
? 10                           (Y/N)? N

                               END OF PROGRAM
```

Fig. 1-5. Sample results from Program 1-5.

Program 1-6

```
100 REM ********************************
102 REM *    1-6                        *
104 REM ********************************
106 REM   AUTHOR
108 REM       COPYRIGHT 1982
110 REM        BY LAWRENCE MCNITT.
112 REM   PURPOSE
114 REM       TIME TO REACH 1320 FEET
116 REM       FOR AN OBJECT TO REACH
118 REM       A SPECIFIED DISTANCE.
120 REM   SYSTEM
122 REM       UNIVERSAL SUBSET
124 REM        OF BASIC.
200 REM ********************************
202 REM *    ORGANIZATION              *
204 REM ********************************
206 REM   900   MAIN ROUTINE
208 REM        1000   INITIAL MESSAGE
210 REM        1100   GET DATA
212 REM        1200   PROCESS
214 REM        1300   FINAL MESSAGE
300 REM ********************************
302 REM *    VARIABLES                 *
304 REM ********************************
306 REM    U$   USER RESPONSE
308 REM    A    ACCELERATION RATE
310 REM    D    REQUIRED DISTANCE
312 REM    T    REQUIRED TIME
900 REM ********************************
902 REM *    MAIN ROUTINE              *
904 REM ********************************
906 REM INITIAL MESSAGE
908 GOSUB 1006
910 REM GET DATA
912 GOSUB 1106
914 REM PROCESS
916 GOSUB 1206
918 REM FINAL MESSAGE
920 GOSUB 1306
922 IF U$ = "Y" THEN 912
924 PRINT
926 PRINT "END OF PROGRAM"
999 STOP
1000 REM ********************************
```

```
1002 REM *    INITIAL MESSAGE           *
1004 REM ******************************
1006 PRINT
1008 PRINT
1010 PRINT
1012 PRINT "PROGRAM 1-6   "
1014 PRINT
1016 PRINT "DETERMINE THE TIME REQUIRED"
1018 PRINT "TO REACH ONE-QUARTER MILE"
1020 PRINT "(1320 FEET) BY AN OBJECT"
1022 PRINT "UNDER CONSTANT ACCELERATION."
1099 RETURN
1100 REM ******************************
1102 REM *    GET DATA               *
1104 REM ******************************
1106 PRINT
1108 PRINT "ACCELERATION RATE (FEET/SEC/SEC)";
1110 INPUT A
1112 LET D = 1320
1199 RETURN
1200 REM ******************************
1202 REM *    PROCESS                *
1204 REM ******************************
1206 LET T = SQR(2 * D / A)
1208 PRINT
1210 PRINT "REQUIRED TIME IN SECONDS",T
1299 RETURN
1300 REM ******************************
1302 REM *    FINAL MESSAGE          *
1304 REM ******************************
1306 PRINT
1308 PRINT "TRY ANOTHER ACCELERATION RATE (Y/N)";
1310 INPUT U$
1312 IF U$ = "Y" THEN 1399
1314 IF U$ = "N" THEN 1399
1316 PRINT
1318 PRINT "INVALID RESPONSE"
1320 GOTO 1306
1399 RETURN
9999 END
```

inventory costs are involved. Each order placed incurs a cost C. Holding costs amount to H per unit per year. Demand consists of D units per year and is constant throughout the year. The average inventory level will be one-half the order quantity, Q. The expression

$$.5 * H * Q$$

gives the annual holding cost. The expression

```
PROGRAM 1-6

DETERMINE THE TIME REQUIRED
TO REACH ONE-QUARTER MILE
(1320 FEET) BY AN OBJECT
UNDER CONSTANT ACCELERATION.

ACCELERATION RATE (FEET/SEC/SEC)? 8

REQUIRED TIME IN SECONDS        18.1659

TRY ANOTHER ACCELERATION RATE (Y/N)? Y

ACCELERATION RATE (FEET/SEC/SEC)? 16

REQUIRED TIME IN SECONDS        12.8452

TRY ANOTHER ACCELERATION RATE (Y/N)? N

END OF PROGRAM
```

Fig. 1-6. Sample results from Program 1-6.

$$D / Q$$

gives the number of orders placed per year, so that

$$C * D / Q$$

gives the annual cost of placing orders. Putting the two annual costs together gives the formula

$$T = .5 * H * Q + C * D / Q$$

giving the total annual inventory costs.

The question now becomes one of determining the order quantity that minimizes the total annual inventory costs. The first derivative of the total cost function is

$$.5 * H - C * D / (Q * Q).$$

The first derivative gives the slope of the total cost function for all values of Q. The slope should be zero for both the maximum and the minimum points of the total cost function. The equation

$$Q = SQR(2 * C * D / H)$$

results from setting the first derivative equal to zero and solving for Q. The second derivative with respect to Q is

$$2 * C * D / (Q * Q * Q).$$

Since the second derivative is positive for all relevant values of C, D, and Q, the solution is the global minimum.

As an example, assume that demand for a product is constant at the rate of 400 units per year. Holding costs are $5.00 per unit per year. Orders cost $10.00 each to place. Determine the optimum order quantity that minimizes total annual inventory costs. Program 1-7 carries out the simple calculation made possible by the analysis. Figure 1-7 shows the results.

As you can see, mathematics provides a rich and powerful set of tools for solving problems needing analytic solutions, but these tools are unable to solve every problem. Sometimes analytic

13

Program 1-7

```
100 REM **********************************
102 REM *    1-7                          *
104 REM **********************************
106 REM   AUTHOR
108 REM       COPYRIGHT 1982
110 REM       BY LAWRENCE MCNITT.
112 REM   PURPOSE
114 REM       SOLVE INVENTORY ECONOMIC
116 REM       ORDER QUANTITY PROBLEMS.
118 REM   SYSTEM
120 REM       UNIVERSAL SUBSET
122 REM       OF BASIC.
200 REM **********************************
202 REM *    ORGANIZATION                 *
204 REM **********************************
206 REM   900   MAIN ROUTINE
208 REM         1000   INITIAL MESSAGE
210 REM         1100   GET DATA
212 REM         1200   PROCESS
214 REM         1300   FINAL MESSAGE
300 REM **********************************
302 REM *    VARIABLES                    *
304 REM **********************************
306 REM    U$   USER RESPONSE
308 REM    D    QUANTITY DEMANDED PER YEAR
310 REM    C    COST PER ORDER PLACED
312 REM    H    HOLDING COST PER UNIT PER YEAR
314 REM    Q    ORDER QUANTITY
900 REM **********************************
902 REM *    MAIN ROUTINE                 *
904 REM **********************************
906 REM INITIAL MESSAGE
908 GOSUB 1006
910 REM GET DATA
912 GOSUB 1106
914 REM PROCESS
916 GOSUB 1206
918 REM FINAL MESSAGE
920 GOSUB 1306
922 IF U$ = "Y" THEN 912
924 PRINT
926 PRINT "END OF PROGRAM"
999 STOP
1000 REM **********************************
```

14

```
1002 REM *    INITIAL MESSAGE          *
1004 REM ****************************
1006 PRINT
1008 PRINT
1010 PRINT
1012 PRINT "PROGRAM 1-7   "
1014 PRINT
1016 PRINT "DETERMINE THE OPTIMUM ORDER"
1018 PRINT "QUANTITY GIVEN THE YEARLY DEMAND,"
1020 PRINT "COST PER ORDER PLACED, AND"
1022 PRINT "HOLDING COST PER UNIT PER YEAR."
1099 RETURN
1100 REM ****************************
1102 REM *    GET DATA                *
1104 REM ****************************
1106 PRINT
1108 PRINT "QUANTITY DEMANDED PER YEAR     ";
1110 INPUT D
1112 PRINT "COST PER ORDER PLACED          ";
1114 INPUT C
1116 PRINT "HOLDING COST PER UNIT PER YEAR";
1118 INPUT H
1199 RETURN
1200 REM ****************************
1202 REM *    PROCESS                 *
1204 REM ****************************
1206 LET Q = SQR(2 * C * D / H)
1208 PRINT
1210 PRINT "OPTIMUM ORDER QUANTITY",Q
1299 RETURN
1300 REM ****************************
1302 REM *    FINAL MESSAGE           *
1304 REM ****************************
1306 PRINT
1308 PRINT "TRY ANOTHER PROBLEM (Y/N)";
1310 INPUT U$
1312 IF U$ = "Y" THEN 1399
1314 IF U$ = "N" THEN 1399
1316 PRINT
1318 PRINT "INVALID RESPONSE"
1320 GOTO 1306
1399 RETURN
9999 END
```

```
PROGRAM 1-7
DETERMINE THE OPTIMUM ORDER
QUANTITY GIVEN THE YEARLY DEMAND,
COST PER ORDER PLACED, AND
HOLDING COST PER UNIT PER YEAR.

QUANTITY DEMANDED PER YEAR     ? 400
COST PER ORDER PLACED          ? 10
HOLDING COST PER UNIT PER YEAR? 5

OPTIMUM ORDER QUANTITY           40

TRY ANOTHER PROBLEM (Y/N)? N

END OF PROGRAM
```

Fig. 1-7. Sample results from Program 1-7.

solutions require greater effort than simulation methods.

Exercise 1-2

1. What interest rate must an initial investment of $12,500 earn in order to grow to $20,000 by the end of two years assuming quarterly compounding?
2. An ancient cannon has a muzzle velocity of 460 feet per second. What angles of elevation are needed for the cannon ball to land 3,450 feet away? Assuming the cannon ball can reach that far, there are two possible angles, a high angle with a high arch and a low angle with a low arch.

SIMULATION MODELS

Simulation models are similar to analytic models in many ways. The difference between them lies more in the method of solution than in the model characteristics. Simulation methods can involve trial and error solution techniques. The systems analyst can monitor the output from several variables over time and then adjust the model slightly and run it again to compare results.

It is not true to say that mathematics is not involved. Mathematical analysis may be needed while setting up the equations used in the model. The distinction between analysis and simulation can become blurred.

Automobile Velocities

As an example of a simulation model consider two automobiles that pass a checkpoint at different times. The faster car is gaining on the slower car that is ahead of it. When and how far down the road will the faster auto overtake the slower one? This problem does have a simple, efficient analytic solution.

Another approach is to develop a model based on the simple formula

$$D = V * T$$

giving the distance D as a function of velocity, V, and time, T. The solution method involves computing the distance traveled by each automobile for various times until a time is found for which the two automobiles have traveled about the same distance. Program 1-8 illustrates this trial and error approach. Figure 1-8 shows the results.

Program 1-8

```
100 REM ********************************
102 REM *     1-8                      *
104 REM ********************************
106 REM    AUTHOR
108 REM        COPYRIGHT 1982
110 REM        BY LAWRENCE MCNITT.
112 REM    PURPOSE
114 REM        ONE AUTO OVERTAKING ANOTHER
116 REM        WITH CONSTANT VELOCITIES.
118 REM    SYSTEM
120 REM        UNIVERSAL SUBSET
122 REM        OF BASIC.
200 REM ********************************
202 REM *    ORGANIZATION              *
204 REM ********************************
206 REM   900    MAIN ROUTINE
208 REM          1000   INITIAL MESSAGE
210 REM          1100   GET DATA
212 REM          1200   PROCESS
214 REM          1300   FINAL MESSAGE
300 REM ********************************
302 REM *    VARIABLES                 *
304 REM ********************************
306 REM    U$    USER RESPONSE
308 REM    V1    VELOCITY OF FIRST AUTO
310 REM    V2    VELOCITY OF SECOND AUTO
312 REM    D1    DISTANCE FOR FIRST AUTO
314 REM    D2    DISTANCE FOR SECOND AUTO
316 REM    H     HEAD START FOR FIRST AUTO
318 REM    T     TIME
900 REM ********************************
902 REM *    MAIN ROUTINE              *
904 REM ********************************
906 REM INITIAL MESSAGE
908 GOSUB 1006
910 REM GET DATA
912 GOSUB 1106
914 REM PROCESS
916 GOSUB 1206
918 REM FINAL MESSAGE
920 GOSUB 1306
922 IF U$ = "Y" THEN 912
924 PRINT
926 PRINT "END OF PROGRAM"
```

```
999 STOP
1000 REM *******************************
1002 REM *    INITIAL MESSAGE         *
1004 REM *******************************
1006 PRINT
1008 PRINT
1010 PRINT
1012 PRINT "PROGRAM 1-8   "
1014 PRINT
1016 PRINT "ONE AUTO PASSES A CHECKPOINT"
1018 PRINT "AT A FIXED VELOCITY. A SECOND"
1020 PRINT "AUTO PASSES LATER AT A HIGHER"
1022 PRINT "VELOCITY. EVALUATE THEIR"
1024 PRINT "RELATIVE LOCATIONS AT SPECIFIED"
1026 PRINT "TIMES."
1099 RETURN
1100 REM *******************************
1102 REM *    GET DATA               *
1104 REM *******************************
1106 PRINT
1108 PRINT "VELOCITY OF FIRST AUTO (MPH)         ";
1110 INPUT V1
1112 PRINT "VELOCITY OF SECOND AUTO (MPH)        ";
1114 INPUT V2
1116 PRINT "HEAD START OF FIRST AUTO (MINUTES)";
1118 INPUT H
1120 LET H = H / 60
1199 RETURN
1200 REM *******************************
1202 REM *    PROCESS                *
1204 REM *******************************
1206 PRINT
1208 PRINT "ELAPSED TIME (MINUTES)";
1210 INPUT T
1212 LET T = T / 60
1214 LET D1 = V1 * (H + T)
1216 LET D2 = V2 * T
1218 PRINT
1220 PRINT "AUTO","DISTANCE IN MILES"
1222 PRINT "FIRST",D1
1224 PRINT "SECOND",D2
1226 PRINT
1228 PRINT "TRY ANOTHER ELAPSED TIME (Y/N)";
1230 INPUT U$
1232 IF U$ = "Y" THEN 1206
1299 RETURN
```

```
1300 REM ********************************
1302 REM *      FINAL MESSAGE           *
1304 REM ********************************
1306 PRINT
1308 PRINT "TRY ANOTHER PROBLEM (Y/N)";
1310 INPUT U$
1312 IF U$ = "Y" THEN 1399
1314 IF U$ = "N" THEN 1399
1316 PRINT
1318 PRINT "INVALID RESPONSE"
1320 GOTO 1306
1399 RETURN
9999 END
```

Economic Order Quantity

The same approach could be used for the inventory economic order quantity problem. Demand is constant at the rate of 400 units per year. Cost per order placed is $10.00. The holding cost is $5.00 per unit per year. Listing 1-9 illustrates the trial and error approach for determining the optimum order quantity. It also measures the sensitivity of the total cost to the choice in order quantity. Figure 1-9 shows the results.

Exercise 1-3

1. Use the trial and error approach to estimate the internal rate of return for the following series of annual cash flows received at the beginning of each year:

$$-25,000 \quad -15,000 \quad 15,000 \quad 10,000.$$

The internal rate of return is that interest rate which will result in a net present value of zero.
2. An ancient cannon has a muzzle velocity of 460 feet per second. Use the trial and error approach to find the angle of elevation needed to place the cannon ball at a distance of 3725 feet plus or minus fifty feet.

MODEL BEHAVIOR

The purpose of a simulation may be to monitor the behavior of a given system under varying conditions rather than to solve for the optimum setting. The simulation may involve moving the model through time, noting the values of selected variables at various times.

This is much like using sensors to monitor a real system. Monitoring the simulated system may be easier than monitoring the real thing. The readings may be printed or they may be graphed. The two programs in this section model the position of a bouncing ball over time and distance.

Listing 1-10 prints the location of the ball over time. Figure 1-10 shows the results. There are several problems evident in this program. One is that a resolution of one second is too large to give a very refined picture of the trajectory of the bouncing ball. Increasing the resolution to one-tenth or one-hundredth of a second would make the burden of interpreting the printed output unbearable.

Model validation poses another problem. The performance of the model should be checked with that of the real system. If the disagreement is great, the model should be refined. In the case of the bouncing ball, the forward velocity will probably decrease with each impact. This decrease in forward momentum will be greatest for the first bounce or two as energy is absorbed in getting the ball to spin.

Program 1-11 provides a graph depicting the position of the bouncing ball using greater resolution. Figure 1-11 shows the results. Note that the LPRINT statement as found in TRS-80 BASIC is used in this program. If you do not want a print out or if you are using another type of computer, change this statement appropriately.

```
PROGRAM 1-8
ONE AUTO PASSES A CHECKPOINT
AT A FIXED VELOCITY. A SECOND
AUTO PASSES LATER AT A HIGHER
VELOCITY. EVALUATE THEIR
RELATIVE LOCATIONS AT SPECIFIED
TIMES.

VELOCITY OF FIRST AUTO (MPH)        ? 55
VELOCITY OF SECOND AUTO (MPH)       ? 70
HEAD START OF FIRST AUTO (MINUTES) ? 2

ELAPSED TIME (MINUTES)? 10

AUTO                DISTANCE IN MILES
FIRST                 11
SECOND                11.6667

TRY ANOTHER ELAPSED TIME (Y/N)? Y

ELAPSED TIME (MINUTES) ? 8

AUTO                DISTANCE IN MILES
FIRST                 9.16667
SECOND                9.33333

TRY ANOTHER ELAPSED TIME (Y/N)? Y

ELAPSED TIME (MINUTES) ? 7
AUTO                DISTANCE IN MILES
FIRST                 8.25
SECOND                8.16667

TRY ANOTHER ELAPSED TIME (Y/N)? Y

ELAPSED TIME (MINUTES) ? 7.5

AUTO                DISTANCE IN MILES
FIRST                 8.70833
SECOND                8.75
TRY ANOTHER ELAPSED TIME (Y/N)? N

END OF PROGRAM
```

Fig. 1-8. Sample results from Program 1-8.

Program 1-9

```
100 REM ********************************
102 REM *    1-9                       *
104 REM ********************************
106 REM   AUTHOR
108 REM       COPYRIGHT 1982
110 REM       BY LAWRENCE MCNITT.
112 REM   PURPOSE
114 REM       EVALUATE INVENTORY ECONOMIC
116 REM       ORDER QUANTITY PROBLEMS.
118 REM   SYSTEM
120 REM       UNIVERSAL SUBSET
122 REM       OF BASIC.
200 REM ********************************
202 REM *    ORGANIZATION              *
204 REM ********************************
206 REM   900    MAIN ROUTINE
208 REM           1000   INITIAL MESSAGE
210 REM           1100   GET DATA
212 REM           1200   PROCESS
214 REM           1300   FINAL MESSAGE
300 REM ********************************
302 REM *    VARIABLES                 *
304 REM ********************************
306 REM    U$   USER RESPONSE
308 REM    D    QUANTITY DEMANDED PER YEAR
310 REM    C    COST PER ORDER PLACED
312 REM    H    HOLDING COST PER UNIT PER YEAR
314 REM    Q    ORDER QUANTITY
316 REM    T1   ANNUAL ORDER COSTS
318 REM    T2   ANNUAL HOLDING COSTS
320 REM    T    TOTAL ANNUAL COSTS
900 REM ********************************
902 REM *    MAIN ROUTINE              *
904 REM ********************************
906 REM INITIAL MESSAGE
908 GOSUB 1006
910 REM GET DATA
912 GOSUB 1106
914 REM PROCESS
916 GOSUB 1206
918 REM FINAL MESSAGE
920 GOSUB 1306
922 IF U$ = "Y" THEN 912
924 PRINT
```

```
926 PRINT "END OF PROGRAM"
999 STOP
1000 REM *******************************
1002 REM *    INITIAL MESSAGE          *
1004 REM *******************************
1006 PRINT
1008 PRINT
1010 PRINT
1012 PRINT "PROGRAM 1-9   "
1014 PRINT
1016 PRINT "EVALUATE THE COSTS FOR ORDER"
1018 PRINT "QUANTITIES GIVEN THE YEARLY DEMAND,"
1020 PRINT "COST PER ORDER PLACED, AND"
1022 PRINT "HOLDING COST PER UNIT PER YEAR."
1099 RETURN
1100 REM *******************************
1102 REM *    GET DATA                 *
1104 REM *******************************
1106 PRINT
1108 PRINT "QUANTITY DEMANDED PER YEAR     ";
1110 INPUT D
1112 PRINT "COST PER ORDER PLACED          ";
1114 INPUT C
1116 PRINT "HOLDING COST PER UNIT PER YEAR";
1118 INPUT H
1199 RETURN
1200 REM *******************************
1202 REM *    PROCESS                  *
1204 REM *******************************
1206 PRINT
1208 PRINT "ORDER QUANTITY";
1210 INPUT Q
1212 LET T1 = C * D / Q
1214 LET T2 = H * Q / 2
1216 LET T = T1 + T2
1218 PRINT
1220 PRINT ,"ANNUAL COST"
1222 PRINT "ORDERING",T1
1224 PRINT "HOLDING",T2
1226 PRINT "TOTAL",T
1228 PRINT
1230 PRINT "TRY ANOTHER ORDER QUANTITY (Y/N)";
1232 INPUT U$
1234 IF U$ = "Y" THEN 1206
1236 IF U$ = "N" THEN 1299
1238 PRINT
```

```
1240 PRINT "INVALID RESPONSE"
1242 GOTO 1206
1299 RETURN
1300 REM ******************************
1302 REM *     FINAL MESSAGE          *
1304 REM ******************************
1306 PRINT
1308 PRINT "TRY ANOTHER PROBLEM (Y/N)";
1310 INPUT U$
1312 IF U$ = "Y" THEN 1399
1314 IF U$ = "N" THEN 1399
1316 PRINT
1318 PRINT "INVALID RESPONSE"
1320 GOTO 1306
1399 RETURN
9999 END
```

Exercise 1-4

1. An ancient cannon has a muzzle velocity of 460 feet per second. For an angle of elevation of 25 degrees give the height and distance of the cannon ball on a second by second basis.
2. Plot the trajectory of the cannon ball for a cannon having a muzzle velocity of 460 feet per second and an angle of elevation of 25 degrees.

SIMULATION METHODS

Methods are more important than the model in simulation. The models themselves are as varied as human experience. Certain tools and techniques have proven useful in developing computer simulation models. There are also proven methods to help analyze these models. This book discusses both aspects.

Trial-and-Error Approach

One approach is to use trial-and-error search strategies. When a model does not lend itself to direct analytic solution or when the analyst wants to compare many different decision values in addition to the optimum settings, he can "play" with the model in a way that would not be practical with the real system, as long as the equations in the model are in a form that permits easy modification and analysis.

The following problem can be dealt with using the trial-and-error approach: the demand for a particular product is given by the formula

$$D = 300 * (20 / P) ** 2.$$

The demand is for 300 units at a price of $20.00. Higher prices result in lower demand. Lower prices result in higher demand. The symbol ** signifies that the following number is an exponent. The symbol used for this operation varies somewhat from system to system with the up-arrow most often used.

The per-unit cost of production decreases with increased production quantities due to economies of scale. The formula

$$C = 200 * D ** .6$$

gives the total production cost for the quantity D.

What unit-price will result in the maximum gross profit computed as the difference between revenue and total cost? Those skilled in mathematics should look for analytic solutions. The simulation approach is also feasible. A by-product of the

```
PROGRAM 1-9

EVALUATE THE COSTS FOR ORDER
QUANTITIES GIVEN THE YEARLY DEMAND,
COST PER ORDER PLACED, AND
HOLDING COST PER UNIT PER YEAR.

QUANTITY DEMANDED PER YEAR     ? 400
COST PER ORDER PLACED          ? 10
HOLDING COST PER UNIT PER YEAR? 5

ORDER QUANTITY? 20

                  ANNUAL COSTS
ORDERING          200
HOLDING           50
TOTAL             250

TRY ANOTHER ORDER QUANTITY (Y/N)? Y

ORDER QUANTITY? 40

                  ANNUAL COSTS
ORDERING          100
HOLDING           100
TOTAL             200

TRY ANOTHER ORDER QUANTITY (Y/N)? Y

ORDER QUANTITY? 60

                  ANNUAL COSTS
ORDERING          66.6667
HOLDING           150
TOTAL             216.667

TRY ANOTHER ORDER QUANTITY (Y/N)? N

TRY ANOTHER PROBLEM (Y/N)? N

END OF PROGRAM
```

Fig. 1-9. Sample results from Program 1-9.

Program 1-10

```
100 REM ********************************
102 REM *    1-10                      *
104 REM ********************************
106 REM   AUTHOR
108 REM       COPYRIGHT 1982
110 REM        BY LAWRENCE MCNITT.
112 REM   PURPOSE
114 REM       BOUNCING BALL BEHAVIOR
116 REM       LISTING POSITION OVER TIME.
118 REM   SYSTEM
120 REM       UNIVERSAL SUBSET
122 REM        OF BASIC.
200 REM ********************************
202 REM *    ORGANIZATION              *
204 REM ********************************
206 REM   900   MAIN ROUTINE
208 REM           1000   INITIAL MESSAGE
210 REM           1100   GET DATA
212 REM           1200   PROCESS
214 REM           1300   FINAL MESSAGE
300 REM ********************************
302 REM *    VARIABLES                 *
304 REM ********************************
306 REM    U$   USER RESPONSE
308 REM    V    HORIZONTAL VELOCITY
310 REM    H1   MAXIMUM HEIGHT OF BOUNCE
312 REM    E    COEFFICIENT OF ELASTICITY
314 REM    G    ACCELERATION DUE TO GRAVITY
316 REM    M    MAXIMUM TIME FOR SIMULATION
318 REM    T    CURRENT TIME
320 REM    D    CURRENT DISTANCE
322 REM    H    CURRENT HEIGHT
324 REM    T1   TIME AT HIGHEST POINT
326 REM    T2   TIME OF NEXT IMPACT
328 REM    T3   TIME IN THE AIR DURING BOUNCE
900 REM ********************************
902 REM *    MAIN ROUTINE              *
904 REM ********************************
906 REM INITIAL MESSAGE
908 GOSUB 1006
910 REM GET DATA
912 GOSUB 1106
914 REM PROCESS
916 GOSUB 1206
```

```
918 REM FINAL MESSAGE
920 GOSUB 1306
922 IF U$ = "Y" THEN 912
924 PRINT
926 PRINT "END OF PROGRAM"
999 STOP
1000 REM *****************************
1002 REM *    INITIAL MESSAGE        *
1004 REM *****************************
1006 PRINT
1008 PRINT
1010 PRINT
1012 PRINT "PROGRAM 1-10"
1014 PRINT
1016 PRINT "SIMULATE THE BEHAVIOR OF"
1018 PRINT "A BOUNCING BALL OVER TIME."
1099 RETURN
1100 REM *****************************
1102 REM *    GET DATA               *
1104 REM *****************************
1106 PRINT
1108 PRINT "COEFFICIENT OF ELASTICITY GIVING"
1110 PRINT "THE RATIO OF THE HEIGHT OF THE"
1112 PRINT "NEXT BOUNCE TO THAT OF THE CURRENT ONE";
1114 INPUT E
1116 PRINT
1118 PRINT "HORIZONTAL VELOCITY (FEET/SEC)";
1120 INPUT V
1122 PRINT
1124 PRINT "STARTING HEIGHT IN FEET";
1126 INPUT H1
1128 PRINT
1130 PRINT "MAXIMUM TIME FOR SIMULATION (SEC)";
1132 INPUT M
1134 LET G = 32.2
1199 RETURN
1200 REM *****************************
1202 REM *    PROCESS                *
1204 REM *****************************
1206 PRINT
1208 PRINT "TIME","DISTANCE","HEIGHT"
1210 LET T1 = 0
1212 LET T2 = SQR(2 * H1 / G)
1214 FOR T = 0 TO M
1216     IF T < T2 THEN 1228
1218     LET H1 = E * H1
```

```
1220    LET T3 = 2 * SQR(2 * H1 / G)
1222    LET T1 = T2 + T3 / 2
1224    LET T2 = T2 + T3
1226    IF H1 > .1 THEN 1216
1228    LET D = V * T
1230    LET H = H1 - .5 * G * (T1 - T) [ 2
1232    IF H1 < .1 THEN 1299
1234    PRINT T,D,H
1236 NEXT T
1299 RETURN
1300 REM *****************************
1302 REM *    FINAL MESSAGE          *
1304 REM *****************************
1306 PRINT
1308 PRINT "TRY ANOTHER PROBLEM (Y/N)";
1310 INPUT U$
1312 IF U$ = "Y" THEN 1399
1314 IF U$ = "N" THEN 1399
1316 PRINT
1318 PRINT "INVALID RESPONSE"
1320 GOTO 1306
1399 RETURN
9999 END
```

simulation approach is the ability to measure the sensitivity of the measure of performance (profit) to the value of the decision variable (price).

Program 1-12 carries out the calculations and allows the user to choose a set of prices to compare in one run. Figure 1-12 shows the results.

The Curse of Dimensionality

Evaluating a model that has only one decision variable is relatively easy. Many models have three or more decision variables. Some computer simulations have more than twenty decision variables plus hundreds of uncontrollable variables representing the state of the external and internal environments.

There are often interdependencies among the decision variables so that they must be analyzed jointly. The problem becomes one of finding the optimum combination of values for the decision variables. If the decision variables are independent, the approach is to analyze each variable by itself while holding the other variables constant. If they are dependent, then they must be analyzed in groups.

Evaluating several decision variables as a group adds enormously to the computational burden. Evaluating ten settings for each of four decision variables gives a table of results having 10,000 entries. Each variable constitutes one dimension. Letting m be the number of settings to evaluate for each variable (resolution) and n be the number of variables (dimension), the expression

$$m ** n$$

gives the number of points to evaluate.

If the model is deterministic, one replication per point is sufficient. If the model is probabilistic, many replications per point may be necessary to determine reliable average measures of performance. The computational burden increases very rapidly with increases in the dimension (number of decision variables). This is the curse of dimensionality.

```
PROGRAM 1-10

SIMULATE THE BEHAVIOR OF
A BOUNCING BALL OVER TIME.

COEFFICIENT OF ELASTICITY GIVING
THE RATIO OF THE HEIGHT OF THE
NEXT BOUND TO THAT OF THE CURRENT ONE? .9

HORIZONTAL VELOCITY (FEET/SEC)? 50

MAXIMUM TIME FOR SIMULATION (SEC)? 12

TIME              DISTANCE          HEIGHT
  0                  0               50
  1                 25               33.9
  2                 50               11.8879
  3                 75               41.966
  4                100               39.8442
  5                125               5.52227
  6                150               32.7907
  7                175               38.9725
  8                200               12.9542
  9                225               26.5875
 10                250               35.6896
 11                275               12.5916
 12                300               24.5797

TRY ANOTHER PROBLEM (Y/N)? N

END OF PROGRAM
```

Fig. 1-10. Sample results from Program 1-10.

Program 1-11

```
100 REM *******************************
102 REM *    1-11                      *
104 REM *******************************
106 REM   AUTHOR
108 REM       COPYRIGHT 1982
110 REM        BY LAWRENCE MCNITT.
112 REM   PURPOSE
114 REM       BOUNCING BALL BEHAVIOR
116 REM       PRINTING GRAPH OF POSITION.
```

```
118 REM   SYSTEM
120 REM       MICROSOFT BASIC
122 REM       RADIO SHACK TRS-80.
200 REM ******************************
202 REM *   ORGANIZATION             *
204 REM ******************************
206 REM   900   MAIN ROUTINE
208 REM         1000   INITIAL MESSAGE
210 REM         1100   GET DATA
212 REM         1200   PROCESS
214 REM         1300   FINAL MESSAGE
300 REM *******************************
302 REM *   VARIABLES                *
304 REM *******************************
306 REM    U$   USER RESPONSE
308 REM    V    HORIZONTAL VELOCITY
310 REM    H1   MAXIMUM HEIGHT OF BOUNCE
312 REM    E    COEFFICIENT OF ELASTICITY
314 REM    G    ACCELERATION DUE TO GRAVITY
316 REM    M    MAXIMUM TIME FOR SIMULATION
318 REM    T    CURRENT TIME
320 REM    D    CURRENT DISTANCE
322 REM    H    CURRENT HEIGHT
324 REM    T1   TIME AT HIGHEST POINT
326 REM    T2   TIME OF NEXT IMPACT
328 REM    T3   TIME IN THE AIR DURING BOUNCE
330 REM    S    STEP SIZE FOR TIME INCREMENT
332 REM    H2   STARTING HEIGHT FOR SCALING GRAPH
900 REM *******************************
902 REM *    MAIN ROUTINE             *
904 REM *******************************
906 REM INITIAL MESSAGE
908 GOSUB 1006
910 REM GET DATA
912 GOSUB 1106
914 REM PROCESS
916 GOSUB 1206
918 REM FINAL MESSAGE
920 GOSUB 1306
922 IF U$ = "Y" THEN 912
924 PRINT
926 PRINT "END OF PROGRAM"
999 STOP
1000 REM ******************************
1002 REM *   INITIAL MESSAGE          *
1004 REM ******************************
```

```
1006 PRINT
1008 PRINT
1010 PRINT
1012 PRINT "PROGRAM 1-11"
1014 PRINT
1016 PRINT "SIMULATE THE BEHAVIOR OF"
1018 PRINT "A BOUNCING BALL OVER TIME."
1099 RETURN
1100 REM ******************************
1102 REM *    GET DATA               *
1104 REM ******************************
1106 PRINT
1108 PRINT "COEFFICIENT OF ELASTICITY GIVING"
1110 PRINT "THE RATIO OF THE HEIGHT OF THE"
1112 PRINT "NEXT BOUNCE TO THAT OF THE CURRENT ONE":
1114 INPUT E
1116 PRINT
1118 PRINT "HORIZONTAL VELOCITY (FEET/SEC)";
1120 INPUT V
1122 PRINT
1124 PRINT "STARTING HEIGHT IN FEET";
1126 INPUT H1
1128 PRINT
1130 PRINT "MAXIMUM TIME FOR SIMULATION (SEC)";
1132 INPUT M
1134 PRINT
1136 PRINT "STEP SIZE FOR TIME INCREMENT";
1138 INPUT S
1140 LET G = 32.2
1142 LET H2 = H1
1199 RETURN
1200 REM ******************************
1202 REM *    PROCESS                *
1204 REM ******************************
1206 LPRINT
1208 LPRINT "DISTANCE","HEIGHT"
1210 LET T1 = 0
1212 LET T2 = SQR(2 * H1 / G)
1214 FOR T = 0 TO M STEP S
1216     IF T < T2 THEN 1228
1218     LET H1 = E * H1
1220     LET T3 = 2 * SQR(2 * H1 / G)
1222     LET T1 = T2 + T3 / 2
1224     LET T2 = T2 + T3
1226     IF H1 > .1 THEN 1216
1228     LET D = V * T
```

30

```
1230     LET H = H1 - .5 * G * (T1 - T) [ 2
1232     IF H1 < .1 THEN 1299
1234     LET P = 20 + INT(40 * H / H2)
1236     LPRINT D;TAB(P);"*"
1238 NEXT T
1299 RETURN
1300 REM *******************************
1302 REM *     FINAL MESSAGE           *
1304 REM *******************************
1306 PRINT
1308 PRINT "TRY ANOTHER PROBLEM (Y/N)";
1310 INPUT U$
1312 IF U$ = "Y" THEN 1399
1314 IF U$ = "N" THEN 1399
1316 PRINT
1318 PRINT "INVALID RESPONSE"
1320 GOTO 1306
1399 RETURN
9999 END
```

```
PROGRAM 1-11



SIMULATE THE BEHAVIOR OF
A BOUNCING BALL OVER TIME.

COEFFICIENT OF ELASTICITY GIVING
THE RATIO OF THE HEIGHT OF THE
NEXT BOUNCE TO THAT OF THE CURRENT ONE? .8

HORIZONTAL VELOCITY (FEET/SEC)? 25

STARTING HEIGHT IN FEET? 20

MAXIMUM TIME FOR SIMULATION (SEC)? 6

STEP SIZE FOR TIME INCREMENT? .2

DISTANCE          HEIGHT
  0                                                              *
  5                                                          *
 10                                                      *
 15                                                  *
```

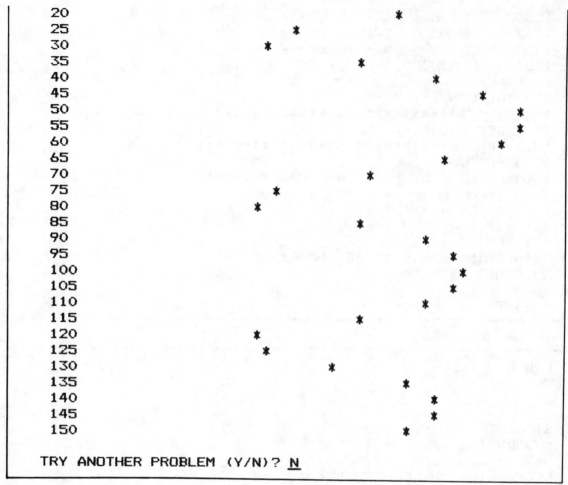

```
20                                           *
25                                  *
30                              *
35                                *
40                                      *
45                                         *
50                                           *
55                                          *
60                                        *
65                                   *
70                            *
75                       *
80                    *
85                          *
90                               *
95                                 *
100                                  *
105                                 *
110                              *
115                         *
120                 *
125                 *
130                    *
135                       *
140                          *
145                          *
150                      *
```

TRY ANOTHER PROBLEM (Y/N)? <u>N</u>

Fig. 1-11. Sample results from Program 1-11.

Program 1-12

```
100 REM *******************************
102 REM *    1-12                      *
104 REM *******************************
106 REM   AUTHOR
108 REM       COPYRIGHT 1982
110 REM       BY LAWRENCE MCNITT.
112 REM   PURPOSE
114 REM       DEMAND FUNCTION AND
116 REM       ECONOMIES OF SCALE.
118 REM   SYSTEM
120 REM       MICROSOFT BASIC
```

```
122 REM        RADIO SHACK TRS-80.
200 REM ********************************
202 REM *    ORGANIZATION             *
204 REM ********************************
206 REM   900   MAIN ROUTINE
208 REM         1000   INITIAL MESSAGE
210 REM         1100   GET DATA
212 REM         1200   PROCESS
214 REM         1300   FINAL MESSAGE
300 REM ********************************
302 REM *    VARIABLES                *
304 REM ********************************
306 REM    U$   USER RESPONSE
308 REM    P    CURRENT PRICE
310 REM    P1   LOWER LIMIT FOR PRICE
312 REM    P2   UPPER LIMIT FOR PRICE
314 REM    P3   STEP SIZE FOR PRICE
316 REM    D    QUANTITY DEMANDED
318 REM    C    TOTAL COST
320 REM    G    GROSS PROFIT
900 REM ********************************
902 REM *    MAIN ROUTINE             *
904 REM ********************************
906 REM INITIAL MESSAGE
908 GOSUB 1006
910 REM GET DATA
912 GOSUB 1106
914 REM PROCESS
916 GOSUB 1206
918 REM FINAL MESSAGE
920 GOSUB 1306
922 IF U$ = "Y" THEN 912
924 PRINT
926 PRINT "END OF PROGRAM"
999 STOP
1000 REM ********************************
1002 REM *    INITIAL MESSAGE          *
1004 REM ********************************
1006 PRINT
1008 PRINT
1010 PRINT
1012 PRINT "PROGRAM 1-12"
1014 PRINT
1016 PRINT "ANALYZE THE EFFECT OF PRICING"
1018 PRINT "ON DEMAND AND ECONOMIES OF"
1020 PRINT "SCALE ON PROFITABILITY."
```

```
1099 RETURN
1100 REM ******************************
1102 REM *     GET DATA               *
1104 REM ******************************
1106 PRINT
1108 PRINT "LIMITS FOR PRICES"
1110 PRINT "LOWER LIMIT";
1112 INPUT P1
1114 PRINT "UPPER LIMIT";
1116 INPUT P2
1118 PRINT "STEP SIZE  ";
1120 INPUT P3
1199 RETURN
1200 REM ******************************
1202 REM *     PROCESS                *
1204 REM ******************************
1206 PRINT
1208 PRINT "PRICE","QUANTITY","COST","PROFIT"
1210 FOR P = P1 TO P2 STEP P3
1212     LET D = 300 * (20 / P) [ 2
1214     LET C = 200 * D [ .6
1216     LET G = P * D - C
1218     PRINT P,D,C,G
1220 NEXT P
1299 RETURN
1300 REM ******************************
1302 REM *     FINAL MESSAGE          *
1304 REM ******************************
1306 PRINT
1308 PRINT "TRY ANOTHER PROBLEM (Y/N)";
1310 INPUT U$
1312 IF U$ = "Y" THEN 1399
1314 IF U$ = "N" THEN 1399
1316 PRINT
1318 PRINT "INVALID RESPONSE"
1320 GOTO 1306
1399 RETURN
9999 END
```

To counterbalance the curse of dimensionality, there are search strategies that can provide good results most of the time. Digital computers can handle problems involving massive numbers of calculations. They are now routinely solving problems that could not have been solved before. Technological advances result in faster and faster computers that can solve more complex problems than those solved five years ago. Computer simulation requires the human element in the choice of efficient search strategies as well as the computing power of computers.

```
PROGRAM 1-12

ANALYZE THE EFFECT OF PRICING
ON DEMAND AND ECONOMIES OF
SCALE ON PROFITABILITY.

LIMITS FOR PRICES

LOWER LIMIT? 10
UPPER LIMIT? 100
STEP SIZE? 10

PRICE           QUANTITY        COST            PROFIT
 10             1200            14077.9         -2077.93
 20             300             6127.78         -127.775
 30             133.333         3766.98          233.02
 40             75              2667.27          332.731
 50             48              2040.68          359.321
 60             33.3333         1639.67          360.327
 70             24.4898         1362.77          351.52
 80             18.75           1161             339.004
 90             14.8148         1007.97          325.363
 100            12              888.257          311.743


TRY ANOTHER PROBLEM (Y/N)? Y

LIMITS FOR PRICES
LOWER LIMIT? 50
UPPER LIMIT? 70
STEP SIZE   ? 2

PRICE           QUANTITY        COST            PROFIT
 50             48.2653         2040.68          359.321
 52             44.3787         1946.86          360.832
 54             41.1523         1860.66          361.566
 56             38.2653         1781.2           361.656
 58             35.6718         1707.75          361.212
 60             33.3333         1639.67          360.327
 62             31.2175         1576.41          359.075
 64             29.2969         1517.48          357.521
 66             27.5482         1462.47          355.715
 68             25.9516         1411             353.702
 70             24.4898         1362.77          351.52
```

Fig. 1-12. Sample results from Program 1-12.

The Insatiable Demand for Computing Power

Computer simulation is one of the leading factors fostering the development of ever faster and more powerful computers. Simulations require this speed and power because of the problem of dimensionality as mentioned above. Power and speed are also required because of the need for finer resolution. To achieve more refined results, the resolution is improved by increasing the number of possible settings for a variable.

Exercise 1-5

1. In Program 1-12, let the function

$$1500 * (20 / P) ** 2$$

represent the demand function. Determine the price that results in the maximum gross profit.

2. In Program 1-12, let the function

$$100 * D ** .8$$

give the total cost function. Determine the price that results in the maximum gross profit.

Chapter 2

Deterministic Models

Simulation models may be deterministic or probabilistic. A *probabilistic* model may assume any one of many states for each set of inputs. A *deterministic* model assumes only one state for a given set of inputs.

Deterministic models are easier to analyze as only one replication (trial) is needed for each set of input parameters. Probably the best known large deterministic simulation models are those representing the United States economy. The largest models of the economy contain hundreds of equations and variables.

One purpose of simulation is to observe the behavior of the model and use the results in prediction. Another purpose of the simulation may be to determine the input settings that will result in optimizing some objective. The purpose of some simulations is to observe the interaction of two or more variables over time. One variable may increase while the other decreases. One variable may lag behind the other. This interaction is evident in biological systems. Some life forms compete for the same resources. Parasites and hosts may have dependencies. One species may depend on another for food.

A PREDATOR-PREY MODEL

Predator-prey models are examples of simulations used for observing the interaction of variables. They represent the simplest aspects of biological systems. One simple model involves wolves, rabbits, and food for the rabbits. The wolves live primarily on rabbits. The rabbits live on plants.

The plants, rabbits, and wolves increase at stated rates. There is an upper limit for the amount of plant life available to be eaten. The rabbit population reflects losses through starvation and from the wolves. The wolf population reflects losses by starvation if there aren't enough rabbits.

Let the variable F be the amount of plant life. Let R be the number of rabbits. Let W be the number of wolves. The coefficient C1 gives the growth factor for plant propagation. C2 gives the number of units of food eaten per rabbit. C3 gives the rabbit population growth rate per period. C4 gives the number of rabbits eaten per wolf. C5 gives the wolf population growth rate.

The formula

$$F = C1 * F - C2 * R$$

gives the new food supply for the rabbits. This cannot exceed a specified upper bound or fall below a specified lower bound. The formula

$$R = C3 * R - C4 * W$$

gives the rabbit population size including normal growth and losses to wolves. If there isn't enough food to support the rabbits, the population size is diminished through starvation. The formula

$$W = C5 * W$$

gives the normal wolf population growth. If there aren't enough rabbits, the wolf population diminishes through starvation.

The coefficients for the equations may be estimated through the use of field data. The model needs initial starting conditions that may also come from experience with an actual population study. An important part of the process is to validate the mathematical model. This involves determining whether the model behaves in the same manner as the actual biological system is observed to behave.

The model is a simplification of the real system. It will not always behave exactly as the real system does. Many potential variables have been left out. The analyst must interpret results of the analysis with caution.

Program 2-1 illustrates a simple predator-prey-food-chain model. Figure 2-1 shows the results.

Exercise 2-1

1. Modify the predator-prey model of this section to include graphical output representing the population levels for each of the three populations.

Program 2-1

```
100 REM ****************************
102 REM *    2-1                  *
104 REM ****************************
106 REM   AUTHOR
108 REM       COPYRIGHT 1982
110 REM       BY LAWRENCE MCNITT.
112 REM   PURPOSE
114 REM       PREDATOR, PREY FOOD CHAIN.
116 REM   SYSTEM
118 REM       UNIVERSAL SUBSET
120 REM       OF BASIC.
200 REM ****************************
202 REM *    ORGANIZATION         *
204 REM ****************************
206 REM   900   MAIN ROUTINE
208 REM         1000   INITIAL MESSAGE
210 REM         1100   PARAMETERS
212 REM         1200   PROCESS
214 REM         1300   FINAL MESSAGE
300 REM ****************************
302 REM *    VARIABLES            *
```

```
304 REM ********************************
306 REM    U$   USER RESPONSE
308 REM    F    FOOD SUPPLY LEVEL
310 REM    R    NUMBER OF RABBITS
312 REM    W    NUMBER OF WOLVES
314 REM    C1   RATE OF GROWTH OF FOOD SUPPLY
316 REM    C2   FOOD CONSUMPTION PER RABBIT
318 REM    C3   RATE OF GROWTH OF RABBIT POPULATION
320 REM    C4   RABBIT CONSUMPTION PER WOLF
322 REM    C5   RATE OF GROWTH OF WOLVES
324 REM    N    NUMBER OF PERIODS TO SIMULATE
326 REM    T    CURRENT TIME PERIOD
900 REM ********************************
902 REM *    MAIN ROUTINE                *
904 REM ********************************
906 REM INITIAL MESSAGE
908 GOSUB 1006
910 REM PARAMETERS
912 GOSUB 1106
914 REM PROCESS
916 GOSUB 1206
918 REM FINAL MESSAGE
920 GOSUB 1306
922 IF U$ = "Y" THEN  916
924 PRINT
926 PRINT "END OF PROGRAM"
999 STOP
1000 REM ********************************
1002 REM *     INITIAL MESSAGE           *
1004 REM ********************************
1006 PRINT
1008 PRINT
1010 PRINT
1012 PRINT "PROGRAM 2-1"
1014 PRINT
1016 PRINT "PREDATOR, PREY, FOOD CHAIN"
1018 PRINT "MODEL DEPICTING POPULATION"
1020 PRINT "INTERACTION OVER TIME."
1099 RETURN
1100 REM ********************************
1102 REM *     PARAMETERS                *
1104 REM ********************************
1106 LET F = 40000
1108 LET R = 250
1110 LET W = 8
1112 LET C1 = 1.7
```

```
1114 LET C2 = 20
1116 LET C3 = 4
1118 LET C4 = 25
1120 LET C5 = 2
1199 RETURN
1200 REM ******************************
1202 REM *    PROCESS                 *
1204 REM ******************************
1206 PRINT
1208 PRINT "NUMBER OF PERIODS TO SIMULATE";
1210 INPUT N
1212 PRINT
1214 PRINT ,"POPULATIONS"
1216 PRINT "FOOD","RABBITS","WOLVES"
1218 FOR T = 1 TO N
1220    LET F = C1 * F - C2 * R
1222    LET F = INT(.5 + F)
1224    IF F > 900000 THEN LET F = 900000
1226    IF F < 500 THEN LET F = 500
1228    LET R = C3 * R - C4 * W
1230    IF F/R > C2 THEN 1234
1232    LET R = R * 2 * (.5 [ (C2 * R / F))
1234    LET R = INT(.5 + R)
1236    IF R < 12 THEN LET R = 12
1238    LET W = C5 * W
1240    IF R/W > C4 THEN 1244
1242    LET W = W * 2 * (.5 [ (C4 * W / R))
1244    LET W = INT(.5 + W)
1246    IF W < 6 THEN LET W = 6
1248    PRINT F,R,W
1250 NEXT T
1299 RETURN
1300 REM ******************************
1302 REM *    FINAL MESSAGE           *
1304 REM ******************************
1306 PRINT
1308 PRINT "CONTINUE SIMULATION (Y/N)";
1310 INPUT U$
1312 IF U$ = "Y" THEN 1399
1314 IF U$ = "N" THEN 1399
1316 PRINT
1318 PRINT "INVALID RESPONSE"
1320 GOTO 1306
1399 RETURN
9999 END
```

```
PROGRAM 2-1

PREDATOR, PREY, FOOD CHAIN
MODEL DEPICTING POPULATION
INTERACTION OVER TIME.

NUMBER OF PERIODS TO SIMULATE? 10
                    POPULATIONS
FOOD                RABBITS         WOLVES
  63000               800             16
  91100              2800             32
  98870              4839             64
  71299              1125             36
  98708              3600             72
  95804              4070            144
  81467              2931            105
  79874              3751            159
  60766              1782             29
  67662              3449             58

CONTINUE SIMULATION (Y/N)? N

END OF PROGRAM
```

Fig. 2-1. Sample results from Program 2-1.

THE GAME OF LIFE

The game of life, invented by John Conway, was first described in *Scientific American* in 1974. It has provided a popular model for computer simulation because of its visual appeal. The game involves the births and deaths of objects located in a rectangular array of cells.

A birth will occur in an empty cell if exactly three of the immediately adjacent cells are occupied. Each cell having exactly two or three adjacent cells occupied will survive to the next generation. A death from isolation occurs if one or fewer adjacent cells are occupied. A death from overpopulation occurs if four or more adjacent cells are occupied. The game requires an initial starting pattern. The game continues for a given number of cycles or until none of the cells are occupied.

Program 2-2 asks for the initial pattern and the number of generations to simulate. Figure 2-2 shows the results.

Exercise 2-2

1. Using techniques similar to that of the game of life develop a model describing the spread of an infectious disease throughout a population. Include considerations of immunity. An individual becomes immune to the disease after having had it once.

MODELS OF THE ECONOMY

Econometrics includes mathematical analysis of the economy. An important part of econometrics involves simulation models of the behavior of the economy over time. Some of these models are large and complex. They have been tested thoroughly

Program 2-2

```
100 REM ********************************
102 REM *    2-2                       *
104 REM ********************************
106 REM   AUTHOR
108 REM       COPYRIGHT 1982
110 REM       BY LAWRENCE MCNITT.
112 REM   PURPOSE
114 REM       GAME OF LIFE.
116 REM   SYSTEM
118 REM       UNIVERSAL SUBSET
120 REM       OF BASIC.
200 REM ********************************
202 REM *    ORGANIZATION              *
204 REM ********************************
206 REM   900   MAIN ROUTINE
208 REM         1000   INITIAL MESSAGE
210 REM         1100   INITIAL PATTERN
212 REM         1200   PROCESS
214 REM         1300   FINAL MESSAGE
300 REM ********************************
302 REM *    VARIABLES                 *
304 REM ********************************
306 REM   A(12,12)   OLD MATRIX
308 REM   B(12,12)   NEW MATRIX
310 REM   U$  USER RESPONSE
312 REM   N   NUMBER IN INITIAL POPULATION
314 REM   R   ROW
316 REM   C   COLUMN
318 REM   I   INDEX
320 REM   J   INDEX
322 REM   C   COUNT OF NEIGHBORS
900 REM ********************************
902 REM *    MAIN ROUTINE              *
904 REM ********************************
905 DIM A(12,12),B(12,12)
906 REM INITIAL MESSAGE
908 GOSUB 1006
910 REM INITIAL PATTERN
912 GOSUB 1106
914 REM PROCESS
916 GOSUB 1206
918 REM FINAL MESSAGE
920 GOSUB 1306
922 IF U$ = "Y" THEN 916
```

42

```
924 PRINT
926 PRINT "END OF PROGRAM"
999 STOP
1000 REM ******************************
1002 REM *    INITIAL MESSAGE         *
1004 REM ******************************
1006 PRINT
1008 PRINT
1010 PRINT
1012 PRINT "PROGRAM 2-2"
1014 PRINT
1016 PRINT "GAME OF LIFE SIMULATION AS"
1018 PRINT "DESCRIBED IN SCIENTIFIC"
1020 PRINT "AMERICAN IN 1974."
1022 LET M = 12
1024 FOR I = 1 TO M
1026    FOR J = 1 TO M
1028       LET B(I,J) = 0
1030    NEXT J
1032 NEXT I
1099 RETURN
1100 REM ******************************
1102 REM *    PARAMETERS              *
1104 REM ******************************
1106 PRINT
1108 PRINT "THIS GAME OF LIFE MATRIX"
1110 PRINT "CAN HAVE UP TO 10 ROWS"
1112 PRINT "AND UP TO 10 COLUMNS."
1114 PRINT
1116 PRINT "NUMBER OF CELLS INITIALLY OCCUPIED ";
1118 INPUT N
1120 FOR I = 1 TO N
1122    PRINT
1124    PRINT "CELL";I
1126    PRINT "ROW LOCATION";
1128    INPUT R
1130    PRINT "COL LOCATION";
1132    INPUT C
1134    LET B(R+1,C+1) = 1
1136 NEXT I
1199 RETURN
1200 REM ******************************
1202 REM *    PROCESS                 *
1204 REM ******************************
1206 FOR I = 1 TO M
1208    FOR J = 1 TO M
```

```
1210        LET A(I,J) = B(I,J)
1214     NEXT J
1216 NEXT I
1218 FOR I = 2 TO M-1
1220     FOR J = 2 TO M-1
1222        LET C = A(I-1,J-1) + A(I-1,J) + A(I-1,J+1)
1224        LET C = C + A(I,J-1) + A(I,J+1)
1226        LET C = C + A(I+1,J-1) + A(I+1,J)
1228        LET C = C + A(I+1,J+1)
1230        IF C <= 1 THEN B(I,J) = 0
1232        IF C = 3 THEN B(I,J) = 1
1234        IF C >= 4 THEN B(I,J) = 0
1236     NEXT J
1240 NEXT I
1242 PRINT
1244 FOR I = 2 TO M-1
1246     FOR J = 2 TO M-1
1248        IF B(I,J) = 0 THEN PRINT "   ";
1250        IF B(I,J) = 1 THEN PRINT " X ";
1252     NEXT J
1254     PRINT
1256 NEXT I
1299 RETURN
1300 REM ****************************
1302 REM *    FINAL MESSAGE         *
1304 REM ****************************
1306 PRINT
1308 PRINT "CONTINUE SIMULATION (Y/N)";
1310 INPUT U$
1312 IF U$ = "Y" THEN 1399
1314 IF U$ = "N" THEN 1399
1316 PRINT
1318 PRINT "INVALID RESPONSE"
1320 GOTO 1306
1399 RETURN
9999 END
```

with historical data and show surprising agreement with reality.

A model is only a model: its predictions are not perfect. Although this is true of models of the economy, they do provide useful tools for study and analysis for those willing to accept their imperfections.

A Simple Model of the Economy

The simple model of the economy shown in this section illustrates the nature of many economic models. This model contains four equations, five variables, and seven constants. Large models of the economy contain hundreds of equations with a corresponding number of variables and constants.

```
PROGRAM 2-2

GAME OF LIFE SIMULATION AS
DESCRIBED IN SCIENTIFIC
AMERICAN IN 1974.

THIS GAME OF LIFE MATRIX
CAN HAVE UP TO 10 ROWS
AND UP TO 10 COLUMNS.

NUMBER OF CELLS OCCUPIED INITIALLY? 5

CELL 1
ROW LOCATION? 1
COL LOCATION? 2

CELL 2
ROW LOCATION? 2
COL LOCATION? 3

CELL 3
ROW LOCATION? 3
COL LOCATION? 1

CELL 4
ROW LOCATION? 3
COL LOCATION? 2

CELL 5
ROW LOCATION? 3
COL LOCATION? 3

   X     X
      X  X
      X

CONTINUE SIMULATION (Y/N)? Y

         X
   X     X
      X

CONTINUE SIMULATION (Y/N)? N

END OF PROGRAM
```

Fig. 2-2. Sample results from Program 2-2.

The variables include income, Y, investment, I, taxes, T, consumption, C, and government expenditures, G. The level of government expenditures is an external variable. The values of the external variables are established from outside the model. The other variables are derived internally. The equations

$$I = 4 + .08 * Y$$
$$Y = 45 + 2.5 * (I + G)$$
$$T = .19 * Y$$
$$C = 70 + .73 * (Y - T)$$

describe the change from one period to the next.

Econometric models utilize *lagged variables* extensively. Lagged variables are those that compute values for the current stage as some function of variables at earlier stages. Investment is the lagged variable for the example in this section because investment for the current period is a function of income for the previous period.

The initial settings for the variables must be selected for the simulation. The observed behavior of the model depends to some extent on its initial state. The initial state is summarized by the value 300 representing the income from the previous period. Here, income is the lagged variable. The initial state reflects the starting point for predicting the subsequent states. Program 2-3 illustrates economic modeling using the simple model of the economy. Figure 2-3 shows the results.

Program 2-3

```
100 REM ******************************
102 REM *    2-3                     *
104 REM ******************************
106 REM   AUTHOR
108 REM       COPYRIGHT 1982
110 REM       BY LAWRENCE MCNITT.
112 REM   PURPOSE
114 REM       MODEL OF THE ECONOMY.
116 REM   SYSTEM
118 REM       UNIVERSAL SUBSET
120 REM       OF BASIC.
200 REM ******************************
202 REM *    ORGANIZATION            *
204 REM ******************************
206 REM   900   MAIN ROUTINE
208 REM         1000   INITIAL MESSAGE
210 REM         1100   PARAMETERS
212 REM         1200   PROCESS
214 REM         1300   FINAL MESSAGE
300 REM ******************************
302 REM *    VARIABLES               *
304 REM ******************************
306 REM    U$   USER RESPONSE
308 REM    Y    INCOME
310 REM    G    GOVERNMENT EXPENDITURES
312 REM    C    CONSUMPTION
314 REM    T    TAXES
316 REM    I    INVESTMENT
```

```
318 REM    C1   CONSTANT FOR INVESTMENT FUNCTION
320 REM    C2   FRACTION OF LAST YEAR INCOME TO INVEST
322 REM    C3   CONSTANT FOR INCOME FUNCTION
324 REM    C4   MULTIPLIER FOR GOVERNMENT AND INVESTMENT
326 REM    C5   FRACTION PAID IN TAXES
328 REM    C6   CONSTANT FOR CONSUMPTION FUNCTION
330 REM    C7   FRACTION OF DISPOSABLE INCOME CONSUMED
900 REM ******************************
902 REM *   MAIN ROUTINE              *
904 REM ******************************
906 REM INITIAL MESSAGE
908 GOSUB 1006
910 REM PARAMETERS
912 GOSUB 1106
914 REM PROCESS
916 GOSUB 1206
918 REM FINAL MESSAGE
920 GOSUB 1306
922 IF U$ = "Y" THEN   916
924 PRINT
926 PRINT "END OF PROGRAM"
999 STOP
1000 REM ******************************
1002 REM *    INITIAL MESSAGE          *
1004 REM ******************************
1006 PRINT
1008 PRINT
1010 PRINT
1012 PRINT "PROGRAM 2-3"
1014 PRINT
1016 PRINT "SIMPLE MODEL OF THE ECONOMY"
1018 PRINT "USING LAGGED VARIABLES."
1099 RETURN
1100 REM ******************************
1102 REM *    PARAMETERS               *
1104 REM ******************************
1106 LET Y = 300
1108 LET C1 = 4
1110 LET C2 = .08
1112 LET C3 = 45
1114 LET C4 = 2.5
1116 LET C5 = .19
1118 LET C6 = 70
1120 LET C7 = .73
1199 RETURN
1200 REM ******************************
```

```
1202 REM *     PROCESS                    *
1204 REM ******************************
1206 PRINT
1208 PRINT "GOVERNMENT EXPENDITURES";
1210 INPUT G
1212 LET I = C1 + C2 * Y
1214 LET Y = C3 + C4 * (I + G)
1216 LET T = C5 * Y
1218 LET C = C6 + C7 * (Y - T)
1220 PRINT
1222 PRINT "INCOME".Y
1224 PRINT "CONSUMPTION",C
1226 PRINT "TAXES",T
1228 PRINT "INVESTMENT",I
1299 RETURN
1300 REM ******************************
1302 REM *     FINAL MESSAGE           *
1304 REM ******************************
1306 PRINT
1308 PRINT "CONTINUE SIMULATION (Y/N)";
1310 INPUT U$
1312 IF U$ = "Y" THEN 1399
1314 IF U$ = "N" THEN 1399
1316 PRINT
1318 PRINT "INVALID RESPONSE"
1320 GOTO 1306
1399 RETURN
9999 END
```

Exercise 2-3

1. Modify the program in this section to include equations and initial settings that better reflect the current U.S. economic situation.
2. Locate a more comprehensive model that includes fifteen or twenty equations. Implement that model using values that reflect the current U.S. situation.

MODELS OF A COMPANY

Decisions involving resources and budgets are made by managers. The purpose of many simulation models is to help managers make such decisions. Some models focus on the behavior of the managers themselves. These models endeavor to model the stimuli that affect managers and the reactions of the managers to those stimuli.

Managers develop expectations of performance based on experience. They formalize the expectations as goals and compare actual performance with the goals. If the actual performance falls behind expectations, they will apply pressure to improve the actual performance. If the performance exceeds expectations, the expectations will be increased accordingly.

An index of pressure is derived from comparing actual performance with expected performance. The result may be a decrease or an increase in pressure depending upon whether or not performance exceeds expectations. The magnitude of the difference between actual performance and ex-

```
PROGRAM 2-3

SIMPLE MODEL OF THE ECONOMY
USING LAGGED VARIBLES.

GOVERNMENT EXPENDITURES? 80

INCOME            315
CONSUMPTION       256.26
TAXES             59.85
INVESTMENT        28

CONTINUE SIMULATION (Y/N)? Y

GOVERNMENT EXPENDITURES? 100

INCOME            368
CONSUMPTION       287.598
TAXES             69.92
INVESTMENT        29.2

CONTINUE SIMULATION (Y/N)? Y

GOVERNMENT EXPENDITURES? 100

INCOME            378.6
CONSUMPTION       293.866
TAXES             71.934
INVESTMENT        33.44

CONTINUE SIMULATION (Y/N)? N
```

Fig. 2-3. Sample results from Program 2-3.

pected performance determines the magnitude of the index of pressure.

Program 2-4 illustrates a model depicting the behavioral aspects of managerial decision making. Figure 2-4 shows the results.

Exercise 2-4

1. Extend the model of this section to more realistically model profit and sales aspiration adjustments if the actual levels are consistently greater than estimates or less than estimates. Also carefully consider the simulated response of the managers to the index of pressure.

PERFORMANCE OBJECTIVES

Simulation modeling has definite goals and objectives. One possible objective is to find a more efficient use of resources. Another is to increase the level of profit. Other possible objectives are to lower the cost of production and to increase sales.

An important aspect of simulation modeling involves defining measures of performance and the functional relationship of these measures to other components of the model. Often the important measures are in monetary terms and reflect cost, revenue, and profit. At other times the measures of performance will be in terms of numbers of items, amount of payload, or throughput for some process.

A simulation experiment involving only one important identifiable measure of performance is the easiest to analyze. The objective is to determine the settings of the controllable variables that optimize that measure. This goal may be to minimize costs or to maximize profits.

Program 2-4

```
100 REM ******************************
102 REM *    2-4                      *
104 REM ******************************
106 REM   AUTHOR
108 REM       COPYRIGHT 1982
110 REM       BY LAWRENCE MCNITT.
112 REM   PURPOSE
114 REM       BEHAVIORAL MODEL
```

```
116 REM      OF THE FIRM.
118 REM   SYSTEM
120 REM      UNIVERSAL SUBSET
122 REM      OF BASIC.
200 REM ******************************
202 REM *   ORGANIZATION             *
204 REM ******************************
206 REM  900  MAIN ROUTINE
208 REM         1000  INITIAL MESSAGE
210 REM         1100  PARAMEERS
212 REM         1200  PROCESS
214 REM         1300  FINAL MESSAGE
300 REM ******************************
302 REM *   VARIABLES                *
304 REM ******************************
306 REM  U$  USER RESPONSE
308 REM  A   ASPIRED PROFIT
310 REM  P1  ESTIMATED PROFIT
312 REM  P2  ACTUAL PROFIT
314 REM  S1  ESTIMATED SALES
316 REM  S2  ACTUAL SALES
318 REM  B1  BUDGETED ADMINISTRATIVE EXPENSE
320 REM  B2  BUDGETED MANUFACTURING EXPENSE
322 REM  B3  BUDGETED SALES EXPENSE
324 REM  C1  ACTUAL ADMINISTRATIVE EXPENSE
326 REM  C2  ACTUAL MANUFACTURING EXPENSE
328 REM  C3  ACTUAL SALES EXPENSE
330 REM  P   INDEX OF PRESSURE
900 REM ******************************
902 REM *   MAIN ROUTINE             *
904 REM ******************************
906 REM INITIAL MESSAGE
908 GOSUB 1006
910 REM PARAMETERS
912 GOSUB 1106
914 REM PROCESS
916 GOSUB 1206
918 REM FINAL MESSAGE
920 GOSUB 1306
922 IF U$ = "Y" THEN 916
924 PRINT
926 PRINT "END OF PROGRAM"
999 STOP
1000 REM *****************************
1002 REM *   INITIAL MESSAGE         *
1004 REM *****************************
```

```
1006 PRINT
1008 PRINT
1010 PRINT
1012 PRINT "PROGRAM 2-4"
1014 PRINT
1016 PRINT "BEHAVIORAL MODEL OF THE FIRM"
1018 PRINT "WITH MANAGERIAL DECISIONS"
1020 PRINT "REFLECTING PROFIT ASPIRATIONS"
1022 PRINT "AND BUDGET LEVELS WITH RESPECT"
1024 PRINT "ACTUAL LEVELS."
1099 RETURN
1100 REM ******************************
1102 REM *     PARAMETERS              *
1104 REM ******************************
1106 LET P2 = 10000
1108 LET S2 = 200000
1110 LET C1 = 10000
1112 LET C2 = 150000
1114 LET C3 = 30000
1116 LET P = 0
1199 RETURN
1200 REM ******************************
1202 REM *     PROCESS                 *
1204 REM ******************************
1206 LET A = 1.05 * P2
1208 LET S1 = 1.03 * S2 + 10000 * P
1210 LET B1 = C1 - 200 * P
1212 LET B2 = .5 * (1.03 * C2 + .7 * S1)
1214 LET B3 = C3 - 600 * P
1216 LET P1 = S1 - B1 - B2 - B3
1218 LET P = .0001 * (A - P1)
1220 LET S2 = 1.03 * S2 + 10000 * P
1222 LET C1 = B1 + 100 * P
1224 LET C2 = 90000 + .3 * S2 - 500 * P
1226 LET C3 = B3 + 300 * P
1228 LET P2 = S2 - C1 - C2 - C3
1230 PRINT
1232 PRINT "PROFIT ASPIRATION LEVEL",A
1234 PRINT "INDEX OF PRESSURE        ",P
1236 PRINT
1238 PRINT ,"ESTIMATED","ACTUAL"
1240 PRINT "PROFIT",P1,P2
1242 PRINT "SALES",S1,S2
1244 PRINT
1246 PRINT "EXPENSE","BUDGETED","ACTUAL"
1248 PRINT "ADMIN",B1,C1
```

```
1250 PRINT "MANUF",B2,C2
1252 PRINT "SALES",B3,C3
1299 RETURN
1300 REM ******************************
1302 REM *    FINAL MESSAGE            *
1304 REM ******************************
1306 PRINT
1308 PRINT "CONTINUE SIMULATION (Y/N)";
1310 INPUT U$
1312 IF U$ = "Y" THEN 1399
1314 IF U$ = "N" THEN 1399
1316 PRINT
1318 PRINT "INVALID RESPONSE"
1320 GOTO 1306
1399 RETURN
9999 END
```

PROGRAM 2-4

BEHAVIORAL MODEL OF A FIRM
WITH MANAGERIAL DECISIONS
REFLECTING PROFIT ASPIRATIONS
AND BUDGET LEVELS WITH RESPECT
TO ACTUAL LEVELS.

PROFIT ASPIRATION LEVEL   10500
INDEX OF PRESSURE   -.615

	ESTIMATED	ACTUAL
PROFIT	16650	9833.5
SALES	206000	199850

EXPENSE	BUDGETED	ACTUAL
ADMIN	10000	9938.5
MANUF	149350	150263
SALES	30000	29815.5

CONTINUE SIMULATION (Y/N)? Y

PROFIT ASPIRATION LEVEL   10325.2
INDEX OF PRESSURE   -.184572

	ESTIMATED	ACTUAL
PROFIT	12170.9	12535.4
SALES	199696	204000

```
EXPENSE            BUDGETED          ACTUAL
ADMIN             10061.5           10043
MANUF             147279            151292
SALES             30184.5           30129.1

CONTINUE SIMULATION (Y/N)? Y

PROFIT ASPIRATION LEVEL            13162.2
INDEX OF PRESSURE                 -.398066

                  ESTIMATED         ACTUAL
PROFIT            17142.8           13937.7
SALES             208274            206139

EXPENSE           BUDGETED          ACTUAL
ADMIN             10080             10040.2
MANUF             150811            152041
SALES             30239.9           30120.5

CONTINUE SIMULATION (Y/N)? N

END OF PROGRAM
```

Fig. 2-4. Sample results from Program 2-4.

Many problem situations cannot be resolved through considering only one goal. Many plausible performance measures are possible. The goal may be to reduce the cost of an item without damaging its quality. The objective may be to juggle many conflicting goals to arrive at a good compromise.

There are several solution methods for problems involving multiple objectives. One method involves weighting the goals according to relative importance and then optimizing the measures of performance according to their assigned weights.

Another method is to select one goal as the most important. This method optimizes the most important goal subject to minimum performance levels in regard to the other goals. Because of technological innovations, the acceptable levels for the other goals are changed from time to time. If these goals are easily attained, the standards are increased. If they are too difficult to achieve, the standards are lowered. Changing environmental conditions can force changes in the choice of a goal for optimization.

Program 2-5 estimates the revenue, profit, and market share for a product assuming linear demand and cost functions. The results are shown in Fig. 2-5.

Exercise 2-5

1. Determine the price that maximizes revenue using the model illustrated in this section. Determine the price that maximizes profit.

GOAL SEEKING METHODS

Often the purpose of modeling is to optimize some particular performance objective. There are several approaches to optimization. The simplest involves brute force enumeration. The decision maker simply tries all relevant decision settings and chooses the one that optimizes the measure of performance. More efficient schemes involve searching for the optimum setting. If the mathematical properties of the model identify the direction of the optimum value, the method of bisec-

Program 2-5

```
100 REM *******************************
102 REM *     2-5                      *
104 REM *******************************
106 REM   AUTHOR
108 REM       COPYRIGHT 1982
110 REM       BY LAWRENCE MCNITT.
112 REM   PURPOSE
114 REM       ESTIMATE REVENUE, COST, AND
116 REM       PROFIT ASSUMING LINEAR DEMAND
118 REM       AND COST FUNCTIONS.
120 REM   SYSTEM
122 REM       UNIVERSAL SUBSET
124 REM       OF BASIC.
200 REM *******************************
202 REM *   ORGANIZATION               *
204 REM *******************************
206 REM   900   MAIN ROUTINE
208 REM         1000   INITIAL MESSAGE
210 REM         1100   PARAMETERS
212 REM         1200   PROCESS
214 REM         1300   FINAL MESSAGE
300 REM *******************************
302 REM *   VARIABLES                  *
304 REM *******************************
306 REM     U$   USER RESPONSE
308 REM     P    SELLING PRICE
310 REM     P1   LOWER LIMIT FOR PRICE
312 REM     P2   UPPER LIMIT FOR PRICE
314 REM     P3   STEP SIZE FOR PRICE
316 REM     Q    QUANTITY DEMANDED
318 REM     Q1   Y-INTERCEPT FOR DEMAND FUNCTION
320 REM     Q2   SLOPE FOR DEMAND FUNCTION
322 REM     C    TOTAL COST
324 REM     C1   Y-INTERCEPT FOR COST FUNCTION
326 REM     C2   SLOPE FOR COST FUNCTION
328 REM     R    REVENUE
330 REM     G    GROSS PROFIT
332 REM     S    SHARE OF MARKET
334 REM     T    TOTAL INDUSTRY DEMAND
900 REM *******************************
902 REM *   MAIN ROUTINE               *
904 REM *******************************
906 REM INITIAL MESSAGE
908 GOSUB 1006
```

```
910 REM PARAMETERS
912 GOSUB 1106
914 REM PROCESS
916 GOSUB 1206
918 REM FINAL MESSAGE
920 GOSUB 1306
922 IF U$ = "Y" THEN 916
924 PRINT
926 PRINT "END OF PROGRAM"
999 STOP
1000 REM ****************************
1002 REM *    INITIAL MESSAGE       *
1004 REM ****************************
1006 PRINT
1008 PRINT
1010 PRINT
1012 PRINT "PROGRAM 2-5"
1014 PRINT
1016 PRINT "FOR EACH OF A SET OF PRICES,"
1018 PRINT "ESTIMATE DEMAND, REVENUE,"
1020 PRINT "COST, AND PROFIT. BOTH DEMAND"
1022 PRINT "AND COST FUNCTIONS ARE LINEAR."
1099 RETURN
1100 REM ****************************
1102 REM *    PARAMETERS            *
1104 REM ****************************
1106 PRINT
1108 PRINT "DEMAND FUNCTION"
1110 PRINT "Y-INTERCEPT";
1112 INPUT Q1
1114 PRINT "SLOPE        ";
1116 INPUT Q2
1118 PRINT
1120 PRINT "COST FUNCTION"
1122 PRINT "Y-INTERCEPT";
1124 INPUT C1
1126 PRINT "SLOPE        ";
1128 INPUT C2
1130 PRINT
1132 PRINT "TOTAL INDUSTRY DEMAND";
1134 INPUT T
1199 RETURN
1200 REM ****************************
1202 REM *    PROCESS               *
1204 REM ****************************
1206 PRINT
```

```
1208 PRINT "LIMITS FOR PRICES"
1210 PRINT "LOWER LIMIT";
1212 INPUT P1
1214 PRINT "UPPER LIMIT";
1216 INPUT P2
1218 PRINT "STEP SIZE   ";
1220 INPUT P3
1222 PRINT
1224 PRINT "PRICE","REVENUE","PROFIT","MARKET SHARE"
1226 FOR P = P1 TO P2 STEP P3
1228    LET Q = Q1 + Q2 * P
1230    LET C = C1 + C2 * Q
1232    LET R = P * Q
1234    LET G = R - C
1236    LET S = Q / T
1238    PRINT P,R,G,S
1240 NEXT P
1299 RETURN
1300 REM ********************************
1302 REM *     FINAL MESSAGE            *
1304 REM ********************************
1306 PRINT
1308 PRINT "TRY ANOTHER SET OF PRICES (Y/N)";
1310 INPUT U$
1312 IF U$ = "Y" THEN 1399
1314 IF U$ = "N" THEN 1399
1316 PRINT
1318 PRINT "INVALID RESPONSE"
1320 GOTO 1306
1399 RETURN
9999 END
```

tion converges to the solution quite rapidly.

Many simulation schemes involve interaction between the computer model and the people analyzing the model. After analyzing the results of one run, the analyst selects the settings for the next run.

If the methods of determining the next settings are well defined, the rules for adjusting the model can be placed within the simulation model itself. The model then attempts to zero in on the solution automatically. This can save much of the human effort involved in searching for the optimum settings.

Optimizing a function with many variables is much more difficult than optimizing a function with one variable. Brute force enumeration becomes impractical when there are a large number of variables. Search strategies also become much more complex.

The theory and methods of optimization from the field of mathematics give insight into optimization with simulation models. One method involves inspecting the surface of the objective function in the neighborhood of a specific point to determine in which direction to move and how far to move in the search for the best point.

A problem with nonlinear optimization problems is the potential existence of multiple local optima. Each local maximum, for example, corresponds to one of many "mountain tops." The efficient search procedures do not guarantee finding the top of the highest mountain. The mathematical characteristics of a local maximum are the same as those of the global maximum, except for the value, of course. There may be no assurance of finding the global optimum without using brute force enumeration. On the other hand, enumeration may not be computationally feasible.

One variation of the enumeration technique involves selecting values for evaluation at fixed intervals. If the optimum point is known to be within

```
PROGRAM 2-5

FOR EACH OF A SET OF PRICES,
ESTIMATE DEMAND, REVENUE,
COST, AND PROFIT. BOTH DEMAND
AND COST FUNCTIONS ARE LINEAR.

DEMAND FUNCTION
Y-INTERCEPT? 70000
SLOPE       ? -40000

COST FUNCTION
Y-INTERCEPT? 10000
SLOPE       ? .50

TOTAL INDUSTRY DEMAND? 200000

LIMITS FOR PRICES
LOWER LIMIT? .7
UPPER LIMIT? 1.4
STEP SIZE   ? .1

PRICE            REVENUE         PROFIT          MARKET SHARE
 .7               29400          -1600            .21
 .8               30400           1400            .19
 .9               30600           3600            .17
1                 30000           5000            .15
1.1               28600           5600            .13
1.2               26400           5400            .11
1.3               23400           4400            .09
1.4               19600           2600            .07

TRY ANOTHER SET OF PRICES (Y/N)? N

END OF PROGRAM
```

Fig. 2-5. Sample results from Program 2-5.

a small subinterval, that subinterval defines a new range to be searched. This process continues using smaller and smaller subintervals in the search process.

Program 2-6 uses this approach for locating the value of X which maximizes the value of the function. Figure 2-6 shows the results.

A Program for a Function of Four Variables

A firm has two similar products that compete with each other for the same customers. Advertising levels affect the demand for the products. The

Program 2-6

```
100 REM **********************************
102 REM *    2-6                          *
104 REM **********************************
106 REM   AUTHOR
108 REM        COPYRIGHT 1982
110 REM        BY LAWRENCE MCNITT.
112 REM   PURPOSE
114 REM        SEARCH FOR MAXIMUM POINT
116 REM        OF A FUNCTION OF ONE
118 REM        VARIABLE USING ENUMERATION.
120 REM   SYSTEM
122 REM        UNIVERSAL SUBSET
124 REM        OF BASIC.
200 REM **********************************
202 REM *    ORGANIZATION                 *
204 REM **********************************
206 REM   900   MAIN ROUTINE
208 REM         1000   INITIAL MESSAGE
210 REM         1100   LIMITS
212 REM         1200   PROCESS
214 REM              2000   EVALUATE
216 REM         1300   FINAL MESSAGE
300 REM **********************************
302 REM *    VARIABLES                    *
304 REM **********************************
306 REM     U$  USER RESPONSE
308 REM     X   ARGUMENT FOR FUNCTION
310 REM     X1  LOWER LIMIT
312 REM     X2  UPPER LIMIT
314 REM     X3  STEP SIZE
316 REM     F   CURRENT VALUE OF FUNCTION
318 REM     B1  BEST VALUE OF FUNCTION SO FAR
320 REM     B2  VALUE OF X FOR BEST VALUE OF FUNCTION
900 REM **********************************
902 REM *    MAIN ROUTINE                 *
904 REM **********************************
906 REM INITIAL MESSAGE
```

```
908 GOSUB 1006
910 REM LIMITS
912 GOSUB 1106
914 REM PROCESS
916 GOSUB 1206
918 REM FINAL MESSAGE
920 GOSUB 1306
922 IF U$ = "Y" THEN 912
924 PRINT
926 PRINT "END OF PROGRAM"
999 STOP
1000 REM ****************************
1002 REM *    INITIAL MESSAGE       *
1004 REM ****************************
1006 PRINT
1008 PRINT
1010 PRINT
1012 PRINT "PROGRAM 2-6"
1014 PRINT
1016 PRINT "SEARCH BY ENUMERATION FOR"
1018 PRINT "MAXIMUM VALUE OF A FUNCTION"
1020 PRINT "OF ONE VARIABLE."
1099 RETURN
1100 REM ****************************
1102 REM *    PARAMETERS            *
1104 REM ****************************
1106 PRINT
1108 PRINT "LIMITS FOR ARGUMENT X"
1110 PRINT "LOWER LIMIT";
1112 INPUT X1
1114 PRINT "UPPER LIMIT";
1116 INPUT X2
1118 PRINT "STEP SIZE   ";
1120 INPUT X3
1122 PRINT
1124 PRINT "DISPLAY TABLE OF RESULTS (Y/N)";
1126 INPUT U$
1128 IF U$ = "Y" THEN 1199
1130 IF U$ = "N" THEN 1199
1132 PRINT
1134 PRINT "INVALID RESPONSE"
1136 GOTO 1122
1199 RETURN
1200 REM ****************************
1202 REM *    PROCESS               *
1204 REM ****************************
```

```
1206 LET B1 = -10E30
1208 IF U$ = "N" THEN 1214
1210 PRINT
1212 PRINT "VALUE OF X","VALUE OF FUNCTION"
1214 FOR X = X1 TO X2 STEP X3
1216    REM FUNCTION
1218    GOSUB 2006
1220    IF F <= B1 THEN 1226
1222    LET B1 = F
1224    LET B2 = X
1226    IF U$ = "N" THEN 1230
1228    PRINT X,F
1230 NEXT X
1232 PRINT
1234 PRINT "OPTIMUM VALUE FOR"
1236 PRINT "X",B2
1238 PRINT "FUNCTION",B1
1299 RETURN
1300 REM ******************************
1302 REM *    FINAL MESSAGE           *
1304 REM ******************************
1306 PRINT
1308 PRINT "TRY ANOTHER SET OF LIMITS (Y/N)";
1310 INPUT U$
1312 IF U$ = "Y" THEN 1399
1314 IF U$ = "N" THEN 1399
1316 PRINT
1318 PRINT "INVALID RESPONSE"
1320 GOTO 1306
1399 RETURN
2000 REM ******************************
2002 REM *    FUNCTION                *
2004 REM ******************************
2006 LET R = 240 * SQR(X)
2008 LET C = 1000 + 2.5 * X [ .95
2010 LET F = R - C
2099 RETURN
9999 END
```

firm must select a price and an advertising level for each of the two products.

The demand for each product is a function of its price, the price of the other product, and the advertising level. A relatively low price on one product will take sales away from the other.

The section starting with line number 2000 in Program 2-7 estimates demand as a function of the price and advertising levels. From the demand level, it computes revenues, costs, and profits for the individual products as well as the total profit for both products together.

PROGRAM 2-6

SEARCH BY ENUMERATION FOR
MAXIMUM VALUE OF A FUNCTION
OF ONE VARIABLE.

LIMITS FOR ARGUMENT X
LOWER LIMIT? 4000
UPPER LIMIT? 10000
STEP SIZE   ? 1000

DISPLAY TABLE OF RESULTS (Y/N)? Y

VALUE OF X	VALUE OF FUNCTION
4000	7573.57
5000	7805.46
6000	7881.12
7000	7839.41
8000	7705.53
9000	7496.88
1000	7226.07

OPTIMUM VALUE FOR
X   6000
FUNCTION   7881.12

TRY ANOTHER SET OF LIMITS (Y/N)? Y

LIMITS FOR ARGUMENT X
LOWER LIMIT? 5000
UPPER LIMIT? 7000
STEP SIZE   ? 100

DISPLAY TABLE OF RESULTS (Y/N)? N

OPTIMUM VALUE FOR
X   6100
FUNCTION   7881.73

TRY ANOTHER SET OF LIMITS (Y/N)? Y

LIMITS FOR ARGUMENT X
LOWER LIMIT? 6000
UPPER LIMIT? 6200
STEP SIZE   ? 1

```
DISPLAY TABLE OF RESULTS (Y/N)? N

OPTIMUM VALUE FOR
X              6103
FUNCTION       7881.73

TRY ANOTHER SET OF LIMITS (Y/N)? N

END OF PROGRAM
```

Fig. 2-6. Sample results from Program 2-6.

The equation

$$D1 = (50*P2 - 20*P1 - 1000)*(100)/P1)**2$$

gives the estimated demand for product 1 assuming an advertising level of 100,000. The equation

$$D1 = D1 + .5 * LOG(A1 / 100000)$$

adjusts the demand to reflect the advertising effect.

The equation

$$C1 = 20000 + 150 * D1 ** .81$$

estimates cost as a function of quantity and includes an economy of the scale factor. Similar equations exist for the second product.

Program 2-7 is an example of a program that performs an analysis using several decision variables. Figure 2-7 shows the results.

Program 2-7

```
100 REM ********************************
102 REM *    2-7                       *
104 REM ********************************
106 REM   AUTHOR
108 REM       COPYRIGHT 1982
110 REM       BY LAWRENCE MCNITT.
112 REM   PURPOSE
114 REM       SEARCH FOR MAXIMUM POINT
116 REM       OF A FUNCTION OF FOUR
118 REM       VARIABLES USING ENUMERATION.
120 REM   SYSTEM
122 REM       UNIVERSAL SUBSET
124 REM       OF BASIC.
200 REM ********************************
202 REM *    ORGANIZATION              *
204 REM ********************************
206 REM   900   MAIN ROUTINE
208 REM         1000   INITIAL MESSAGE
210 REM         1100   LIMITS
212 REM         1200   PROCESS
214 REM               2000   EVALUATE
```

```
216 REM          1300  FINAL MESSAGE
300 REM ******************************
302 REM *    VARIABLES               *
304 REM ******************************
306 REM    U$   USER RESPONSE
308 REM    P1   PRICE FOR PRODUCT 1
310 REM    P2   PRICE FOR PRODUCT 2
312 REM    A1   ADVERTISING FOR PRODUCT 1
314 REM    A2   ADVERTISING FOR PRODUCT 2
316 REM    D1   DEMAND FOR PRODUCT 1
318 REM    D2   DEMAND FOR PRODUCT 2
320 REM    R1   REVENUE FOR PRODUCT 1
322 REM    R2   REVENUE FOR PRODUCT 2
324 REM    C1   COST FOR PRODUCT 1
326 REM    C2   COST FOR PRODUCT 2
328 REM    G1   GROSS PROFIT FOR PRODUCT 1
330 REM    G2   GROSS PROFIT FOR PRODUCT 2
332 REM    G    TOTAL GROSS PROFIT
334 REM    B    BEST GROSS PROFIT FOUND SO FAR
336 REM    B1   BEST PRICE FOR PRODUCT 1
338 REM    B2   BEST PRICE FOR PRODUCT 2
340 REM    B3   BEST ADVERTISING FOR PRODUCT 1
342 REM    B4   BEST ADVERTISING FOR PRODUCT 2
344 REM    L1   LOWER LIMIT PRICE FOR PRODUCT 1
346 REM    L2   LOWER LIMIT PRICE FOR PRODUCT 2
348 REM    L3   LOWER LIMIT ADVERTISING FOR PRODUCT 1
350 REM    L4   LOWER LIMIT ADVERTISING FOR PRODUCT 2
352 REM    M1   UPPER LIMIT PRICE FOR PRODUCT 1
354 REM    M2   UPPER LIMIT PRICE FOR PRODUCT 2
356 REM    M3   UPPER LIMIT ADVERTISING FOR PRODUCT 1
358 REM    M4   UPPER LIMIT ADVERTISING FOR PRODUCT 2
360 REM    S1   STEP SIZE FOR PRICE FOR PRODUCT 1
362 REM    S2   STEP SIZE FOR PRICE FOR PRODUCT 2
364 REM    S3   STEP SIZE FOR ADVERTISING FOR PRODUCT 1
366 REM    S4   STEP SIZE FOR ADVERTISING FOR PRODUCT 2
900 REM ******************************
902 REM *    MAIN ROUTINE             *
904 REM ******************************
906 REM INITIAL MESSAGE
908 GOSUB 1006
910 REM LIMITS
912 GOSUB 1106
914 REM PROCESS
916 GOSUB 1206
918 REM FINAL MESSAGE
920 GOSUB 1306
```

```
922 IF U$ = "Y" THEN 912
924 PRINT
926 PRINT "END OF PROGRAM"
999 STOP
1000 REM *****************************
1002 REM *    INITIAL MESSAGE        *
1004 REM *****************************
1006 PRINT
1008 PRINT
1010 PRINT
1012 PRINT "PROGRAM 2-7"
1014 PRINT
1016 PRINT "SEARCH BY ENUMERATION FOR"
1018 PRINT "MAXIMUM VALUE OF A FUNCTION"
1020 PRINT "OF FOUR VARIABLES."
1099 RETURN
1100 REM *****************************
1102 REM *    PARAMETERS             *
1104 REM *****************************
1106 PRINT
1108 PRINT "LIMITS FOR PRICE FOR PRODUCT 1"
1110 PRINT "LOWER LIMIT";
1112 INPUT L1
1114 PRINT "UPPER LIMIT";
1116 INPUT M1
1118 PRINT "STEP SIZE   ";
1120 INPUT S1
1122 PRINT
1124 PRINT "LIMITS FOR PRICE FOR PRODUCT 2"
1126 PRINT "LOWER LIMIT";
1128 INPUT L2
1130 PRINT "UPPER LIMIT";
1132 INPUT M2
1134 PRINT "STEP SIZE   ";
1136 INPUT S2
1138 PRINT
1140 PRINT "LIMITS FOR ADVERTISING FOR PRODUCT 1"
1142 PRINT "LOWER LIMIT";
1144 INPUT L3
1146 PRINT "UPPER LIMIT";
1148 INPUT M3
1150 PRINT "STEP SIZE   ";
1152 INPUT S3
1154 PRINT
1156 PRINT "LIMITS FOR ADVERTISING FOR PRODUCT 2"
1158 PRINT "LOWER LIMIT";
```

```
1160 INPUT L4
1164 PRINT "UPPER LIMIT";
1166 INPUT M4
1168 PRINT "STEP SIZE   ";
1170 INPUT S4
1199 RETURN
1200 REM ******************************
1202 REM *    PROCESS                 *
1204 REM ******************************
1206 LET B = -10E30
1208 FOR P1 = L1 TO M1 STEP S1
1210    FOR P2 = L2 TO M2 STEP S2
1212      FOR A1 = L3 TO M3 STEP S3
1214        FOR A2 = L4 TO M4 STEP S4
1216          REM FUNCTION
1218          GOSUB 2006
1220          IF G <= B THEN 1232
1222          LET B = G
1224          LET B1 = P1
1226          LET B2 = P2
1228          LET B3 = A1
1230          LET B4 = A2
1232        NEXT A2
1234      NEXT A1
1236    NEXT P2
1238 NEXT P1
1240 PRINT
1242 PRINT "BEST RESULT SO FAR"
1244 PRINT "TOTAL PROFIT",B
1246 LET P1 = B1
1248 LET P2 = B2
1250 LET A1 = B3
1252 LET A2 = B4
1254 REM FUNCTION
1256 GOSUB 2006
1258 PRINT
1260 PRINT ,"PRODUCT 1","PRODUCT 2"
1262 PRINT "PRICE",P1,P2
1264 PRINT "ADVERTISING",A1,A2
1266 PRINT "DEMAND",D1,D2
1268 PRINT
1270 PRINT "REVENUE",R1,R2
1272 PRINT "COST",C1,C2
1274 PRINT "PROFIT",G1,G2
1299 RETURN
1300 REM ******************************
```

```
1302 REM *    FINAL MESSAGE           *
1304 REM ******************************
1306 PRINT
1308 PRINT "TRY ANOTHER SET OF LIMITS (Y/N)";
1310 INPUT U$
1312 IF U$ = "Y" THEN 1399
1314 IF U$ = "N" THEN 1399
1316 PRINT
1318 PRINT "INVALID RESPONSE"
1320 GOTO 1306
1399 RETURN
2000 REM ******************************
2002 REM *    FUNCTION               *
2004 REM ******************************
2006 LET D1 = 50 * P2 - 20 * P1 - 1000
2007 LET D1 = D1 * (100 / P1) [ 2
2008 LET D2 = 100 * P1 - 60 * P2 - 500
2009 LET D2 = D2 * (100 / P2) [ 2
2010 LET D1 = D1 + .5 * D1 * LOG(A1 / 100000)
2012 LET D2 = D2 + .5 * D2 * LOG(A2 / 100000)
2013 IF D1 < 0 THEN LET D1 = 1
2014 LET R1 = P1 * D1
2015 IF D2 < 0 THEN LET D2 = 1
2016 LET R2 = P2 * D2
2018 LET C1 = 20000 + 150 * D1 [ .81
2020 LET C2 = 50000 + 300 * D2 [ .84
2022 LET G1 = R1 - A1 - C1
2024 LET G2 = R2 - A2 - C2
2026 LET G = G1 + G2
2099 RETURN
9999 END
```

```
PROGRAM 2-7

SEARCH BY ENUMERATION FOR
MAXIMUM VALUE OF A FUNCTION
OF FOUR VARIABLES.

LIMITS FOR PRICE FOR PRODUCT 1
LOWER LIMIT? 100
UPPER LIMIT? 150
STEP SIZE   ? 50

LIMITS FOR PRICE FOR PRODUCT 2
```

```
LOWER LIMIT? 100
UPPER LIMIT? 150
STEP SIZE  ? 50

LIMITS FOR ADVERTISING FOR PRODUCT 1
LOWER LIMIT? 50000
UPPER LIMIT? 150000
STEP SIZE  ? 50000

LIMITS FOR ADVERTISING FOR PRODUCT 2
LOWER LIMIT? 50000
UPPER LIMIT? 150000
STEP SIZE  ? 50000

BEST RESULT SO FAR
TOTAL PROFIT       114831

                  PRODUCT 1        PRODUCT 2
PRICE             100              150
ADVERTISING       150000           50000
DEMAND            5412.3           145.206

REVENUE           541230           21780.9
COST              178537           69642.1
PROFIT            212693           -97861.2

TRY ANOTHER SET OF LIMITS (Y/N)? Y

LIMITS FOR PRICE FOR PRODUCT 1
LOWER LIMIT? 150
UPPER LIMIT? 200
STEP SIZE  ? 50

LIMITS FOR PRICE FOR PRODUCT 2
LOWER LIMIT? 150
UPPER LIMIT? 200
STEP SIZE  ? 50

LIMITS FOR ADVERTISING FOR PRODUCT 1
LOWER LIMIT? 50000
UPPER LIMIT? 150000
STEP SIZE  ? 50000

LIMITS FOR ADVERTISING FOR PRODUCT 2
LOWER LIMIT? 50000
UPPER LIMIT? 150000
```

```
STEP SIZE   ? 50000

BEST RESULT SO FAR
TOTAL PROFIT       210959

                   PRODUCT 1        PRODUCT 2
PRICE              200              150
ADVERTISING        50000            150000
DEMAND             408.395          5612.75

REVENUE            81678.3          841913
COST               39586.3          473086
PROFIT             -7867.95         218827

TRY ANOTHER SET OF LIMITS (Y/N)? N

END OF PROGRAM
```

Fig. 2-7. Sample results from Program 2-7.

Simulation modeling requires care. Models involving the pricing and advertising levels for two products may be valid for only a limited range of prices and advertising levels. The model should be validated by comparing its behavior with that of the real system. Extrapolating a model beyond the limits for which its validity is proven is unwise.

Exercise 2-6

1. Modify Listing 2-6 to include nonlinear functions. Search one of those functions for the optimum value of X.
2. Continue the search using Listing 2-7 to find the best combination of product prices and advertising levels.

Chapter 3

Random Events

Many simulation models incorporate methods for representing random events. These random events involve factors outside the control of the decision maker and outside the sphere of measurement. Physics and engineering models of well-known phenomena are quite accurate. Many models, however, do not give an exact description of the actual system behavior. The random element represents the degree of uncertainty.

This chapter discusses methods of representing random values using pseudorandom number generators. Uniform random numbers form the backbone of random number generation. Statistical tests help in validating the randomness of a series of random numbers.

STOCHASTIC PROCESSES

A *stochastic process* produces chance outcomes. The term stochastic is a technical term for probabilistic. As far as the model is concerned, the values are uncertain. The computer generates the random values as needed. This generation scheme is transparent to the policy rules controlling the behavior of the model. These rules are an important part of the model. For example, one inventory ordering policy is to choose an order quantity that brings the inventory level up to 110 percent of the demand for the last period. Program 3-1 models this simple inventory ordering policy. Figure 3-1 shows the results.

The model starts at an initial state and passes through transient stages for a few periods until it stabilizes. A change in demand destabilizes the system resulting in a period of transition before the model behavior settles down to a steady rate.

A change in demand results in a greater change in order quantity. The ordering policy in the listing is particularly susceptible to this type of amplification. Amplification is a problem within the entire distribution chain. Products pass through a distribution chain from production to the warehouse, to the distribution center, to the wholesaler, to the retailer, and finally to the consumer. Demand ripples back from the consumer to the producer.

If aggregate demand is stable and consumers

Program 3-1

```
100 REM *********************************
102 REM *    3-1                        *
104 REM *********************************
106 REM   AUTHOR
108 REM       COPYRIGHT 1982
110 REM        BY LAWRENCE MCNITT.
112 REM   PURPOSE
114 REM       OBSERVE BEHAVIOR OF SYSTEM
116 REM        WITH VARIABLE INPUT OVER TIME.
118 REM   SYSTEM
120 REM       UNIVERSAL SUBSET
122 REM        OF BASIC.
200 REM *********************************
202 REM *    ORGANIZATION               *
204 REM *********************************
206 REM   900   MAIN ROUTINE
208 REM         1000   INITIAL MESSAGE
210 REM         1100   INITIAL CONDITIONS
212 REM         1200   PROCESS
214 REM         1300   FINAL MESSAGE
300 REM *********************************
302 REM *    VARIABLES                  *
304 REM *********************************
306 REM    U$   USER RESPONSE
308 REM    D    DEMAND
310 REM    R    FRACTION OF DEMAND FOR FORECAST
312 REM    F    FORECAST
314 REM    V    INVENTORY LEVEL
316 REM    Q    ORDER QUANTITY
318 REM    N    NUMBER OF PERIODS
320 REM    I    COUNTER
322 REM    S    UNITS SOLD
324 REM    L    LOST SALES
900 REM *********************************
902 REM *    MAIN.ROUTINE               *
904 REM *********************************
906 REM INITIAL MESSAGE
908 GOSUB 1006
910 REM INITIAL CONDITIONS
912 GOSUB 1106
914 REM PROCESS
916 GOSUB 1206
918 REM FINAL MESSAGE
920 GOSUB 1306
```

```
922 IF U$ = "Y" THEN 912
924 PRINT
926 PRINT "END OF PROGRAM"
999 STOP
1000 REM *****************************
1002 REM *    INITIAL MESSAGE        *
1004 REM *****************************
1006 PRINT
1008 PRINT
1010 PRINT
1012 PRINT "PROGRAM 3-1"
1014 PRINT
1016 PRINT "EVALUATE INVENTORY ORDERING POLICY"
1018 PRINT "THAT SELECTS THE ORDER QUANTITY"
1020 PRINT "NEEDED TO RAISE THE INVENTORY LEVEL"
1022 PRINT "TO A STATED FRACTION ABOVE THE DEMAND"
1024 PRINT "FOR THE PREVIOUS PERIOD."
1099 RETURN
1100 REM ******************************
1102 REM *    INITIAL CONDITIONS      *
1104 REM ******************************
1106 PRINT
1108 PRINT "MULTIPLIER GIVING THE INVENTORY"
1110 PRINT "LEVEL NEEDED FOR THE FOLLOWING"
1112 PRINT "PERIOD FROM THE CURRENT DEMAND";
1114 INPUT R
1116 PRINT
1118 PRINT "BEGINNING","DEMAND","LOST","ORDER"
1120 PRINT "INVENTORY",,"SALES","QUANTITY"
1199 RETURN
1200 REM *******************************
1202 REM *    PROCESS                 *
1204 REM *******************************
1206 READ V
1208 READ N
1210 FOR I = 1 TO N
1212     READ D
1214     LET S = D
1216     LET L = 0
1218     IF S <= V THEN 1224
1220     LET S = V
1222     LET L = D - V
1224     LET Q = R * D - V + S
1226     PRINT V,D,L,Q
1228     LET V = V - S + Q
1230 NEXT I
```

```
1299 RETURN
1300 REM *****************************
1302 REM *    FINAL MESSAGE          *
1304 REM *****************************
1306 PRINT
1308 PRINT "TRY ANOTHER MULTIPLIER (Y/N)";
1310 INPUT U$
1312 IF U$ = "Y" THEN 1322
1314 IF U$ = "N" THEN 1399
1316 PRINT
1318 PRINT "INVALID RESPONSE"
1320 GOTO 1306
1322 RESTORE
1399 RETURN
8000 REM *****************************
8002 REM *    INITIAL INVENTORY LEVEL *
8004 REM *    NUMBER OF PERIODS        *
8006 REM *    DEMAND FOR PERIOD 1      *
8008 REM *    DEMAND FOR PERIOD 2      *
8010 REM *    ETC.                     *
8012 REM *    DEMAND FOR PERIOD N      *
8014 REM *****************************
9000 DATA 120
9002 DATA 10
9004 DATA 100,100,120,120,120
9006 DATA 100,100,100,120,120
9999 END
```

PROGRAM 3-1

EVALUATE THE INVENTORY ORDERING POLICY
THAT SELECTS THE ORDER QUANTITY
NEEDED TO RAISE THE INVENTORY LEVEL
TO A STATED FRACTION ABOVE THE DEMAND
FOR THE PREVIOUS PERIOD.

MULTIPLIER GIVING THE INVENTORY
LEVEL NEEDED FOR THE FOLLOWING
PERIOD FROM THE CURRENT DEMAND? 1.1

BEGINNING INVENTORY	DEMAND	LOST SALES	ORDER QUANTITY
120	100	0	90
110	100	0	100

```
       110              120              10              132
       132              120               0              120
       132              120               0              120
       132              100               0               78
       110              100               0              100
       110              100               0              100
       110              120              10              132
       132              120               0              120

 TRY ANOTHER MULTIPLIER (Y/N)? Y

 MULTIPLIER GIVING THE INVENTORY
 LEVEL NEEDED FOR THE FOLLOWING
 PERIOD FROM THE CURRENT DEMAND? 1.2

 BEGINNING          DEMAND           LOST            ORDER
 INVENTORY                           SALES           QUANTITY
       120              100               0              100
       120              100               0              100
       120              120               0              144
       144              120               0              120
       144              120               0              120
       144              100               0               76
       120              100               0              100
       120              100               0              100
       120              120               0              144
       144              120               0              120

 TRY ANOTHER MULTIPLIER (Y/N)? N

 END OF PROGRAM
```

Fig. 3-1. Sample results from Program 3-1.

act independently, the aggregate demand for the product remains relatively stable. If economic conditions bring changes in aggregate demand on the consumer level, these swings may be amplified on each level as they pass through the distribution chain.

Exercise 3-1

1. Modify the model of this section to include a profit of $12.75 for each unit sold, a holding cost per period of $2.30 for each item held in inventory until the next period, and a stockout cost of $8.40 for each unit of lost sales. Determine the optimum multiplier to use in order to maximize the net income computed as gross profit less inventory holding cost and stockout cost. Use the demand levels given in the model.

UNIFORM RANDOM NUMBERS

Uniform random numbers form the backbone of random number generation. Each possible value is equally likely. There must be no discernible pattern in a sequence of uniform random numbers. Because uniform random numbers represent probabilistic phenomena, they are often represented as fractional numbers (probabilities) within the range from zero to one.

If a certain event has a .25 probability, then a random number within the range 0 to .25 can represent that event. Suppose one of the unique events A, B, and C can occur with probabilities .2, .5, and .3, respectively. A random number within the interval (0– .2) can represent event A. A random number within the interval (.2– .7) can represent event B. A random number within the interval (.7– 1) can represent event C. The probability that any given random number falls exactly on any of the boundaries, .200000 . . ., for example, is essentially zero.

Pseudorandom Number Generators

Pseudorandom numbers result from a mechanical or programmed process. Even though the process generating the next random number from the current random number is known, the resulting pseudorandom numbers exhibit the properties of randomness to the model.

Pseudorandom number generators will eventually begin to cycle. The pseudorandom numbers may be biased in that they give preference to some subsets of the intended range or exhibit a nonrandom pattern. The essential question is whether or not the pseudorandom numbers generated are suitable for the simulation model and its analysis. There are numerous tests for nonrandomness.

BASIC translators include the built-in function RND to generate uniform pseudorandom numbers. The specific use of this function varies from system to system. Some systems do not require an argument with the RND function. Other systems use an argument to specify desired properties of the random number or a starting seed for the random number generation.

The random number seed determines the starting point for the sequence of pseudorandom numbers. For certain experiments, results are better if the simulation model uses the same sequence of random numbers for each run. Other experiments require a different sequence of random numbers for each replication of the experiment for a given setting.

A special command, random or randomize is available with many BASIC systems to provide a randomly generated seed for the random number sequence. This may involve reading the last few digits of the internal clock.

Program 3-2 uses the RND function to generate a sequence of pseudorandom numbers. Figure 3-2 shows the results.

One method for generating pseudorandom

Program 3-2

```
100 REM *******************************
102 REM *   3-2                        *
104 REM *******************************
106 REM   AUTHOR
108 REM       COPYRIGHT 1982
110 REM       BY LAWRENCE MCNITT.
112 REM   PURPOSE
114 REM       GENERATE RANDOM NUMBERS
116 REM       USING BUILT-IN FUNCTION.
118 REM   SYSTEM
120 REM       UNIVERSAL SUBSET
122 REM       OF BASIC.
200 REM *******************************
202 REM *   ORGANIZATION               *
```

```
204 REM *******************************
206 REM   900   MAIN ROUTINE
208 REM         1000   INITIAL MESSAGE
210 REM         1100   INITIAL CONDITIONS
212 REM         1200   PROCESS
214 REM         1300   FINAL MESSAGE
300 REM *******************************
302 REM *   VARIABLES                 *
304 REM *******************************
306 REM   U$   USER RESPONSE
308 REM   N    NUMBER OF RANDOM NUMBERS
310 REM   I    COUNTER
312 REM   R    RANDOM NUMBER
900 REM *******************************
902 REM *   MAIN ROUTINE              *
904 REM *******************************
906 REM INITIAL MESSAGE
908 GOSUB 1006
910 REM INITIAL CONDITIONS
912 GOSUB 1106
914 REM PROCESS
916 GOSUB 1206
918 REM FINAL MESSAGE
920 GOSUB 1306
922 IF U$ = "Y" THEN 912
924 PRINT
926 PRINT "END OF PROGRAM"
999 STOP
1000 REM *****************************
1002 REM *    INITIAL MESSAGE        *
1004 REM *****************************
1006 PRINT
1008 PRINT
1010 PRINT
1012 PRINT "PROGRAM 3-2"
1014 PRINT
1016 PRINT "GENERATE A SERIES OF UNIFORM"
1018 PRINT "RANDOM NUMBERS USING THE"
1020 PRINT "BUILT-IN FUNCTION."
1099 RETURN
1100 REM *****************************
1102 REM *    INITIAL CONDITIONS     *
1104 REM *****************************
1106 PRINT
1108 PRINT "NUMBER OF RANDOM NUMBERS";
1110 INPUT N
```

```
1112 PRINT
1114 PRINT "INDEX","RANDOM NUMBER"
1199 RETURN
1200 REM *******************************
1202 REM *    PROCESS                  *
1204 REM *******************************
1206 FOR I = 1 TO N
1208    LET R = RND(0)
1210    PRINT I,R
1212 NEXT I
1299 RETURN
1300 REM *******************************
1302 REM *    FINAL MESSAGE            *
1304 REM *******************************
1306 PRINT
1308 PRINT "TRY ANOTHER SET (Y/N)";
1310 INPUT U$
1312 IF U$ = "Y" THEN 1399
1314 IF U$ = "N" THEN 1399
1316 PRINT
1318 PRINT "INVALID RESPONSE"
1320 GOTO 1306
1399 RETURN
9999 END
```

numbers involves multiplying the current random number by a constant to obtain the next random number. The best approach is to perform the multiplication with binary integers keeping only part of the product. For example, the product of two 32-bit integers contains 64 bits. The righthand or middle 32 bits can constitute the result. This method works well in machine language but not for most higher-level languages such as BASIC.

A similar approach is possible with BASIC. The randomization will involve only 24 bits of precision because the standard BASIC variable is in scientific notation form consisting of a mantissa and an exponent. The randomization involves the mantissa (fraction) portion.

Program 3-3 uses a subroutine to generate the next random number from the current random number. Figure 3-3 shows the results.

Exercise 3-2

1. Use the built-in RND function to generate twenty uniform random numbers. Try the program with and without the initial randomization of the seed. Read the instructions for the RND function found in your BASIC language reference manual and try the options that are available.

STATISTICAL TESTS

There are a number of statistical tests that can be used to determine whether or not a set of pseudorandom numbers are adequately random for a given purpose. These tests include the frequency test and the runs test.

The chi square test for goodness of fit tests whether the observed frequencies deviate significantly from the expected frequencies. For uniform random numbers, numbers from subintervals of equal width should be produced at the same relative frequency. Fifty percent of the random numbers should fall in the interval $0-.5$ and fifty percent in the interval $.5-1$. Because of sampling error, the

```
PROGRAM 3-2

GENERATE A SERIES OF UNIFORM
RANDOM NUMBERS USING THE
BUILT-IN FUNCTION.

NUMBER OF RANDOM NUMBERS? 10

INDEX           RANDOM NUMBER
1               .221245
2               .713147
3               .0254784
4               .403587
5               .771907
6               .0810247
7               .992322
8               .587953
9               .437448
10              .40596

TRY ANOTHER SET (Y/N)? N

END OF PROGRAM
```

Fig. 3-2. Sample results from Program 3-2.

observed number will not be exactly fifty percent. If the interval 0−1 contains ten subintervals 0−.1, .1−.2, etc., ten percent should fall in each subinterval subject, of course, to sampling error. The chi square test of goodness of fit tests whether or not the observed deviation from what is expected is too great to attribute to sampling error.

A standard statistics textbook will describe the chi square test of goodness of fit and how to use it. The formula

$$E = N / K$$

gives the expected frequency for each of K subintervals. The variable N is the number of random numbers involved in the test. If $F(i)$ is the observed frequency for the subinterval i, the formula

$$C = Sum((F(i) - E)**2) / (E)$$

gives the chi square value for the test. There are k-1 degrees of freedom.

Program 3-4 is used to test the frequencies for one hundred numbers using two subintervals and then four hundred numbers using ten subintervals. Figure 3-4 shows the results.

Program 3-3

```
100 REM ******************************
102 REM *    3-3                     *
104 REM ******************************
106 REM   AUTHOR
108 REM       COPYRIGHT 1982
110 REM       BY LAWRENCE MCNITT.
112 REM   PURPOSE
114 REM       GENERATE RANDOM NUMBERS
116 REM       USING SPECIAL SUBROUTINE.
118 REM   SYSTEM
120 REM       UNIVERSAL SUBSET
122 REM       OF BASIC.
200 REM ******************************
202 REM *    ORGANIZATION            *
204 REM ******************************
206 REM   900   MAIN ROUTINE
208 REM         1000   INITIAL MESSAGE
```

```
210 REM          1100   INITIAL CONDITIONS
212 REM          1200   PROCESS
214 REM                   2000   RANDOM NUMBER
216 REM          1300   FINAL MESSAGE
300 REM *****************************
302 REM *    VARIABLES               *
304 REM *****************************
306 REM    U$   USER RESPONSE
308 REM    N    NUMBER OF RANDOM NUMBERS
310 REM    I    COUNTER
312 REM    R    RANDOM NUMBER
900 REM *****************************
902 REM *    MAIN ROUTINE            *
904 REM *****************************
906 REM INITIAL MESSAGE
908 GOSUB 1006
910 REM INITIAL CONDITIONS
912 GOSUB 1106
914 REM PROCESS
916 GOSUB 1206
918 REM FINAL MESSAGE
920 GOSUB 1306
922 IF U$ = "Y" THEN 912
924 PRINT
926 PRINT "END OF PROGRAM"
999 STOP
1000 REM *****************************
1002 REM *     INITIAL MESSAGE        *
1004 REM *****************************
1006 PRINT
1008 PRINT
1010 PRINT
1012 PRINT "PROGRAM  3-3"
1014 PRINT
1016 PRINT "GENERATE A SERIES OF UNIFORM"
1018 PRINT "RANDOM NUMBERS USING A"
1020 PRINT "SPECIAL SUBROUTINE."
1022 LET R = .355429
1099 RETURN
1100 REM *****************************
1102 REM *     INITIAL CONDITIONS      *
1104 REM *****************************
1106 PRINT
1108 PRINT "NUMBER OF RANDOM NUMBERS";
1110 INPUT N
1112 PRINT
```

```
1114 PRINT "INDEX","RANDOM NUMBER"
1199 RETURN
1200 REM ******************************
1202 REM *      PROCESS                *
1204 REM ******************************
1206 FOR I = 1 TO N
1208     REM RANDOM NUMBER
1210     GOSUB 2006
1212     PRINT I,R
1214 NEXT I
1299 RETURN
1300 REM ******************************
1302 REM *      FINAL MESSAGE          *
1304 REM ******************************
1306 PRINT
1308 PRINT "TRY ANOTHER SET (Y/N)";
1310 INPUT U$
1312 IF U$ = "Y" THEN 1399
1314 IF U$ = "N" THEN 1399
1316 PRINT
1318 PRINT "INVALID RESPONSE"
1320 GOTO 1306
1399 RETURN
2000 REM ******************************
2002 REM *      RANDOM NUMBER          *
2004 REM ******************************
2006 LET R = 124.321 * R
2008 LET R = R - INT(R)
2099 RETURN
9999 END
```

Runs Tests

The simple frequency test will not show patterns in a sequence of random numbers. The runs test is capable of showing nonrandom patterns. A pattern consists of a repeated cycling of values or their properties. A sequence of three increasing values is a run of size three. A decreasing sequence of three in a row is also a run of size three.

For a set of N random numbers, the formula

$$(2N - 1) / 3$$

gives the expected number of runs of all sizes. The formula

$$(2 * (k*k+3*k+1)* \\ N - (k*k*k+3*k*k-k-4)) / ((k+3)!)$$

gives the expected number of runs of size k for k less than N−1. The formula

$$2 / N!$$

gives the expected number of runs of length N−1.

Program 3-5 carries out the runs test on a sequence of pseudorandom numbers. Figure 3-5 shows the results.

Exercise 3-3

1. Use the frequency test for the pseudorandom

79

```
PROGRAM 3-3

GENERATE A SERIES OF UNIFORM
RANDOM NUMBERS USING A
SPECIAL SUBROUTINE.

NUMBER OF RANDOM NUMBERS? 5

INDEX           RANDOM NUMBER
 1               .187286
 2               .28363
 3               .261211
 4               .47406
 5               .935619


TRY ANOTHER SET (Y/N)? N

END OF PROGRAM
```

Fig. 3-3. Sample results from Program 3-3.

numbers generated by the RND function.
2. Use the runs test to test for patterns in the pseudorandom numbers generated by the RND function.

SAMPLINGS FOR USE IN SIMULATIONS

A population is the set of all possible observations of interest. Probability distributions describe the characteristics of the populations. Simulated sampling from the population involves random values selected from the probability distribution describing that population.

The most common probability distributions include the binomial, exponential, and normal. There are a host of other probability distributions available to describe populations.

The Normal Distribution

The normal distribution is the most important single distribution in statistics and probability

Program 3-4

```
100 REM ******************************
102 REM *    3-4                     *
104 REM ******************************
106 REM   AUTHOR
108 REM       COPYRIGHT 1982
110 REM        BY LAWRENCE MCNITT.
112 REM   PURPOSE
114 REM       CHI SQUARE FREQUENCY TEST
116 REM       FOR UNIFORM RANDOM NUMBERS.
118 REM   SYSTEM
120 REM       UNIVERSAL SUBSET
122 REM       OF BASIC.
200 REM ******************************
202 REM *    ORGANIZATION            *
204 REM ******************************
206 REM   900   MAIN ROUTINE
208 REM         1000  INITIAL MESSAGE
210 REM         1100  INITIALIZE
212 REM         1200  PROCESS
214 REM         1300  OUTPUT
216 REM         1400  FINAL MESSAGE
300 REM ******************************
302 REM *    VARIABLES               *
```

```
304 REM ********************************
306 REM    F(100)    FREQUENCIES
308 REM    U$    USER RESPONSE
310 REM    N     NUMBER OF RANDOM NUMBERS
312 REM    I     COUNTER
314 REM    K     CATEGORY
316 REM    R     RANDOM NUMBER
318 REM    E     EXPECTED FREQUENCY
320 REM    C     CHI SQUARE VALUE
322 REM    K1    NUMBER OF CATEGORIES
324 REM    D     DIFFERENCE BETWEEN OBSERVED AND EXPECTED
900 REM ********************************
902 REM *     MAIN ROUTINE              *
904 REM ********************************
906 DIM F(100)
908 REM INITIAL MESSAGE
910 GOSUB 1006
912 REM INITIALIZE
914 GOSUB 1106
916 REM PROCESS
918 GOSUB 1206
920 REM OUTPUT
922 GOSUB 1306
924 REM FINAL MESSAGE
926 GOSUB 1406
928 IF U$ = "Y" THEN 914
930 PRINT
932 PRINT "END OF PROGRAM"
999 STOP
1000 REM ********************************
1002 REM *      INITIAL MESSAGE           *
1004 REM ********************************
1006 PRINT
1008 PRINT
1010 PRINT
1012 PRINT "PROGRAM 3-4"
1014 PRINT
1016 PRINT "TEST OF UNIFORM RANDOM NUMBERS"
1018 PRINT "USING THE CHI SQUARE GOODNESS"
1020 PRINT "OF FIT TEST FOR EQUAL FREQUENCIES."
1099 RETURN
1100 REM ********************************
1102 REM *      INITIALIZE                *
1104 REM ********************************
1106 PRINT
1108 PRINT "NUMBER OF RANDOM NUMBERS";
```

```
1110 INPUT N
1112 PRINT
1114 PRINT "NUMBER OF CATEGORIES";
1116 INPUT K1
1118 FOR K = 1 TO K1
1120    LET F(K) = 0
1122 NEXT K
1199 RETURN
1200 REM *****************************
1202 REM *     PROCESS                *
1204 REM *****************************
1206 FOR I = 1 TO N
1208    LET R = RND(0)
1210    LET K = 1 + INT(K1 * R)
1212    LET F(K) = F(K) + 1
1214 NEXT I
1216 LET C = 0
1218 LET E = N / K1
1220 FOR K = 1 TO K1
1222    LET D = F(K) - E
1224    LET C = C + D * D / E
1226 NEXT K
1299 RETURN
1300 REM *****************************
1302 REM *     OUTPUT                 *
1304 REM *****************************
1306 PRINT
1308 PRINT "CHI SQUARE",C
1310 PRINT "DEG OF FR",K1-1
1312 PRINT
1314 PRINT "DISPLAY FREQUENCIES (Y/N)";
1316 INPUT U$
1318 IF U$ = "Y" THEN 1328
1320 IF U$ = "N" THEN 1399
1322 PRINT
1324 PRINT "INVALID RESPONSE"
1326 GOTO 1312
1328 PRINT
1330 PRINT "CATEGORY","FREQUENCY"
1332 FOR K = 1 TO K1
1334    PRINT K,F(K)
1336 NEXT K
1399 RETURN
1400 REM *****************************
1402 REM *     FINAL MESSAGE          *
1404 REM *****************************
```

```
1406 PRINT
1408 PRINT "TRY ANOTHER TEST (Y/N)";
1410 INPUT U$
1412 IF U$ = "Y" THEN 1499
1414 IF U$ = "N" THEN 1499
1416 PRINT
1418 PRINT "INVALID RESPONSE"
1420 GOTO 1406
1499 RETURN
9999 END
```

PROGRAM 3-4

```
TEST OF UNIFORM RANDOM NUMBERS
USING THE CHI SQUARE GOODNESS
OF FIT TEST FOR EQUAL FREQUENCIES.
NUMBER OF RANDOM NUMBERS? 100

NUMBER OF CATEGORIES? 2

CHI SQUARE          1
DEG OF FR           1

DISPLAY FREQUENCIES (Y/N)? Y

CATEGORY            FREQUENCY
  1                    45
  2                    55


TRY ANOTHER TEST (Y/N)? Y

NUMBER OF RANDOM NUMBERS? 400

NUMBER OF CATEGORIES? 10

CHI SQUARE          6.35
DEG OF FR           9

DISPLAY FREQUENCIES (Y/N)? Y

CATEGORY            FREQUENCY
  1                    41
  2                    44
```

```
             3                 32
             4                 32
             5                 38
             6                 49
             7                 44
             8                 40
             9                 38
            10                 42

        TRY  ANOTHER  TEST  (Y/N)?  N

        END  OF  PROGRAM
```

Fig. 3-4. Sample results from Program 3-4.

Program 3-5

```
100 REM ******************************
102 REM *    3-5                      *
104 REM ******************************
106 REM   AUTHOR
108 REM      COPYRIGHT 1982
110 REM       BY LAWRENCE MCNITT.
112 REM   PURPOSE
114 REM      RUNS TEST FOR
116 REM      UNIFORM RANDOM NUMBERS.
118 REM   SYSTEM
120 REM      UNIVERSAL SUBSET
122 REM      OF BASIC.
200 REM ********************************
202 REM *    ORGANIZATION              *
204 REM ********************************
206 REM   900   MAIN ROUTINE
208 REM         1000   INITIAL MESSAGE
210 REM         1100   INITIALIZE
212 REM         1200   PROCESS
214 REM         1300   OUTPUT
216 REM         1400   FINAL MESSAGE
300 REM ********************************
302 REM *    VARIABLES                 *
304 REM ********************************
306 REM   F(100)   FREQUENCIES
308 REM   U$   USER RESPONSE
310 REM   N    NUMBER OF RANDOM NUMBERS
312 REM   I    COUNTER
314 REM   K    CATEGORY
```

```
316 REM    R    RANDOM NUMBER
318 REM    E    EXPECTED FREQUENCY
320 REM    C    CHI SQUARE VALUE
322 REM    K1   NUMBER OF CATEGORIES
324 REM    D    DIFFERENCE BETWEEN OBSERVED AND EXPECTED
326 REM    T    TYPE OF RUN (1 = UP, -1 = DOWN)
328 REM    L    LAST RANDOM NUMBER
330 REM    D1   DENOMINATOR TERM FOR FACTORIAL
332 REM    F1   FACTORIAL FOR DENOMINATOR
334 REM    M    EXPECTED NUMBER OF RUNS OF ALL LENGTHS
336 REM    X    OBSERVED NUMBER OF RUNS OF ALL LENGTHS
338 REM    M1   CUMULATIVE EXPECTED NUMBER
340 REM    X1   CUMULATIVE OBSERVED NUMBER
900 REM ******************************
902 REM *    MAIN ROUTINE             *
904 REM ******************************
906 DIM F(100)
908 REM INITIAL MESSAGE
910 GOSUB 1006
912 REM INITIALIZE
914 GOSUB 1106
916 REM PROCESS
918 GOSUB 1206
920 REM OUTPUT
922 GOSUB 1306
924 REM FINAL MESSAGE
926 GOSUB 1406
928 IF U$ = "Y" THEN 914
930 PRINT
932 PRINT "END OF PROGRAM"
999 STOP
1000 REM ******************************
1002 REM *    INITIAL MESSAGE           *
1004 REM ******************************
1006 PRINT
1008 PRINT
1010 PRINT
1012 PRINT "PROGRAM 3-5"
1014 PRINT
1016 PRINT "TEST OF UNIFORM RANDOM NUMBERS"
1018 PRINT "USING THE RUNS TESTS OF VARIOUS"
1020 PRINT "LENGTHS AND THE CHI SQUARE TEST"
1022 PRINT "OF FREQUENCIES."
1099 RETURN
1100 REM ******************************
1102 REM *    INITIALIZE                *
```

```
1104 REM ****************************
1106 PRINT
1108 PRINT "NUMBER OF RANDOM NUMBERS";
1110 INPUT N
1112 FOR K = 1 TO 100
1114    LET F(K) = 0
1116 NEXT K
1199 RETURN
1200 REM *****************************
1202 REM *    PROCESS              *
1204 REM *****************************
1206 LET L = RND(0)
1208 LET R = RND(0)
1210 LET T = SGN(R - L)
1212 LET K = 1
1214 LET L = R
1216 FOR I = 3 TO N
1218    LET R = RND(0)
1220    IF (R-L)*T > 0 THEN 1228
1222    LET F(K) = F(K) + 1
1224    LET T = SGN(R - L)
1226    LET K = 0
1228    LET K = K + 1
1230    LET L = R
1232 NEXT I
1299 RETURN
1300 REM *****************************
1302 REM *    OUTPUT                 *
1304 REM *****************************
1306 LET M = (2 * N - 1) / 3
1308 LET X = 0
1310 FOR K = 1 TO 100
1312    LET X = X + F(K)
1314 NEXT K
1316 PRINT
1318 PRINT "EXPECTED NUMBER OF RUNS",M
1320 PRINT "OBSERVED NUMBER OF RUNS",X
1322 PRINT
1324 PRINT "SIZE OF RUN","OBSERVED","EXPECTED"
1326 LET C = 0
1328 LET F1 = 6
1330 LET D1 = 3
1332 LET E1 = 0
1333 LET X1 = 0
1334 FOR K = 1 TO 100
1336    LET D1 = D1 + 1
```

```
1338    LET F1 = F1 * D1
1340    LET E = (K*K+3*K+1)*N - (K*K*K+3*K*K-K-4)
1342    LET E = 2 * E / F1
1344    PRINT K,F(K),E
1346    LET D = F(K) - E
1348    LET C = C + D * D / E
1350    LET E1 = E1 + E
1351    LET X1 = X1 + F(K)
1352     IF M-E1 < 2 THEN 1356
1354 NEXT K
1356 PRINT "OVER";K,X-X1,M-E1
1358 LET D = (X-X1) - (M-E1)
1360 LET C = C + D * D / (M - M1)
1362 PRINT
1364 PRINT "CHI SQUARE",C
1366 PRINT "DEG OF FR",K+1
1399 RETURN
1400 REM ****************************
1402 REM *    FINAL MESSAGE         *
1404 REM ****************************
1406 PRINT
1408 PRINT "TRY ANOTHER TEST (Y/N)";
1410 INPUT U$
1412 IF U$ = "Y" THEN 1499
1414 IF U$ = "N" THEN 1499
1416 PRINT
1418 PRINT "INVALID RESPONSE"
1420 GOTO 1406
1499 RETURN
9999 END
```

theory. Many natural phenomena exhibit its characteristics. The normal distribution has the familiar bell shape. It is symmetric about the mode (most likely value) with the greatest concentration near that point.

There are several methods for generating normally distributed values. The method that is the easiest to understand uses the central limit theorem. The central limit theorem implies that the sum of a set of independently drawn values tends toward the normal as the number of the values increases. This occurs regardless of the shape of the populations from which those values are selected.

The normal distribution is determined by its mean (average) and standard deviation (measure of variability or spread). One common method of generating normally distributed values is to find the sum of twelve uniform random numbers selected within the interval (0–1) a number of times. These sums have a mean of six and a standard deviation of one. Subtracting the value six from any of the sums results in a standard normal value drawn from a population having a mean of zero and a standard deviation of one.

The formula

$$Z = Sum\ (Rnd(0)) - 6$$

```
PROGRAM  3-5

TEST OF UNIFORM RANDOM NUMBERS
USING THE RUNS TESTS OF VARIOUS
LENGTHS AND THE CHI SQUARE TEST
OF FREQUENCIES.

NUMBER OF RANDOM NUMBERS? 100

EXPECTED NUMBER OF RUNS          66.3333
OBSERVED NUMBER OF RUNS          65

SIZE OF RUN        OBSERVED        EXPECTED


   1                40             41.75
   2                19             18.1
   3                5              5.14722
OVER 3              1              1.33611

CHI SQUARE         .124019
DEG OF FR          4

TRY ANOTHER TEST (Y/N)? Y

NUMBER OF RANDOM NUMBERS? 400

EXPECTED NUMBER OF RUNS          266.333
OBSERVED NUMBER OF RUNS          264

SIZE OF RUN        OBSERVED        EXPECTED
   1                169            166.75
   2                68             73.1
   3                19             20.9806
   4                6              4.5619
OVER 4              2              .940857

CHI SQUARE         1.03069
DEG OF FR          5

TRY ANOTHER TEST (Y/N)? N

END OF PROGRAM
```

Fig. 3-5. Sample results from Program 3-5.

gives the standard score. The transformation

$$X = M + Z*S$$

gives the random value drawn from a population having a mean of M and a standard deviation of S because sets of the sums of twelve uniform random numbers are almost normally distributed.

Program 3-6 generates normally distributed values. Figure 3-6 shows the results.

Program 3-6

```
100 REM ****************************
102 REM *   3-6                    *
104 REM ****************************
106 REM   AUTHOR
108 REM       COPYRIGHT 1982
110 REM       BY LAWRENCE MCNITT.
112 REM   PURPOSE
114 REM       GENERATE NORMALLY DISTRIBUTED
116 REM       RANDOM NUMBERS.
118 REM   SYSTEM
120 REM       UNIVERSAL SUBSET
122 REM       OF BASIC.
200 REM *****************************
202 REM *   ORGANIZATION            *
204 REM *****************************
206 REM   900    MAIN ROUTINE
208 REM          1000   INITIAL MESSAGE
210 REM          1100   PARAMETERS
212 REM          1200   PROCESS
214 REM          1300   FINAL MESSAGE
300 REM *****************************
302 REM *   VARIABLES               *
304 REM *****************************
306 REM   U$   USER RESPONSE
308 REM   N    NUMBER OF VALUES
310 REM   I    COUNTER
312 REM   M    MEAN OF POPULATION
314 REM   S    STANDARD DEVIATION
316 REM   Z    STANDARD SCORE
318 REM   X    VALUE FROM NORMAL POPULATION
320 REM   J    COUNTER
900 REM *****************************
902 REM *   MAIN ROUTINE            *
904 REM *****************************
906 REM INITIAL MESSAGE
908 GOSUB 1006
910 REM PARAMETERS
912 GOSUB 1106
```

```
914 REM PROCESS
916 GOSUB 1206
918 REM FINAL MESSAGE
920 GOSUB 1306
922 IF U$ = "Y" THEN 912
924 PRINT
926 PRINT "END OF PROGRAM"
999 STOP
1000 REM ******************************
1002 REM *    INITIAL MESSAGE        *
1004 REM ******************************
1006 PRINT
1008 PRINT
1010 PRINT
1012 PRINT "PROGRAM 3-6 "
1014 PRINT
1016 PRINT "GENERATE NORMALLY DISTRIBUTED"
1018 PRINT "RANDOM NUMBERS FROM THE SUM"
1020 PRINT "OF TWELVE UNIFORM RANDOM NUMBERS"
1022 PRINT "FOR EACH VALUE."
1099 RETURN
1100 REM ******************************
1102 REM *    PARAMETERS             *
1104 REM ******************************
1106 PRINT
1108 PRINT "POPULATION"
1110 PRINT "MEAN    ";
1112 INPUT M
1114 PRINT "STD DEV ";
1116 INPUT S
1118 PRINT
1120 PRINT "NUMBER OF VALUES";
1122 INPUT N
1199 RETURN
1200 REM ******************************
1202 REM *    PROCESS                *
1204 REM ******************************
1206 PRINT
1208 FOR I = 1 TO N
1210     LET Z = -6
1212     FOR J = 1 TO 12
1214         LET Z = Z + RND(0)
1216     NEXT J
1218     LET X = M + Z * S
1220     PRINT X
1222 NEXT I
```

```
1299 RETURN
1300 REM *******************************
1302 REM *     FINAL MESSAGE           *
1304 REM *******************************
1306 PRINT
1308 PRINT "GENERATE ANOTHER SET OF VALUES (Y/N)";
1310 INPUT U$
1312 IF U$ = "Y" THEN 1399
1314 IF U$ = "N" THEN 1399
1316 PRINT
1318 PRINT "INVALID RESPONSE"
1320 GOTO 1306
1399 RETURN
9999 END
```

The Exponential Distribution

The exponential distribution is highly skewed to the right. One parameter, the mean, specifies the exponential distribution. The equation

$$X = -M *LOG (RND (0))$$

gives the random value selected from an exponential distribution having a mean of M.

Program 3-7 generates exponentially distributed random values. Figure 3-7 shows the results.

Arbitrary Discrete Distributions

The characteristics of a population are given by its probability distribution. The following table gives the values and probabilities for a discrete probability distribution:

```
PROGRAM 3-6

GENERATE NORMALLY DISTRIBUTED
RANDOM NUMBERS FROM THE SUM
OF TWELVE UNIFORM RANDOM NUMBERS
FOR EACH VALUE.

POPULATION
MEAN    ? 100
STD DEV ? 20

NUMBER OF VALUES? 5

   110.258
   118.973
   78.1672
   87.8457
   98.8728

GENERATE ANOTHER SET OF VALUES (Y/N)? N

END OF PROGRAM
```

Fig. 3-6. Sample results from Program 3-6.

Program 3-7

```
100 REM *******************************
102 REM *   3-7                       *
104 REM *******************************
106 REM   AUTHOR
108 REM       COPYRIGHT 1982
110 REM       BY LAWRENCE MCNITT.
112 REM   PURPOSE
114 REM       GENERATE EXPONENTIALLY
116 REM       DISTRIBUTED RANDOM NUMBERS.
118 REM   SYSTEM
120 REM       UNIVERSAL SUBSET
122 REM       OF BASIC.
200 REM *******************************
202 REM *   ORGANIZATION              *
204 REM *******************************
206 REM   900   MAIN ROUTINE
208 REM         1000   INITIAL MESSAGE
210 REM         1100   PARAMETERS
212 REM         1200   PROCESS
214 REM         1300   FINAL MESSAGE
300 REM *******************************
302 REM *   VARIABLES                 *
304 REM *******************************
306 REM   U$   USER RESPONSE
308 REM   N    NUMBER OF VALUES
310 REM   I    COUNTER
312 REM   M    MEAN OF POPULATION
314 REM   X    VALUE FROM EXPONENTIAL DISTRIBUTION
900 REM *******************************
902 REM *   MAIN ROUTINE              *
904 REM *******************************
906 REM INITIAL MESSAGE
908 GOSUB 1006
910 REM PARAMETERS
912 GOSUB 1106
914 REM PROCESS
916 GOSUB 1206
918 REM FINAL MESSAGE
920 GOSUB 1306
922 IF U$ = "Y" THEN 912
924 PRINT
926 PRINT "END OF PROGRAM"
999 STOP
```

```
1000 REM *****************************
1002 REM *    INITIAL MESSAGE        *
1004 REM *****************************
1006 PRINT
1008 PRINT
1010 PRINT
1012 PRINT "PROGRAM 3-7   "
1014 PRINT
1016 PRINT "GENERATE EXPONENTIALLY"
1018 PRINT "DISTRIBUTED RANDOM NUMBERS."
1099 RETURN
1100 REM *****************************
1102 REM *    PARAMETERS            *
1104 REM *****************************
1106 PRINT
1108 PRINT "POPULATION"
1110 PRINT "MEAN       ";
1112 INPUT M
1114 PRINT
1116 PRINT "NUMBER OF VALUES";
1118 INPUT N
1199 RETURN
1200 REM *****************************
1202 REM *    PROCESS               *
1204 REM *****************************
1206 PRINT
1208 FOR I = 1 TO N
1210    LET X = -M * LOG(RND(0))
1212    PRINT X
1214 NEXT I
1299 RETURN
1300 REM *****************************
1302 REM *    FINAL MESSAGE         *
1304 REM *****************************
1306 PRINT
1308 PRINT "GENERATE ANOTHER SET OF VALUES (Y/N)";
1310 INPUT U$
1312 IF U$ = "Y" THEN 1399
1314 IF U$ = "N" THEN 1399
1316 PRINT
1318 PRINT "INVALID RESPONSE"
1320 GOTO 1306
1399 RETURN
9999 END
```

```
PROGRAM 3-7

GENERATE EXPONENTIALLY
DISTRIBUTED RANDOM NUMBERS.

POPULATION
MEAN      ? 10

NUMBER OF VALUES? 5

  13.714
  4.30645E-03
  9.6032
  36.9485
  8.64928

GENERATE ANOTHER SET OF VALUES (Y/N)? N

END OF PROGRAM
```

Fig. 3-7. Sample results from Program 3-7.

Value	Probability
10	.2
20	.5
30	.3

The cumulative probabilities are .2, .7 and 1.0.

The cumulative probabilities form the boundaries for the subintervals within the range (0–1) for uniform random numbers. A random number falling within the subinterval (.2–.7), for example, designates the value 20.

Program 3-8 generates values randomly from a discrete probability distribution. Figure 3-8 shows the results.

Exercise 3-4

1. Generate one hundred values from a normal population having a mean of 400 and a standard deviation of 40. Compare the mean and standard deviation of the one hundred values with the expected population mean and standard deviation.
2. Generate one hundred values from an exponential population having a mean of 5. Compare the mean of the one hundred random values with the population mean of 5.
3. Generate one hundred random values from the following discrete probability distribution:

Value	Probability
20	.1
21	.2
22	.3
23	.4

Compare the observed frequencies with the expected frequencies.

SIMULATING PROCESSES USING RANDOM SAMPLING

A process generates outcomes, usually representing values over time. The process may be deterministic or probabilistic. The process itself may be independent or dependent. An independent process is one for which the outcome of the ith trial is independent of the outcomes that have transpired earlier.

94

Program 3-8

```
100 REM *******************************
102 REM *    3-8                       *
104 REM *******************************
106 REM   AUTHOR
108 REM       COPYRIGHT 1982
110 REM       BY LAWRENCE MCNITT.
112 REM   PURPOSE
114 REM       GENERATE ARBITRARILY
116 REM       DISTRIBUTED RANDOM NUMBERS.
118 REM   SYSTEM
120 REM       UNIVERSAL SUBSET
122 REM       OF BASIC.
200 REM *********************************
202 REM *    ORGANIZATION               *
204 REM *********************************
206 REM   900   MAIN ROUTINE
208 REM         1000   INITIAL MESSAGE
210 REM         1100   PARAMETERS
212 REM         1200   PROCESS
214 REM               2000   GENERATE VALUE
216 REM         1300   FINAL MESSAGE
300 REM *********************************
302 REM *    VARIABLES                  *
304 REM *********************************
306 REM    X(50)    VALUES FOR DISTRIBUTION
308 REM    P(50)    PROBABILITIES
310 REM    U$   USER RESPONSE
312 REM    K    NUMBER OF CATEGORIES
314 REM    N    NUMBER OF VALUES TO GENERATE
316 REM    I    COUNTER
318 REM    J    INDEX
320 REM    R    RANDOM NUMBER
322 REM    V    VALUE GENERATED
324 REM    S    CUMULATIVE PROBABILITY
900 REM *********************************
902 REM *    MAIN ROUTINE               *
904 REM *********************************
906 REM INITIAL MESSAGE
908 GOSUB 1006
910 REM PARAMETERS
912 GOSUB 1106
914 REM PROCESS
916 GOSUB 1206
918 REM FINAL MESSAGE
```

```
920 GOSUB 1306
922 IF U$ = "Y" THEN 912
924 PRINT
926 PRINT "END OF PROGRAM"
999 STOP
1000 REM *****************************
1002 REM *    INITIAL MESSAGE         *
1004 REM *****************************
1006 PRINT
1008 PRINT
1010 PRINT
1012 PRINT "PROGRAM 3-8"
1014 PRINT
1016 PRINT "GENERATE VALUES FROM AN"
1018 PRINT "ARBITRARY DISCRETE"
1020 PRINT "PROBABILITY DISTRIBUTION."
1099 RETURN
1100 REM *****************************
1102 REM *    PARAMETERS              *
1104 REM *****************************
1106 PRINT
1108 PRINT "PROBABILITY DISTRIBUTION"
1110 PRINT
1112 PRINT "NUMBER OF STATES";
1114 INPUT K
1116 PRINT
1118 PRINT "VALUE, PROBABILITY FOR"
1120 LET S = 0
1122 FOR J = 1 TO K
1124     PRINT "STATE";J;
1126     INPUT X(J),P(J)
1128     LET S = S + P(J)
1130     LET P(J) = S
1132 NEXT J
1134 IF ABS(S-1) < .00001 THEN 1142
1136 PRINT
1138 PRINT "INVALID PROBABILITIES, MUST SUM TO 1.0"
1140 GOTO 1116
1142 PRINT
1144 PRINT "NUMBER OF VALUES TO GENERATE";
1146 INPUT N
1199 RETURN
1200 REM *****************************
1202 REM *    PROCESS                 *
1204 REM *****************************
1206 PRINT
```

```
1208 FOR I = 1 TO N
1210    REM GENERATE VALUE
1212    GOSUB 2006
1214    PRINT V
1216 NEXT I
1299 RETURN
1300 REM *****************************
1302 REM *    FINAL MESSAGE          *
1304 REM *****************************
1306 PRINT
1308 PRINT "GENERATE ANOTHER SET OF VALUES (Y/N)";
1310 INPUT U$
1312 IF U$ = "Y" THEN 1399
1314 IF U$ = "N" THEN 1399
1316 PRINT
1318 PRINT "INVALID RESPONSE"
1320 GOTO 1306
1399 RETURN
2000 REM *****************************
2002 REM *    GENERATE VALUE         *
2004 REM *****************************
2006 LET R = RND(0)
2008 FOR J = 1 TO K
2010    IF R > P(J) THEN 2016
2012    LET V = X(J)
2014    LET J = K
2016 NEXT J
2099 RETURN
9999 END
```

```
PROGRAM 3-8

GENERATE VALUES FROM AN
ARBITRARY DISCRETE
PROBABILITY DISTRIBUTION.

PROBABILITY DISTRIBUTION

NUMBER OF STATES? 3

VALUE, PROBABILITY FOR
STATE 1 ? 10,.2
STATE 2 ? 20,.5
STATE 3 ? 30,.3
```

```
20
30
20
10
10
20
10
20
30
20

GENERATE ANOTHER SET OF VALUES (Y/N)? N

END OF PROGRAM
```

Fig. 3-8. Sample results from Program 3-8.

The simulation of an independent process is the same as drawing randomly from a probability distribution. The simulation of a dependent process will be as complex as the complexity of the dependencies among the outcomes.

Arbitrary Continuous Probability Distribution

Items drawn from a continuous population can, in theory, be any value within the specified range. Items drawn from a discrete population can take only the permissible discrete values. A simple modification of the discrete distribution allows it to represent continuous populations having similar shapes.

This method involves two random numbers. The first random number determines the subinterval within which the value falls. The second random number determines the location within that subinterval for the value. This assumes that the possible values within a given subinterval are uniformly distributed.

Program 3-9 samples randomly from the continuous distribution described below:

Boundaries	Probability
5 - 15	.2
15 - 25	.5
25 - 35	.3

Figure 3-9 shows the results.

Exercise 3-5

1. A process generates values that are normally distributed with a mean of 25 and a standard deviation of 5. Simulate the process for the next twenty items.
2. The number of hours between traffic accidents for a city is known to be exponentially distributed with a mean of 4.5 hours. Generate the times between accidents for the next ten accidents.

THE NORMALITY ASSUMPTION OF CLASSICAL STATISTICS

The t distribution, as described in standard texts on statistics, is useful for testing hypotheses about population means. The procedure is to select a sample, compute its mean and standard deviation, compute the standard score, and from the standard score draw conclusions concerning whether the sample mean and t score could have come from a population having a specified mean.

One of the assumptions is that the population is normally distributed. Not all populations are normally distributed, however. How robust is the t test in regard to the normality assumption?

Program 3-9

```
100 REM *******************************
102 REM *    3-9                       *
104 REM *******************************
106 REM   AUTHOR
108 REM      COPYRIGHT 1982
110 REM      BY LAWRENCE MCNITT.
112 REM   PURPOSE
114 REM      GENERATE ARBITRARILY
116 REM      DISTRIBUTED RANDOM NUMBERS.
118 REM   SYSTEM
120 REM      UNIVERSAL SUBSET
122 REM      OF BASIC.
200 REM *******************************
202 REM *    ORGANIZATION              *
204 REM *******************************
206 REM   900   MAIN ROUTINE
208 REM         1000   INITIAL MESSAGE
210 REM         1100   PARAMETERS
212 REM         1200   PROCESS
214 REM             2000   GENERATE VALUE
216 REM         1300   FINAL MESSAGE
300 REM *******************************
302 REM *    VARIABLES                 *
304 REM *******************************
306 REM    X(50)    VALUES FOR DISTRIBUTION
308 REM    P(50)    PROBABILITIES
310 REM    U$    USER RESPONSE
312 REM    K     NUMBER OF CATEGORIES
314 REM    N     NUMBER OF VALUES TO GENERATE
316 REM    I     COUNTER
318 REM    J     INDEX
320 REM    R     RANDOM NUMBER
322 REM    V     VALUE GENERATED
324 REM    S     CUMULATIVE PROBABILITY
900 REM *******************************
902 REM *    MAIN ROUTINE              *
904 REM *******************************
906 REM INITIAL MESSAGE
908 GOSUB 1006
910 REM PARAMETERS
912 GOSUB 1106
914 REM PROCESS
916 GOSUB 1206
918 REM FINAL MESSAGE
```

```
920 GOSUB 1306
922 IF U$ = "Y" THEN 912
924 PRINT
926 PRINT "END OF PROGRAM"
999 STOP
1000 REM *****************************
1002 REM *    INITIAL MESSAGE         *
1004 REM *****************************
1006 PRINT
1008 PRINT
1010 PRINT
1012 PRINT "PROGRAM 3-9"
1014 PRINT
1016 PRINT "GENERATE VALUES FROM AN"
1018 PRINT "ARBITRARY CONTINUOUS"
1020 PRINT "PROBABILITY DISTRIBUTION."
1099 RETURN
1100 REM *****************************
1102 REM *    PARAMETERS              *
1104 REM *****************************
1106 PRINT
1108 PRINT "PROBABILITY DISTRIBUTION"
1110 PRINT
1112 PRINT "NUMBER OF STATES";
1114 INPUT K
1116 PRINT
1118 PRINT "LOWEST BOUNDARY, PROBABILITY FOR"
1120 LET S = 0
1122 FOR J = 1 TO K
1124    PRINT "STATE";J;
1126    INPUT X(J),P(J)
1128    LET S = S + P(J)
1130    LET P(J) = S
1132 NEXT J
1134 PRINT "UPPER BOUNDARY FOR STATE";K;
1136 INPUT X(K+1)
1138 IF ABS(S-1) < .00001 THEN 1146
1140 PRINT
1142 PRINT "PROBABILITIES MUST SUM TO 1.0"
1144 GOTO 1116
1146 PRINT
1148 PRINT "NUMBER OF VALUES TO GENERATE";
1150 INPUT N
1199 RETURN
1200 REM *****************************
1202 REM *    PROCESS                 *
```

```
1204 REM ****************************
1206 PRINT
1208 FOR I = 1 TO N
1210     REM GENERATE VALUE
1212     GOSUB 2006
1214     PRINT V
1216 NEXT I
1299 RETURN
1300 REM ****************************
1302 REM *    FINAL MESSAGE         *
1304 REM ****************************
1306 PRINT
1308 PRINT "GENERATE ANOTHER SET OF VALUES (Y/N)";
1310 INPUT U$
1312 IF U$ = "Y" THEN 1399
1314 IF U$ = "N" THEN 1399
1316 PRINT
1318 PRINT "INVALID RESPONSE"
1320 GOTO 1306
1399 RETURN
2000 REM ****************************
2002 REM *    GENERATE VALUE        *
2004 REM ****************************
2006 LET R = RND(0)
2008 FOR J = 1 TO K
2010     IF R > P(J) THEN 2016
2012     LET V = X(J) + RND(0) * (X(J+1) - X(J))
2014     LET J = K
2016 NEXT J
2018 LET V = .01 * INT(.5 + 100 * V)
2099 RETURN
9999 END
```

One method of testing the normality assumption is through simulated sampling. Choose some population that is nonnormal and observe the results.

Tests of hypotheses involve sampling distributions having known properties. A sampling distribution is defined assuming that the null hypothesis is true. As long as the outcome represented by the sample is not in the extreme tail area of the sampling distribution, the null hypothesis is accepted; otherwise it is rejected. Common tail areas are .05 and .01. For samples of size 9, the critical standard scores are 1.86 and 2.90 having .05 and .01 for their righthand areas. The t distribution is symmetric, hence the standard scores -1.86 and -2.90 have .05 and .01 as their lefthand tail areas.

The exponential distribution is highly skewed to the right. Most of the values are small. A few of the values are very large relative to the mean.

Program 3-10 determines the fractions falling outside the four critical t scores assuming an exponentially distributed population. Figure 3-10 shows the results. As you can see, skewed distributions do have an effect on the normality assumption. The

```
PROGRAM 3-9

GENERATE VALUES FROM AN
ARBITRARY CONTINUOUS
PROBABILITY DISTRIBUTION.

PROBABILITY DISTRIBUTION

NUMBER OF STATES? 3

LOWEST BOUNDARY, PROBABILITY FOR
STATE 1 ? 5,.2
STATE 2 ? 15,.5
STATE 3 ? 25,.3
UPPER BOUNDARY FOR STATE 3 ? 35

NUMBER OF VALUES TO GENERATE? 10

 20.76
 26.76
 26.84
 17.36
 16.04
 30.99
 34.16
 22.5
 27.86
 24.05


GENERATE ANOTHER SET OF VALUES (Y/N)? N

END OF PROGRAM

The output values are rounded to the nearest hundredth.
```

Fig. 3-9. Sample results from Program 3-9.

sampling distribution is still skewed for samples of size n = 9.

Exercise 3-6

1. Test the normality assumption using a uniform population. The population mean is .5 for a uniform random number selected from the interval 0—1. Use sample sizes of 4, 10, and 30.

2. Test the normality assumption using values drawn from the population described by the following probability distribution:

Value	Probability
10	.2
20	.5
30	.3

Program 3-10

```
100 REM *******************************
102 REM *    3-10                      *
104 REM *******************************
106 REM   AUTHOR
108 REM      COPYRIGHT 1982
110 REM      BY LAWRENCE MCNITT.
112 REM   PURPOSE
114 REM      ESTIMATE TAIL AREA FOR T DIST
116 REM      USING EXPONENTIAL POPULATION.
118 REM   SYSTEM
120 REM      UNIVERSAL SUBSET
122 REM      OF BASIC.
200 REM *******************************
202 REM *    ORGANIZATION              *
204 REM *******************************
206 REM   900   MAIN ROUTINE
208 REM         1000   INITIAL MESSAGE
210 REM         1100   PARAMETERS
212 REM         1200   PROCESS
214 REM         1300   FINAL MESSAGE
300 REM *******************************
302 REM *    VARIABLES                 *
304 REM *******************************
306 REM   U$   USER RESPONSE
308 REM   N    SAMPLE SIZE
310 REM   I    COUNTER
312 REM   M    MEAN OF POPULATION
314 REM   X    VALUE FROM EXPONENTIAL DISTRIBUTION
316 REM   T1   T SCORE FOR .05 LEVEL
318 REM   T2   T SCORE FOR .01 LEVEL
320 REM   S1   SUM
322 REM   S2   SUM OF SQUARES
324 REM   A    SAMPLE MEAN
326 REM   T    SAMPLE T SCORE
328 REM   L1   NUMBER OF SAMPLES
330 REM   L    CURRENT SAMPLE
332 REM   F1   FREQUENCY FOR T SCORE
334 REM   F2   FREQUENCY FOR T SCORE
336 REM   F3   FREQUENCY FOR T SCORE
338 REM   F4   FREQUENCY FOR T SCORE
340 REM   S    STANDARD DEVIATION
900 REM *******************************
902 REM *    MAIN ROUTINE              *
904 REM *******************************
```

```
906 REM INITIAL MESSAGE
908 GOSUB 1006
910 REM PARAMETERS
912 GOSUB 1106
914 REM PROCESS
916 GOSUB 1206
918 REM FINAL MESSAGE
920 GOSUB 1306
922 IF U$ = "Y" THEN 912
924 PRINT
926 PRINT "END OF PROGRAM"
999 STOP
1000 REM ******************************
1002 REM *    INITIAL MESSAGE        *
1004 REM ******************************
1006 PRINT
1008 PRINT
1010 PRINT
1012 PRINT "PROGRAM 3-10"
1014 PRINT
1016 PRINT "ESTIMATE TAIL AREA FOR T DIST"
1018 PRINT "FOR SAMPLES DRAWN FROM A NONNORMAL"
1020 PRINT "POPULATION USING THE EXPONENTIAL"
1022 PRINT "DISTRIBUTION FOR THE POPULATION."
1099 RETURN
1100 REM ******************************
1102 REM *    PARAMETERS             *
1104 REM ******************************
1106 PRINT
1108 PRINT "POPULATION"
1110 PRINT "MEAN     ";
1112 INPUT M
1114 PRINT
1116 PRINT "SAMPLE SIZE";
1118 INPUT N
1120 PRINT
1122 PRINT "NUMBER OF SAMPLES";
1124 INPUT L1
1126 PRINT
1128 PRINT "T SCORE FOR"
1130 PRINT ".05 LEVEL";
1132 INPUT T1
1134 PRINT ".01 LEVEL";
1136 INPUT T2
1199 RETURN
1200 REM ******************************
```

```
1202 REM *    PROCESS                          *
1204 REM ******************************
1206 LET F1 = 0
1208 LET F2 = 0
1210 LET F3 = 0
1212 LET F4 = 0
1214 FOR L = 1 TO L1
1216    LET S1 = 0
1218    LET S2 = 0
1220    FOR I = 1 TO N
1222       LET X = -M * LOG(RND(0))
1224       LET S1 = S1 + X
1226       LET S2 = S2 + X * X
1228    NEXT I
1230    LET A = S1 / N
1232    LET S = SQR((S2-S1*S1/N)/(N-1))
1234    LET T = (A - M) / (S / SQR(N))
1236    IF T < -T1 THEN F1 = F1 + 1
1238    IF T < -T2 THEN F2 = F2 + 1
1240    IF T > T1 THEN F3 = F3 + 1
1242    IF T > T2 THEN F4 = F4 + 1
1244 NEXT L
1246 PRINT
1248 PRINT "T SCORE","ESTIMATED TAIL AREA"
1250 PRINT -T1,F1/L1
1252 PRINT -T2,F2/L1
1254 PRINT T1,F3/L1
1256 PRINT T2,F4/L1
1299 RETURN
1300 REM ******************************
1302 REM *    FINAL MESSAGE            *
1304 REM ******************************
1306 PRINT
1308 PRINT "GENERATE ANOTHER SET OF VALUES (Y/N)";
1310 INPUT U$
1312 IF U$ = "Y" THEN 1399
1314 IF U$ = "N" THEN 1399
1316 PRINT
1318 PRINT "INVALID RESPONSE"
1320 GOTO 1306
1399 RETURN
9999 END
```

Use sample sizes of 4, 10, and 30.

3. Test the normality assumption using values drawn from the exponential distribution having a mean of ten. Use sample sizes of 4, 10, and 30.

4. The statistic computed as the sum of the squares of n values randomly selected from a normal

```
PROGRAM 3-10

ESTIMATE TAIL AREA FOR T DIST
FOR SAMPLES DRAWN FROM A NONNORMAL
POPULATION USING THE EXPONENTIAL
DISTRIBUTION FOR THE POPULATION.

POPULATION
MEAN      ? 10

SAMPLE SIZE? 9

NUMBER OF SAMPLES? 1000

T SCORE FOR
.05 LEVEL? 1.86
.01 LEVEL? 2.90

T SCORE            ESTIMATED TAIL AREA
-1.86                  .162
-2.9                   .067
 1.86                  .015
 2.9                   2E-03

GENERATE ANOTHER SET OF VALUES (Y/N)? N

END OF PROGRAM
```

Fig. 3-10. Sample results from Program 3-10.

population having a mean of 0 and a standard deviation of 1 will be chi square distributed with n degrees of freedom. Use a published chi square table to determine the righthand and lefthand tail areas (.05 and .01). Generate a large number of samples of 10 each and compute the relative frequencies for the four tail areas.

Chapter 4
Probabilistic Models

One of the primary purposes of simulation models is to simulate random events. This chapter discusses random number generators and their use in simulated sampling from probability distributions.

In some cases Monte Carlo methods using simulated sampling apply in the solution of deterministic models, but this chapter discusses Monte Carlo methods in the context of numerical integration and constrained optimization problems.

COINS, DICE, AND RANDOM WALKS

Tossing coins and dice and taking random numbers of steps in random directions are all examples of random events that may be simulated using a computerized model.

Tossing a Coin

Tossing a coin and observing whether the result is a head or a tail is a familiar random phenomenon. The experiment is easy to perform. The results are clear and unambiguous. There is little argument in regard to the equitable probabilities. If the coin is tossed in a fair manner the probability of a head on any one toss is .5.

Simulating the coin toss on the computer involves the random number generator. Most BASIC translators include the RND function, which generates random numbers within the range from zero to one. The values are distributed randomly throughout the range.

If the random number falls within the interval 0-.5, the simulated result is a head. If the value falls within the range .5-1, the simulated result is a tail. The advantage of simulated coin tossing is a result of the speed of the computer. The computer can simulate one thousand tosses in a few seconds. This is far less than the time needed to toss an actual coin one thousand times and to record the outcomes. Program 4-1 simulates tossing a coin while counting the number of heads. Figure 4-1 shows the results.

Tossing Dice

A similar problem concerns tossing dice. Each die has six sides numbered 1, 2, . . ., 6. Some games

Program 4-1

```
100 REM ********************************
102 REM *    4-1                      *
104 REM ********************************
106 REM   AUTHOR
108 REM       COPYRIGHT 1982
110 REM        BY LAWRENCE MCNITT.
112 REM   PURPOSE
114 REM        SIMULATE TOSSING A COIN
116 REM        COUNTING HEADS AND TAILS.
118 REM   SYSTEM
120 REM        UNIVERSAL SUBSET
122 REM        OF BASIC.
200 REM ********************************
202 REM *    ORGANIZATION             *
204 REM ********************************
206 REM   900   MAIN ROUTINE
208 REM         1000   INITIAL MESSAGE
210 REM         1100   PARAMETERS
212 REM         1200   PROCESS
214 REM         1300   OUTPUT
216 REM         1400   FINAL MESSAGE
300 REM ********************************
302 REM *    VARIABLES                *
304 REM ********************************
306 REM    U$   USER RESPONSE
308 REM    N    NUMBER OF TOSSES
310 REM    I    COUNTER
312 REM    H    NUMBER OF HEADS
314 REM    R    RANDOM NUMBER
900 REM ********************************
902 REM *    MAIN ROUTINE             *
904 REM ********************************
906 REM INITIAL MESSAGE
908 GOSUB 1006
910 REM PARAMETERS
912 GOSUB 1106
914 REM PROCESS
916 GOSUB 1206
918 REM OUTPUT
920 GOSUB 1306
922 REM FINAL MESSAGE
924 GOSUB 1406
926 IF U$ = "Y" THEN 912
928 PRINT
```

```
930 PRINT "END OF PROGRAM"
999 STOP
1000 REM *****************************
1002 REM *    INITIAL MESSAGE       *
1004 REM *****************************
1006 PRINT
1008 PRINT
1010 PRINT
1012 PRINT "PROGRAM 4-1"
1014 PRINT
1016 PRINT "SIMULATE TOSSING A COIN"
1018 PRINT "COUNTING THE NUMBER OF HEADS."
1099 RETURN
1100 REM *****************************
1102 REM *    PARAMETERS           *
1104 REM *****************************
1106 PRINT
1108 PRINT "NUMBER OF TOSSES";
1110 INPUT N
1199 RETURN
1200 REM *****************************
1202 REM *    PROCESS              *
1204 REM *****************************
1206 LET H = 0
1208 FOR I = 1 TO N
1210    LET R = RND(0)
1212    IF R > .5 THEN 1216
1214    LET H = H + 1
1216 NEXT I
1299 RETURN
1300 REM *****************************
1302 REM *    OUTPUT               *
1304 REM *****************************
1306 PRINT
1308 PRINT "NUMBER OF HEADS",H
1310 PRINT "FRACTION HEADS",H/N
1399 RETURN
1400 REM *****************************
1402 REM *    FINAL OUTPUT         *
1404 REM *****************************
1406 PRINT
1408 PRINT "TRY ANOTHER SET OF TOSSES (Y/N)";
1410 INPUT U$
1412 IF U$ = "Y" THEN 1499
1414 IF U$ = "N" THEN 1499
1416 PRINT
```

```
1418 PRINT "INVALID RESPONSE"
1420 GOTO 1406
1499 RETURN
9999 END
```

involve tossing two dice and recording the sum of the two dice.

The RND function returns values randomly distributed within the interval (0-1). Multiplying these values by six gives values randomly distributed within the interval (0-6). The INT function gives the largest integer less than or equal to the argument. The expression

$$INT~(6*RND(0)~)$$

returns one of the values $0, 1, \ldots, 5$. The expression

$$1 + INT~(6*RND(0)~)$$

selects one of the values $1, 2, \ldots, 6$ randomly. Using each possible sum S as a subscript in the expression

$$F~(S) = F~(S) + 1$$

accumulates the frequency distribution for each sum.

Program 4-2 simulates the tossing of two dice and accumulating the frequencies for the sums. Figure 4-2 shows the results.

Random Walks

Random walk problems are easy to simulate with the computer. The simplest models involve equally likely steps in any one of two or four directions. A common question asked is the expected distance obtained by the nth step. Somewhat more complex random walk problems involve biased steps in which steps in some directions are more likely than others. Also, the size of the step may be a random variable.

```
PROGRAM 4-1

SIMULATE TOSSING A COIN
COUNTING THE NUMBER OF HEADS.

NUMBER OF TOSSES? 10

NUMBER OF HEADS   3
FRACTION HEADS    .3

TRY ANOTHER SET OF TOSSES (Y/N)? Y

NUMBER OF TOSSES? 500

NUMBER OF HEADS   240
FRACTION HEADS    .48

TRY ANOTHER SET OF TOSSES (Y/N)? N

END OF PROGRAM
```

Fig. 4-1. Sample results from Program 4-1.

Program 4-2

```
100 REM *********************************
102 REM *    4 - 2                       *
104 REM *********************************
106 REM   AUTHOR
108 REM       COPYRIGHT 1982
110 REM       BY LAWRENCE MCNITT.
112 REM   PURPOSE
114 REM       SIMULATE TOSSING DICE
116 REM       COUNTING SUM OF OUTCOMES.
118 REM   SYSTEM
120 REM       UNIVERSAL SUBSET
122 REM       OF BASIC.
200 REM *********************************
202 REM *    ORGANIZATION               *
204 REM *********************************
206 REM   900   MAIN ROUTINE
208 REM         1000   INITIAL MESSAGE
210 REM         1100   PARAMETERS
212 REM         1200   PROCESS
214 REM         1300   OUTPUT
216 REM         1400   FINAL MESSAGE
300 REM *********************************
302 REM *    VARIABLES                  *
304 REM *********************************
306 REM    F(12)    FREQUENCIES FOR SUMS
308 REM    U$   USER RESPONSE
310 REM    N    NUMBER OF TOSSES
312 REM    I    COUNTER
314 REM    X1   OUTCOME FOR FIRST DIE
316 REM    X2   OUTCOME FOR SECOND DIE
318 REM    S    SUM OF OUTCOMES
900 REM *********************************
902 REM *    MAIN ROUTINE               *
904 REM *********************************
905 DIM F(12)
906 REM INITIAL MESSAGE
908 GOSUB 1006
910 REM PARAMETERS
912 GOSUB 1106
914 REM PROCESS
916 GOSUB 1206
918 REM OUTPUT
920 GOSUB 1306
922 REM FINAL MESSAGE
```

```
924 GOSUB 1406
926 IF U$ = "Y" THEN 912
928 PRINT
930 PRINT "END OF PROGRAM"
999 STOP
1000 REM ******************************
1002 REM *    INITIAL MESSAGE         *
1004 REM ******************************
1006 PRINT
1008 PRINT
1010 PRINT
1012 PRINT "PROGRAM 4-2"
1014 PRINT
1016 PRINT "SIMULATE TOSSING DICE FORMING"
1018 PRINT "THE FREQUENCY DISTRIBUTION"
1020 PRINT "FOR THE SUM OF THE OUTCOMES."
1099 RETURN
1100 REM ******************************
1102 REM *    PARAMETERS              *
1104 REM ******************************
1106 PRINT
1108 PRINT "NUMBER OF TOSSES";
1110 INPUT N
1199 RETURN
1200 REM ******************************
1202 REM *    PROCESS                 *
1204 REM ******************************
1206 FOR I = 1 TO 12
1208    LET F(I) = 0
1210 NEXT I
1212 FOR I = 1 TO N
1214    LET X1 = 1 + INT(6 * RND(0))
1216    LET X2 = 1 + INT(6 * RND(0))
1218    LET S = X1 + X2
1220    LET F(S) = F(S) + 1
1222 NEXT I
1299 RETURN
1300 REM ******************************
1302 REM *    OUTPUT                  *
1304 REM ******************************
1306 PRINT
1308 PRINT "SUM","FREQUENCY","FRACTION"
1310 FOR S = 2 TO 12
1312    PRINT S,F(S),F(S)/N
1314 NEXT S
1399 RETURN
```

```
1400 REM ******************************
1402 REM *    FINAL OUTPUT            *
1404 REM ******************************
1406 PRINT
1408 PRINT "TRY ANOTHER SET OF TOSSES (Y/N)";
1410 INPUT U$
1412 IF U$ = "Y" THEN 1499
1414 IF U$ = "N" THEN 1499
1416 PRINT
1418 PRINT "INVALID RESPONSE"
1420 GOTO 1406
1499 RETURN
9999 END
```

Program 4-3 simulates a biased random walk in two-dimensions (four directions). Figure 4-3 shows the results.

Exercise 4-1

1. Simulate tossing a biased coin having a probability of .7 of showing a head on any one toss.
2. Simulate the tossing of two dice and accumulating the frequencies for the product of the two values.
3. Replicate the random walk simulation for one hundred steps in each trial. Use the results to predict the average distance from the origin after one hundred steps.

```
PROGRAM P4-2

SIMULATE TOSSING DICE FORMING
THE FREQUENCY DISTRIBUTION
FOR THE SUM OF THE OUTCOMES.

NUMBER OF TOSSES? 1000

SUM               FREQUENCY        FRACTION
  2                   27             .027
  3                   52             .052
  4                   81             .081
  5                  104             .104
  6                  154             .154
  7                  172             .172
  8                  155             .155
  9                   96             .096
 10                   74             .074
 11                   63             .063
 12                   22             .022

TRY ANOTHER SET OF TOSSES (Y/N)? N

END OF PROGRAM
```

Fig. 4-2. Sample results from Program 4-2.

Program 4-3

```
100 REM *******************************
102 REM *    4 - 3                     *
104 REM *******************************
106 REM   AUTHOR
108 REM      COPYRIGHT 1982
110 REM       BY LAWRENCE MCNITT.
112 REM   PURPOSE
114 REM      SIMULATE TWO-DIMENSIONAL
116 REM      BIASED RANDOM WALK.
118 REM   SYSTEM
120 REM      UNIVERSAL SUBSET
122 REM      OF BASIC.
200 REM *******************************
202 REM *    ORGANIZATION              *
204 REM *******************************
206 REM   900   MAIN ROUTINE
208 REM         1000   INITIAL MESSAGE
210 REM         1100   PARAMETERS
212 REM         1200   PROCESS
214 REM         1300   OUTPUT
216 REM         1400   FINAL MESSAGE
300 REM *******************************
302 REM *    VARIABLES                 *
304 REM *******************************
306 REM    U$   USER RESPONSE
308 REM    P1   PROBABILITY FOR NORTH
310 REM    P2   PROBABILITY FOR SOUTH
312 REM    P3   PROBABILTIY FOR WEST
314 REM    P4   PROBABILITY FOR EAST
316 REM    N    NUMBER OF STEPS
318 REM    I    COUNTER
320 REM    X    LOCATION ON X-AXIS
322 REM    Y    LOCATION ON Y-AXIS
324 REM    D    DISTANCE FROM ORIGIN
326 REM    R    RANDOM NUMBER
900 REM *******************************
902 REM *    MAIN ROUTINE              *
904 REM *******************************
906 REM INITIAL MESSAGE
908 GOSUB 1006
910 REM PARAMETERS
912 GOSUB 1106
914 REM PROCESS
916 GOSUB 1206
918 REM OUTPUT
```

```
920 GOSUB 1306
922 REM FINAL MESSAGE
924 GOSUB 1406
926 IF U$ = "Y" THEN 912
928 PRINT
930 PRINT "END OF PROGRAM"
999 STOP
1000 REM *****************************
1002 REM *    INITIAL MESSAGE         *
1004 REM *****************************
1006 PRINT
1008 PRINT
1010 PRINT
1012 PRINT "PROGRAM 4 - 3"
1014 PRINT
1016 PRINT "SIMULATE TWO-DIMENSIONAL"
1018 PRINT "BIASED RANDOM WALK OF A"
1020 PRINT "FIXED NUMBER OF STEPS."
1099 RETURN
1100 REM *****************************
1102 REM *    PARAMETERS              *
1104 REM *****************************
1106 PRINT
1108 PRINT "NUMBER OF STEPS";
1110 INPUT N
1112 PRINT
1114 PRINT "PROBABILITY FOR STEP TOWARD THE"
1116 PRINT "NORTH";
1118 INPUT P1
1120 PRINT "SOUTH";
1122 INPUT P2
1124 PRINT "WEST";
1126 INPUT P3
1128 PRINT "EAST";
1130 INPUT P4
1132 IF ABS(P1+P2+P3+P4-1) < .00001 THEN 1140
1134 PRINT
1136 PRINT "SUM MUST EQUAL 1"
1138 GOTO 1112
1140 LET P2 = P1 + P2
1142 LET P3 = P2 + P3
1144 LET P4 = P3 + P4
1199 RETURN
1200 REM *****************************
1202 REM *    PROCESS                 *
1204 REM *****************************
```

```
1206 LET X = 0
1208 LET Y = 0
1210 FOR I = 1 TO N
1212    LET R = RND(0)
1214    IF R > P1 THEN 1220
1216    LET Y = Y + 1
1218    GOTO 1234
1220    IF R > P2 THEN 1226
1222    LET Y = Y - 1
1224    GOTO 1234
1226    IF R > P3 THEN 1232
1228    LET X = X - 1
1230    GOTO 1234
1232    LET X = X + 1
1234 NEXT I
1299 RETURN
1300 REM *****************************
1302 REM *    OUTPUT                 *
1304 REM *****************************
1306 LET D = SQR(Y*Y + X*X)
1308 PRINT
1310 PRINT "FINAL LOCATION"
1312 IF Y < 0 THEN 1318
1314 PRINT Y;"NORTH"
1316 GOTO 1320
1318 PRINT -Y;"SOUTH"
1320 IF X < 0 THEN 1326
1322 PRINT X;"EAST"
1324 GOTO 1328
1326 PRINT -X;"WEST"
1328 PRINT
1330 PRINT "DISTANCE FROM ORIGIN",D
1399 RETURN
1400 REM *****************************
1402 REM *    FINAL OUTPUT           *
1404 REM *****************************
1406 PRINT
1408 PRINT "TRY ANOTHER RANDOM WALK (Y/N)";
1410 INPUT U$
1412 IF U$ = "Y" THEN 1499
1414 IF U$ = "N" THEN 1499
1416 PRINT
1418 PRINT "INVALID RESPONSE"
1420 GOTO 1406
1499 RETURN
9999 END
```

```
PROGRAM P4-3

SIMULATE TWO-DIMENSIONAL
BIASED RANDOM WALK OF A
FIXED NUMBER OF STEPS.

NUMBER OF STEPS? 100

PROBABILITY FOR STEP TOWARD THE
NORTH? .4
SOUTH? .1
WEST? .3
EAST? .2

FINAL LOCATION
  35 NORTH
  15 WEST

DISTANCE FROM ORIGIN          38.0789

TRY ANOTHER RANDOM WALK (Y/N)? N
END OF PROGRAM
```

Fig. 4-3. Sample results from Program 4-3.

INDUSTRIAL PROCESSES

A process produces output that may be continuous or discrete. The process producing wire is continuous. Building washing machines is a discrete process.

If sufficient history of a real process exists, mathematical processes can be derived to describe characteristics of the output. Simulation modeling uses these characteristics.

Mistakes do happen. Defective output is produced. Even under the best of conditions, some output will be defective. A certain process forming ball bearings results in an expected five percent failure rate under the best conditions. The ball bearings are formed in batches of one hundred at a time. From time to time the process will slip out of adjustment resulting in a higher level of defective product. The following probability distribution describes the value of the process fraction defective as a random walk.

Change in fraction defective	Probability
.00	.4
.01	.5
.05	.1

Program 4-4 simulates the quality of production of several batches assuming a random walk of the process fraction defective with each batch. Figure 4-4 shows the results.

Exercise 4-2

1. Use the model in this section to estimate the average number of defectives produced in ten batches of one hundred each. Run the model for several replications to make the estimate.
2. Adjusting the process costs $15.00 and brings the process back to the initial five percent defective rate. Defective ball bearings cost $.075 each.

117

Program 4-4

```
100 REM ********************************
102 REM *    4-4                       *
104 REM ********************************
106 REM   AUTHOR
108 REM       COPYRIGHT 1982
110 REM         BY LAWRENCE MCNITT.
112 REM   PURPOSE
114 REM       SIMULATE RANDOM WALK
116 REM       OF BINOMIAL PARAMETER.
118 REM   SYSTEM
120 REM       UNIVERSAL SUBSET
122 REM       OF BASIC.
200 REM ********************************
202 REM *    ORGANIZATION              *
204 REM ********************************
206 REM   900    MAIN ROUTINE
208 REM          1000   INITIAL MESSAGE
210 REM          1100   PARAMETERS
212 REM          1200   PROCESS
214 REM          1300   OUTPUT
216 REM          1400   FINAL MESSAGE
300 REM ********************************
302 REM *    VARIABLES                 *
304 REM ********************************
306 REM   A(20)    ADJUSTMENT TO BINOMIAL PARAMETER
308 REM   C(20)    CUMULATIVE PROBABILITY OF ADJUSTMENT
310 REM   U$   USER RESPONSE
312 REM   N    LOT SIZE
314 REM   M    NUMBER OF LOTS
316 REM   P    CURRENT FRACTION DEFECTIVE
318 REM   D    NUMBER DEFECTIVE IN CURRENT LOT
320 REM   I    COUNTER
322 REM   J    COUNTER
324 REM   T    TOTAL
326 REM   R    RANDOM NUMBER
328 REM   N1   NUMBER OF STATES FOR RANDOM WALK
900 REM ********************************
902 REM *    MAIN ROUTINE              *
904 REM ********************************
905 DIM A(20),C(20)
906 REM INITIAL MESSAGE
908 GOSUB 1006
910 REM PARAMETERS
912 GOSUB 1106
```

```
914 REM PROCESS
916 GOSUB 1206
918 REM FINAL MESSAGE
920 GOSUB 1306
922 IF U$ = "Y" THEN 912
924 PRINT
926 PRINT "END OF PROGRAM"
999 STOP
1000 REM *******************************
1002 REM *     INITIAL MESSAGE         *
1004 REM *******************************
1006 PRINT
1008 PRINT
1010 PRINT
1012 PRINT "PROGRAM 4-4"
1014 PRINT
1016 PRINT "SIMULATE OUTPUT FROM BERNOULLI"
1018 PRINT "(BINOMIAL) PROCESS WITH PARAMETER"
1020 PRINT "UNDERGOING RANDOM WALK."
1099 RETURN
1100 REM *******************************
1102 REM *     PARAMETERS              *
1104 REM ****!**************************
1106 PRINT
1108 PRINT "LOT SIZE";
1110 INPUT N
1112 PRINT
1114 PRINT "NUMBER OF LOTS";
1116 INPUT M
1118 PRINT
1120 PRINT "PROBABILITY DISTRIBUTION FOR"
1122 PRINT "RANDOM WALK OF PARAMETER"
1124 PRINT
1126 PRINT "NUMBER OF STATES";
1128 INPUT N1
1130 PRINT
1132 PRINT "ADJUSTMENT, PROBABILITY FOR"
1134 LET T = 0
1136 FOR I = 1 TO N1
1138     PRINT "STATE";I;
1140     INPUT A(I),C(I)
1142     LET T = T + C(I)
1144     LET C(I) = T
1146 NEXT I
1148 IF ABS(T - 1) < .00001 THEN 1156
1150 PRINT
```

```
1152 PRINT "SUM OF PROBABILITIES IS NOT 1.0"
1154 GOTO 1130
1156 PRINT
1158 PRINT "INITIAL FRACTION DEFECTIVE";
1160 INPUT P
1162 RANDOM
1199 RETURN
1200 REM ********************************
1202 REM *     PROCESS                  *
1204 REM ********************************
1206 LET X = 0
1208 PRINT
1210 PRINT "LOT","BERNOULLI","NUMBER"
1212 PRINT ,"PARAMETER","OBSERVED"
1214 FOR I = 1 TO M
1216    LET R = RND(0)
1218    FOR J = 1 TO N1
1220       IF R > C(J) THEN 1226
1222       LET P = P + A(J)
1224       LET J = N1
1226    NEXT J
1228    LET D = 0
1230    FOR J = 1 TO N
1232       LET R = RND(0)
1234       IF R > P THEN 1238
1236       LET D = D + 1
1238    NEXT J
1240    PRINT I,P,D
1242 NEXT I
1299 RETURN
1300 REM ****************************** 
1302 REM *     FINAL MESSAGE           *
1304 REM ****************************** 
1306 PRINT
1308 PRINT "TRY ANOTHER SIMULATION RUN (Y/N)";
1310 INPUT U$
1312 IF U$ = "Y" THEN 1399
1314 IF U$ = "N" THEN 1399
1316 PRINT
1318 PRINT "INVALID RESPONSE"
1320 GOTO 1306
1399 RETURN
9999 END
```

```
PROGRAM P4-4

SIMULATE OUTPUT FROM BERNOULLI
(BINOMIAL) PROCESS WITH PARAMETER
UNDERGOING RANDOM WALK.
LOT SIZE? 100

NUMBER OF LOTS? 10

PROBABILITY DISTRIBUTION FOR
RANDOM WALK OF PARAMETER

NUMBER OF STATES? 3

ADJUSTMENT, PROBABILITY FOR
STATE 1 ? 0,.4
STATE 2 ? .01,.5
STATE 3 ? .05,.1

INITIAL FRACTION DEFECTIVE? .05

LOT               BERNOULLI        NUMBER
                  PARAMETER        OBSERVED
  1                 .06              5
  2                 .06              7
  3                 .07              7
  4                 .08              6
  5                 .08             12
  6                 .08             11
  7                 .09             11
  8                 .1              12
  9                 .1               9
 10                 .15             16
TRY ANOTHER SIMULATION RUN (Y/N)? N

END OF PROGRAM
```

Fig. 4-4. Sample results from Program 4-4.

How many batches should be run before making the adjustment? What number of batches per setting will minimize the total cost consisting of the cost of adjusting and the cost of defective ball bearings?

SIMULATED DEMAND

Price and demand for a product are related. Higher prices result in lower demand. Lower prices result in higher demand. Production and distribution costs place a floor under the price. Competition effectively puts a lid on the price. Many mathematical functions are candidates for representing demand functions.

The choice of demand function can be made subjectively, reflecting the opinion of those familiar with the market. At other times experimental evidence and statistical analysis determine an appropriate demand function. In either situation, the mathematical representation of the demand function will be valid only within a limited range of prices.

Sample Demand Functions

The simplest linear demand function is of the form

$$D = A + B * P$$

in which D is the demand, A is the Y-intercept, and B is the slope of the demand function. The variable P is the price. The slope will usually be negative denoting a decrease in demand with an increase in price.

The demand function is not always linear. The function

$$D = A * B / P$$

also decreases as P increases. The function

$$D = A * (B / P) ** 2$$

is another example of a demand function. Introductory college math textbooks describe many such functions and their properties.

Simulating Demand Over Time

Another aspect of simulating demand involves the time element. The demand may be undergoing a general up or down trend. It may be following a seasonal pattern. There will also be a random component to the demand. This represents the uncertainty resulting from an imperfect forecast.

Program 4-5 simulates demand over time assuming a linear trend and normally distributed deviations from that trend. Figure 4-5 shows the results.

Program 4-5

```
100 REM ******************************
102 REM *    4-5                      *
104 REM ******************************
106 REM   AUTHOR
108 REM       COPYRIGHT 1982
110 REM       BY LAWRENCE MCNITT.
112 REM   PURPOSE
114 REM       SIMULATE DEMAND RANDOMLY DISTRIBUTED
116 REM       AROUND A LINEAR TREND LINE.
118 REM   SYSTEM
120 REM       UNIVERSAL SUBSET
122 REM       OF BASIC.
200 REM ******************************
202 REM *    ORGANIZATION             *
204 REM ******************************
206 REM   900   MAIN ROUTINE
208 REM          1000   INITIAL MESSAGE
210 REM          1100   PARAMETERS
212 REM          1200   PROCESS
214 REM          1300   FINAL MESSAGE
```

```
300 REM ****************************
302 REM *    VARIABLES              *
304 REM ****************************
306 REM    U$  USER RESPONSE
308 REM    A   Y-INTERCEPT FOR TREND LINE
310 REM    B   SLOPE FOR TREND LINE
312 REM    S   STANDARD ERROR FOR RANDOM COMPONENT
314 REM    N   NUMBER OF PERIODS TO SIMULATE
316 REM    I   COUNTER
318 REM    E   EXPECTED VALUE FROM TREND LINE
320 REM    X   OBSERVED VALUE FOR DEMAND
322 REM    J   COUNTER
324 REM    Z   STANDARD SCORE FOR NORMAL
900 REM ****************************
902 REM *    MAIN ROUTINE            *
904 REM ****************************
906 REM INITIAL MESSAGE
908 GOSUB 1006
910 REM PARAMETERS
912 GOSUB 1106
914 REM PROCESS
916 GOSUB 1206
918 REM FINAL MESSAGE
920 GOSUB 1306
922 IF U$ = "Y" THEN 912
924 PRINT
926 PRINT "END OF PROGRAM"
999 STOP
1000 REM ****************************
1002 REM *    INITIAL MESSAGE         *
1004 REM ****************************
1006 PRINT
1008 PRINT
1010 PRINT
1012 PRINT "PROGRAM 4-5"
1014 PRINT
1016 PRINT "SIMULATE DEMAND THAT IS NORMALLY"
1018 PRINT "DISTRIBUTED AROUND A LINEAR"
1020 PRINT "TREND LINE."
1099 RETURN
1100 REM ****************************
1102 REM *    PARAMETERS              *
1104 REM ****************************
1106 PRINT
1107 PRINT "Y-INTERCEPT FOR TREND LINE";
1108 INPUT A
```

```
1110 PRINT
1112 PRINT "SLOPE FOR TREND LINE";
1114 INPUT B
1116 PRINT
1118 PRINT "STANDARD ERROR AROUND TREND";
1120 INPUT S
1122 PRINT
1124 PRINT "NUMBER OF PERIODS TO SIMULATE";
1126 INPUT N
1199 RETURN
1200 REM ******************************
1202 REM *     PROCESS                *
1204 REM ******************************
1206 PRINT
1208 PRINT "PERIOD","EXPECTED","OBSERVED"
1210 FOR I = 1 TO N
1212    LET E = A + B * I
1214    LET Z = -6
1216    FOR J = 1 TO 12
1218       LET Z = Z + RND(0)
1220    NEXT J
1222    LET X = E + Z * S
1224    PRINT I,E,X
1226 NEXT I
1299 RETURN
1300 REM ******************************
1302 REM *     FINAL MESSAGE          *
1304 REM ******************************
1306 PRINT
1308 PRINT "TRY ANOTHER SIMULATION RUN (Y/N)";
1310 INPUT U$
1312 IF U$ = "Y" THEN 1399
1314 IF U$ = "N" THEN 1399
1316 PRINT
1318 PRINT "INVALID RESPONSE"
1320 GOTO 1306
1399 RETURN
9999 END
```

Exercise 4-3

1. Model demand over time using the trend equation

$$D = 100 * SQR(T)$$

and a normally distributed random component.

Make the standard error equal to ten percent of the expected demand for that period.

2. Model demand as a function of price using the equation

$$D = 2000 - 5 * P$$

with a random component that is normally distri-

```
PROGRAM 4-5

SIMULATE DEMAND THAT IS NORMALLY
DISTRIBUTED AROUND A LINEAR
TREND LINE.

Y-INTERCEPT FOR TREND LINE? 100

SLOPE FOR TREND LINE? 5

STANDARD ERROR AROUND TREND? 10

NUMBER OF PERIODS TO SIMULATE? 10

PERIOD              EXPECTED           OBSERVED
   1                  105              118.604
   2                  110              106.949
   3                  115               98.964
   4                  120              133.362
   5                  125              125.56
   6                  130              132.732
   7                  135              121.538
   8                  140              122.332
   9                  145              142.773
  10                  150              163.448

TRY ANOTHER SIMULATION RUN (Y/N)? N
```

Fig. 4-5. Sample results from Program 4-5.

buted. Use a standard error of 50. Generate 10 values for each of the prices $100, $200, and $300.

INTEGRATION BY SIMULATION

Integral calculus is one of the important areas of analytical problem solving in mathematics. If the function f(x) is positive throughout the range from a to b, the definite integral of f(x) from a to b gives the area under the curve between those two points.

Analytic solutions abound for many common functions and should be used if known. Because some functions have no known analytic solutions, other methods may be necessary.

Numerical analysis is the branch of mathematics concerned with the numerical estimation of mathematical operations. Numerical integration methods that give estimates of the value of the definite integral are available. These methods typically involve summing areas for subintervals defined over the region of interest.

Monte Carlo integration is a special form of numerical integration that uses random sampling. It involves generating random points in the interval and computing the average value of the function f(x) over that interval. The average height times the interval width provides an estimate of the definite integral. For example, consider the function

$$X**3 + 2*X**2 + X + 5$$

and its definite integral defined over the interval

125

(0-2). Since the function is positive for all values X within the interval, the definite integral gives the area under the curve from X=0 to X=2. Analytical methods give the answer 21.3333.

Program 4-6 uses Monte Carlo techniques to estimate the definite integral of the function. Figure 4-6 shows the results.

Using numerical integration on a function having a known solution gives an idea of the accuracy of the method for estimating definite integrals.

Program 4-6

```
100 REM *******************************
102 REM *    4-6                       *
104 REM *******************************
106 REM   AUTHOR
108 REM       COPYRIGHT 1982
110 REM       BY LAWRENCE MCNITT.
112 REM   PURPOSE
114 REM       NUMERICAL INTEGRATION USING
116 REM       MONTE CARLO TECHNIQUE.
118 REM   SYSTEM
120 REM       UNIVERSAL SUBSET
122 REM       OF BASIC.
200 REM *******************************
202 REM *    ORGANIZATION              *
204 REM *******************************
206 REM   900   MAIN ROUTINE
208 REM         1000   INITIAL MESSAGE
210 REM         1100   PARAMETERS
212 REM         1200   PROCESS
214 REM                2000   FUNCTION
216 REM         1300   OUTPUT
218 REM         1400   FINAL MESSAGE
300 REM *******************************
302 REM *    VARIABLES                 *
304 REM *******************************
306 REM    U$   USER RESPONSE
308 REM    A    ESTIMATED AREA
310 REM    N    NUMBER OF TRIALS
312 REM    Y    VALUE OF FUNCTION
314 REM    S    SUM OF THE HEIGHTS
316 REM    I    COUNTER
318 REM    L1   LOWER BOUND FOR X
320 REM    L2   UPPER BOUND FOR X
322 REM    X    CURRENT VALUE FOR X
900 REM *******************************
902 REM *    MAIN ROUTINE              *
904 REM *******************************
906 REM INITIAL MESSAGE
```

```
908 GOSUB 1006
910 REM PARAMETERS
912 GOSUB 1106
914 REM PROCESS
916 GOSUB 1206
918 REM OUTPUT
920 GOSUB 1306
922 REM FINAL MESSAGE
924 GOSUB 1406
926 IF U$ = "Y" THEN 912
928 PRINT
930 PRINT "END OF PROGRAM"
999 STOP
1000 REM *******************************
1002 REM *    INITIAL MESSAGE          *
1004 REM *******************************
1006 PRINT
1008 PRINT
1010 PRINT
1012 PRINT "PROGRAM 4-6"
1014 PRINT
1016 PRINT "NUMERICAL INTEGRATION USING"
1018 PRINT "MONTE CARLO SIMULATION."
1099 RETURN
1100 REM *******************************
1102 REM *    PARAMETERS               *
1104 REM *******************************
1106 PRINT
1108 PRINT "NUMBER OF TRIALS";
1110 INPUT N
1112 PRINT
1114 PRINT "LIMITS OF X FOR INTEGRATION"
1116 PRINT "LOWER LIMIT";
1118 INPUT L1
1120 PRINT "UPPER LIMIT";
1122 INPUT L2
1199 RETURN
1200 REM *******************************
1202 REM *    PROCESS                  *
1204 REM *******************************
1206 LET S = 0
1208 FOR I = 1 TO N
1210    LET X = L1 + (L2 - L1) * RND(0)
1212    REM FUNCTION
1213    GOSUB 2006
1214    LET S = S + Y
```

```
1216 NEXT I
1218 LET A = (L2 - L1) * S / N
1299 RETURN
1300 REM *******************************
1302 REM *    OUTPUT                    *
1304 REM *******************************
1306 PRINT
1308 PRINT "ESTIMATED AREA",A
1399 RETURN
1400 REM *******************************
1402 REM *    FINAL OUTPUT              *
1404 REM *******************************
1406 PRINT
1408 PRINT "TRY ANOTHER SIMULATION RUN (Y/N)";
1410 INPUT U$
1412 IF U$ = "Y" THEN 1499
1414 IF U$ = "N" THEN 1499
1416 PRINT
1418 PRINT "INVALID RESPONSE"
1420 GOTO 1406
1499 RETURN
2000 REM *******************************
2002 REM *    FUNCTION                  *
2004 REM *******************************
2006 LET Y = X*X*X + 2*X*X + X + 5
2099 RETURN
9999 END
```

```
PROGRAM 4-6

NUMERICAL INTEGRATION USING
MONTE CARLO SIMULATION.

NUMBER OF TRIALS? 100

LIMITS OF X FOR INTEGRATION
LOWER LIMIT? 0
UPPER LIMIT? 2

ESTIMATED AREA    21.2136

TRY ANOTHER SIMULATION RUN (Y/N)? N

END OF PROGRAM
```

Fig. 4-6. Sample results from Program 4-6.

Exercise 4-4

1. Use Monte Carlo integration to estimate the definite integral for the function

$$.389* 2.73 ** (-.5 * X ** 2)$$

for X in the interval from 0 to 1.5.

2. Multiple definite integrals extend to the concept of volume for two variables. Extend the concept of Monte Carlo integration to include two variables. Test using the function

$$SQR (X**2 + 3*X*Y + .5*Y**2)$$

and the interval 1-3 for X and the interval 2-4 for Y.

MATHEMATICAL PROGRAMMING SIMULATION

Optimization involves maximizing or minimizing a function. The simplest problems involve the optimization of the functions of one variable. The tools of mathematics provide analytic solutions for some functions, but other functions are difficult to solve analytically.

Optimizing functions of many variables greatly increases the complexity of the problem. Even though formal mathematics gives insight into solution methods, increasing numbers of variables compound the problem.

Allowing the variable in the function to take on any mathematically feasible solution is not practical for many problem situations. The possible variables are constrained by laws of nature, common sense, or financial considerations. Incorporating feasibility constraints adds to the burden of finding the optimum value.

Consider the problem of finding the maximum value of the function

$$X**3 - 5*X*X + 3*X - 10$$

within the interval X = 0-6. Monte Carlo optimization involves evaluating the function for a large number of values of X chosen from the interval in question. The larger the number selected the more likely the maximum value found will be at or near the optimum point.

Program 4-7 uses Monte Carlo simulation to search for the optimum value of the functions. Figure 4-7 shows the results.

Program 4-7

```
100 REM **********************************
102 REM *    4-7                          *
104 REM **********************************
106 REM   AUTHOR
108 REM       COPYRIGHT 1982
110 REM       BY LAWRENCE MCNITT.
112 REM   PURPOSE
114 REM       MONTE CARLO OPTIMIZATION OF
116 REM       FUNCTION OF ONE VARIABLE.
118 REM   SYSTEM
120 REM       UNIVERSAL SUBSET
122 REM       OF BASIC.
200 REM **********************************
202 REM *    ORGANIZATION                 *
204 REM **********************************
206 REM   900   MAIN ROUTINE
208 REM         1000   INITIAL MESSAGE
210 REM         1100   PARAMETERS
```

```
212 REM          1200   PROCESS
214 REM                 2000   FUNCTION
216 REM          1300   OUTPUT
218 REM          1400   FINAL MESSAGE
300 REM **********************************
302 REM *    VARIABLES                   *
304 REM **********************************
306 REM    U$   USER RESPONSE
308 REM    T    TYPE OF OPTIMIZATION
310 REM    N    NUMBER OF TRIALS
312 REM    I    COUNTER
314 REM    L1   LOWER BOUND FOR X
316 REM    L2   UPPER BOUND FOR X
318 REM    X    CURRENT VALUE FOR X
320 REM    Y    VALUE OF FUNCTION AT X
322 REM    Y1   BEST VALUE OF Y SO FAR
324 REM    X1   VALUE FOR X FOR BEST Y SO FAR
900 REM **********************************
902 REM *    MAIN ROUTINE                *
904 REM **********************************
906 REM INITIAL MESSAGE
908 GOSUB 1006
910 REM PARAMETERS
912 GOSUB 1106
914 REM PROCESS
916 GOSUB 1206
918 REM OUTPUT
920 GOSUB 1306
922 REM FINAL MESSAGE
924 GOSUB 1406
926 IF U$ = "Y" THEN 912
928 PRINT
930 PRINT "END OF PROGRAM"
999 STOP
1000 REM **********************************
1002 REM *    INITIAL MESSAGE             *
1004 REM **********************************
1006 PRINT
1008 PRINT
1010 PRINT
1012 PRINT "PROGRAM 4-7"
1014 PRINT
1016 PRINT "MONTE CARLO OPTIMIZATION"
1018 PRINT "OF FUNCTION OF ONE VARIABLE."
1099 RETURN
1100 REM **********************************
```

```
1102 REM *    PARAMETERS                *
1104 REM ******************************
1106 PRINT
1108 PRINT "NUMBER OF TRIALS";
1110 INPUT N
1112 PRINT
1114 PRINT "LIMITS OF X FOR SEARCH"
1116 PRINT "LOWER LIMIT";
1118 INPUT L1
1120 PRINT "UPPER LIMIT";
1122 INPUT L2
1199 RETURN
1200 REM ******************************
1202 REM *    PROCESS                  *
1204 REM ******************************
1206 LET Y1 = -10E30
1208 FOR I = 1 TO N
1210    LET X = L1 + (L2 - L1) * RND(0)
1212    REM FUNCTION
1214    GOSUB 2006
1216    IF Y <= Y1 THEN 1222
1218    LET Y1 = Y
1220    LET X1 = X
1222 NEXT I
1299 RETURN
1300 REM ******************************
1302 REM *    OUTPUT                   *
1304 REM ******************************
1306 PRINT
1308 PRINT "BEST RESULT FOUND SO FAR"
1310 PRINT "Y = F(X)",Y1
1312 PRINT "X",X1
1399 RETURN
1400 REM ******************************
1402 REM *    FINAL OUTPUT             *
1404 REM ******************************
1406 PRINT
1408 PRINT "TRY ANOTHER SIMULATION RUN (Y/N)";
1410 INPUT U$
1412 IF U$ = "Y" THEN 1499
1414 IF U$ = "N" THEN 1499
1416 PRINT
1418 PRINT "INVALID RESPONSE"
1420 GOTO 1406
1499 RETURN
2000 REM ******************************
```

```
2002 REM *    FUNCTION                    *
2004 REM ******************************
2006 LET Y = X*X*X - 5*X*X + 3*X - 10
2099 RETURN
9999 END
```

Linear and Nonlinear Programming

Linear programming is a well-known technique for optimizing a linear objective function subject to linear constraints. The methods of solution are efficient and easily programmed for computer solution. The following is a typical problem statement:

$$\text{Max } Y = 10X1 + 25X2$$

Subject to

$$2X1 + 3X2 <= 150$$
$$5X1 + 4X2 <= 200$$
$$X1 \qquad >= 0$$
$$X2 >= 0$$

The function

```
            PROGRAM 4-7

            MONTE CARLO OPTIMIZATION
            OF FUNCTION OF ONE VARIABLE.

            NUMBER OF TRIALS? 100

            LIMITS OF X FOR SEARCH
            LOWER LIMIT? 0
            UPPER LIMIT? 6

            BEST RESULT FOUND SO FAR
            Y = F(X)          41.9291
            X                 5.95897
            TRY ANOTHER SIMULATION RUN (Y/N)? Y

            NUMBER OF TRIALS? 100

            LIMITS OF X FOR SEARCH
            LOWER LIMIT? 5.9
            UPPER LIMIT? 6

            BEST RESULT FOUND SO FAR
            Y = F(X)          43.9537
            X                 5.99909

            TRY ANOTHER SIMULATION RUN (Y/N)? N

            END OF PROGRAM
```

Fig. 4-7. Sample results from Program 4-7.

10X1 + 25X2

is the objective function. The other functions are the constraints.

Unfortunately, the equations are not always linear. Nonlinearities in the objective function or the constraints makes finding a solution more difficult. Monte Carlo simulation involves generating a large number of potential solutions for X1 and X2, testing them for feasibility, and comparing the objective function values to find the one with the optimum value.

Integer solutions are required for some variables. Although integer programming is much more difficult than standard linear programming, the computational burden of adding the integer requirement to a Monte Carlo simulation is minor.

Consider the following problem:

$$\text{Max } X1{*}{*}2 + X2{*}{*}2 + 3X3{*}{*}2 + 4X4{*}{*}2 + 2X5{*}{*}2 - 8X1 - 2X2 - 3X3 - X4 - 2X5$$

Subject to

$$
\begin{aligned}
X1 + X2 + X3 + X4 + X5 &<= 400 \\
X1 + 2X2 + 2X3 + X4 + 6X5 &<= 800 \\
2X1 + X2 + 6X3 &<= 200 \\
X3 + X4 + 5X5 &<= 200 \\
X1{*}{*}2 + X2X3 + 10\text{Log}(1+X5) &>= 100 \\
0 <= X1 <= 99 \quad &\text{Integer} \\
0 <= X2 <= 99 & \\
0 <= X3 <= 50 & \\
50 <= X4 <= 99 & \\
10 <= X5 <= 40 \quad &\text{Integer}
\end{aligned}
$$

Program 4-8 carries out the analysis. The constraints and objective function are isolated in subroutines for easy modification for use in solving

Program 4-8

```
100 REM *******************************
102 REM *    4-8                      *
104 REM *******************************
106 REM   AUTHOR
108 REM      COPYRIGHT 1982
110 REM      BY LAWRENCE MCNITT.
112 REM   PURPOSE
114 REM      MONTE CARLO TECHNIQUE
116 REM      FOR NONLINEAR PROGRAMMING.
118 REM   SYSTEM
120 REM      UNIVERSAL SUBSET
122 REM      OF BASIC.
200 REM *******************************
202 REM *    ORGANIZATION             *
204 REM *******************************
206 REM   900   MAIN ROUTINE
208 REM         1000   INITIAL MESSAGE
210 REM         1100   PARAMETERS
212 REM         1200   PROCESS
214 REM               2000   FEASIBILITY
216 REM               2100   EVALUATE
218 REM               2200   OUTPUT
220 REM         1300   FINAL MESSAGE
300 REM *******************************
302 REM *    VARIABLES                *
```

```
304 REM **************************
305 REM    L(I,2)    LOWER AND UPPER LIMITS FOR VARIABLES
306 REM    X(100)    CURRENT VARIABLE VALUES
308 REM    B(100)    VARIABLE VALUES FOR BEST SO FAR
310 REM    U$  USER RESPONSE
312 REM    N    NUMBER OF VARIABLES
314 REM    M    MAXIMUM NUMBER OF ITERATIONS
316 REM    I    INDEX FOR VARIABLE
318 REM    J    COUNTER
320 REM    C    CONSTRAINT VALUE
322 REM    F    OBJECTIVE FUNCTION VALUE
324 REM    B1   MAXIMUM VALUE FOUND SO FAR
900 REM ******************************
902 REM *    MAIN ROUTINE             *
904 REM ******************************
906 DIM X(100),B(100),L(100,2)
908 REM INITIAL MESSAGE
910 GOSUB 1006
912 REM PARAMETERS
914 GOSUB 1106
916 REM PROCESS
918 GOSUB 1206
920 REM FINAL MESSAGE
922 GOSUB 1306
924 IF U$ = "Y" THEN 918
926 PRINT
928 PRINT "END OF PROGRAM"
999 STOP
1000 REM ******************************
1002 REM *    INITIAL MESSAGE          *
1004 REM ******************************
1006 PRINT
1008 PRINT
1010 PRINT
1012 PRINT "PROGRAM 4-8"
1014 PRINT
1016 PRINT "MONTE CARLO OPTIMIZATION"
1018 PRINT "OF A NONLINEAR OBJECTIVE"
1020 PRINT "FUNCTION SUBJECT TO NONLINEAR"
1022 PRINT "AND INTEGER CONSTRAINTS."
1099 RETURN
1100 REM ******************************
1102 REM *    PARAMETERS               *
1104 REM ******************************
1106 READ N
1108 FOR I = 1 TO N
```

```
1110     READ L(I,1),L(I,2)
1112 NEXT I
1114 LET B1 = -10E30
1199 RETURN
1200 REM ****************************
1202 REM *    PROCESS
1204 REM ****************************
1206 PRINT
1207 PRINT "NUMBER OF ITERATIONS";
1208 INPUT M
1210 FOR J = 1 TO M
1212     REM FEASIBILITY
1214     GOSUB 2006
1216     IF G = 0 THEN 1228
1218     REM EVALUATE
1220     GOSUB 2106
1222     IF F <= B1 THEN 1228
1224     REM OUTPUT
1226     GOSUB 2206
1228 NEXT J
1299 RETURN
1300 REM ****************************
1302 REM *    FINAL MESSAGE          *
1304 REM ****************************
1306 PRINT
1308 PRINT "CONTINUE SIMULATION (Y/N)";
1310 INPUT U$
1312 IF U$ = "Y" THEN 1399
1314 IF U$ = "N" THEN 1399
1316 PRINT
1318 PRINT "INVALID RESPONSE"
1320 GOTO 1306
1399 RETURN
2000 REM ****************************
2002 REM *    FEASIBILITY            *
2004 REM ****************************
2006 LET G = 0
2008 FOR I = 1 TO N
2010     LET X(I) = L(I,1) + RND(0) * (L(I,2) - L(I,1))
2012 NEXT I
2014 LET X(1) = INT(1 + X(1))
2016 LET X(5) = INT(1 + X(5))
2018 LET C = X(1) + X(2) + X(3) + X(4) + X(5)
2020 IF C > 400 THEN 2099
2022 LET C = X(1) + 2*X(2) + 2*X(3) + X(4) + 6*X(5)
2024 IF C > 800 THEN 2099
```

```
2026 LET C = 2*X(1) + X(2) + 6*X(3)
2028 IF C > 200 THEN 2099
2030 LET C = X(3) + X(4) + 5*X(5)
2032 IF C > 200 THEN 2099
2034 LET C = X(1) * X(1) + X(2) * X(3) + 10*LOG(1+X(5))
2036 IF C < 100 THEN 2099
2038 LET G = 1
2099 RETURN
2100 REM ******************************
2102 REM *     EVALUATE               *
2104 REM ******************************
2106 LET F = X(1)*X(1) + X(2)*X(2) + 3*X(3)*X(3)
2108 LET F = F + 4*X(4)*X(4) + 2*X(5)*X(5)
2110 LET F = F - 8*X(1) - 2*X(2) - 3*X(3) - X(4) - 2*X(5)
2199 RETURN
2200 REM ******************************
2202 REM *     OUTPUT                 *
2204 REM ******************************
2206 FOR I = 1 TO N
2208     LET B(I) = X(I)
2210 NEXT I
2212 LET B1 = F
2214 PRINT
2216 PRINT "ITERATION",J
2218 PRINT
2220 PRINT "F(X) =",F
2222 PRINT
2224 PRINT "VARIABLE","VALUE"
2226 FOR I = 1 TO N
2228     PRINT I,X(I)
2230 NEXT I
2299 RETURN
8000 REM ******************************
8002 REM *     NUMBER OF VARIABLES     *
8004 REM *     LIMITS FOR VARIABLE 1   *
8006 REM *     LIMITS FOR VARIABLE 2   *
8008 REM *     THROUGH                 *
8010 REM *     LIMITS FOR VARIABLE N   *
8012 REM ******************************
9000 DATA 5
9001 DATA 0,99
9002 DATA 0,99
9003 DATA 0,50
9004 DATA 50,99
9006 DATA 10,40
9999 END
```

```
PROGRAM 4-8                         2              55.878
                                    3              1.18707
MONTE CARLO OPTIMIZATION            4              61.8506
OF A NONLINEAR OBJECTIVE            5              23
FUNCTION SUBJECT TO NONLINEAR
AND INTEGER CONSTRAINTS.        ITERATION          52

NUMBER OF ITERATIONS? 100       F(X) =             42720.4

ITERATION          6            VARIABLE        VALUE
                                    1              25
F(X) =             13950.3          2              66.0132
                                    3              13.475
VARIABLE        VALUE               4              96.4908
    1              11               5              15
    2              46.6948
    3              10.4758      CONTINUE SIMULATION (Y/N)? Y
    4              50.4453
    5              27           NUMBER OF ITERATIONS? 1000

ITERATION          24           ITERATION          257
F(X) =             17913
                                F(X) =             43355.7
VARIABLE        VALUE
    1              3            VARIABLE        VALUE
    2              50.2049          1              34
    3              1.81505          2              68.4742
    4              60.4979          3              5.90828
    5              22               4              96.9767
                                    5              13
ITERATION          50
                                CONTINUE SIMULATION (Y/N)? N
F(X) =             19248.4
VARIABLE        VALUE            END OF PROGRAM
    1              3
```

Fig. 4-8. Sample results from Program 4-8.

other problems. The results are shown in Fig. 4-8.

Exercise 4-5

1. Use the Monte Carlo optimization approach to estimate the minimum value of the function

$$12 / X**2 + 4*X**.8 - 5*X$$

within the limits .5 to 1.5.

2. Modify the nonlinear constrained optimization program to include only integer solutions for all five variables.

3. Modify the limits for the nonlinear constrained optimization program to provide a more thorough search for the best answer using one thousand interactions. Tighten the upper and lower limits of the search area for each variable to reflect the region giving the best results.

Chapter 5
Statistical Analysis

Statistical analysis is important in estimating the equations that make up the simulation model, in modeling the random events included in the model, and in the evaluation of the results of the simulation experiment.

This chapter reviews some of the most important methods of statistical analysis including regression analysis and analysis of variance. Included are simple programs to aid in the analysis.

A REVIEW OF CLASSICAL STATISTICS

Classical statistical procedures that are useful in dealing with simulation models include the determining of summary measures such as the mean, median, and mode; the testing of hypotheses, and the summarizing of simulation results.

Some areas of human endeavor have too little data to make meaningful judgments. Other areas have too much data. The purpose of statistical data is to draw valid conclusions from masses of data.

Summary measures are important tools for reducing masses of data to meaningful relationships.

Common measures include the arithmetic mean (average), the median, and the mode for the central tendency of the data. They also include the standard deviation and the range indicating the variability (spread) of the data. Still others measure such characteristics as skewness, which refers to the degree of asymmetry of the data about its center.

Tests of Hypotheses

An important use of classical statistics is in testing hypotheses. The hypotheses are usually given in terms of values describing the characteristics of a population. The test focuses on a particular value of the population parameter (summary measure). The null hypothesis is that the population parameter takes on that value. The alternative hypothesis is that the value of the population parameter differs from the value assumed by the null hypothesis.

The benefit of the doubt is always given to the null hypothesis. If a random sample contains a sample result that is close to that described by the null hypothesis, the null hypothesis is accepted.

The burden of proof is on the alternative hypothesis. Only if the sample evidence is completely out of line with that suggested by the null hypothesis is the alternative hypothesis accepted.

Many classical tests of hypotheses concern questions about the population mean. If a sample of size 16 has a mean of 106.4 and a standard deviation of 8, can you conclude that the population mean differs significantly from 100? The standard score is

$$T = (106.4 - 100) / (8 / SQR(16))$$
$$= 3.2.$$

Assuming that the standard deviation came from the sample, the transformed T score is distributed according to the t distribution with $n-1=15$ degrees of freedom.

The critical t scores, at a .05 level of significance, are -2.131 and 2.131. The critical t scores at a .01 level of significance are -2.947 and 2.947. These critical scores come from the t table found in the appendices of most introductory statistics textbooks.

The conclusion is to reject the null hypothesis that the population mean is 100 and conclude that the population mean is greater than 100. The decision to accept or reject the null hypothesis results from comparing the sample result with the expected result if the null hypothesis is true. In this case the sample mean is 106.4. The null hypothesis is that the population mean is 100. The t score gives a relative measure of the distance of the observed sample mean from the population mean assumed by the null hypothesis.

The level of significance gives the tail area defining the critical point at which to begin rejecting the null hypothesis. It is the probability of rejecting the null hypothesis if it is true. For samples of size $n=16$, the fraction of t scores falling between -2.131 and 2.131 is .05. The fraction falling between -2.947 and 2.947 is .01. Choosing a small level of significance, such as .01, gives the null hypothesis greater benefit of the doubt. It places a greater burden of proof on the alternative hypothesis.

Most established computing centers have large libraries of computer programs for statistical analysis. Packages of statistical programs are also available for inexpensive personal computers. Program 5-1, which calculates the mean and the standard deviation for a set of sample data, is a typical statistical program. Figure 5-1 shows the results.

Program 5-1

```
100 REM **********************************
102 REM *    5-1                         *
104 REM **********************************
106 REM   AUTHOR
108 REM      COPYRIGHT 1982
110 REM      BY LAWRENCE MCNITT.
112 REM   PURPOSE
114 REM      SAMPLE MEAN AND
116 REM      STANDARD DEVIATION.
118 REM   SYSTEM
120 REM      UNIVERSAL SUBSET
122 REM      OF BASIC.
200 REM **********************************
202 REM *    ORGANIZATION                *
204 REM **********************************
206 REM   900   MAIN ROUTINE
```

```
208 REM        1000   INITIAL MESSAGE
210 REM        1100   INPUT
212 REM        1200   PROCESS
214 REM        1300   OUTPUT
216 REM        1400   FINAL MESSAGE
300 REM ******************************
302 REM *   VARIABLES                *
304 REM ******************************
306 REM    X(200)   VALUES
308 REM    U$   USER RESPONSE
310 REM    N    NUMBER OF VALUES
312 REM    I    INDEX
314 REM    T1   SUM
315 REM    T2   SUM OF SQUARES
316 REM    M    ARITHMETIC MEAN
318 REM    S    STANDARD DEVIATION
900 REM ******************************
902 REM *   MAIN ROUTINE             *
904 REM ******************************
906 DIM X(200)
908 REM INITIAL MESSAGE
910 GOSUB 1006
912 REM INPUT
914 GOSUB 1106
916 REM PROCESS
918 GOSUB 1206
920 REM OUTPUT
922 GOSUB 1306
924 REM FINAL MESSAGE
926 GOSUB 1406
928 IF U$ = "Y" THEN 914
930 PRINT
932 PRINT "END OF PROGRAM"
999 STOP
1000 REM ******************************
1002 REM *   INITIAL MESSAGE          *
1004 REM ******************************
1006 PRINT
1008 PRINT
1010 PRINT
1012 PRINT "PROGRAM 5-1"
1014 PRINT
1016 PRINT "COMPUTE THE MEAN AND"
1018 PRINT "STANDARD DEVIATION FOR"
1020 PRINT "ONE OR MORE SAMPLES."
1099 RETURN
```

```
1100 REM ******************************
1102 REM *    INPUT                   *
1104 REM ******************************
1106 PRINT
1108 PRINT "NUMBER OF OBSERVATIONS";
1110 INPUT N
1112 PRINT
1114 PRINT "VALUE FOR"
1116 FOR I = 1 TO N
1118    PRINT "OBS";I;
1120    INPUT X(I)
1122 NEXT I
1199 RETURN
1200 REM ******************************
1202 REM *    PROCESS                 *
1204 REM ******************************
1206 LET T1 = 0
1208 LET T2 = 0
1210 FOR I = 1 TO N
1212    LET T1 = T1 + X(I)
1214    LET T2 = T2 + X(I) * X(I)
1216 NEXT I
1218 LET M = T1 / N
1220 LET S = SQR((T2 - T1 * T1 / N) / (N - 1))
1299 RETURN
1300 REM ******************************
1302 REM *    OUTPUT                  *
1304 REM ******************************
1306 PRINT
1308 PRINT "MEAN",M
1310 PRINT "STD DEV",S
1399 RETURN
1400 REM ******************************
1402 REM *    FINAL MESSAGE           *
1404 REM ******************************
1406 PRINT
1408 PRINT "TRY ANOTHER SET OF DATA (Y/N)";
1410 INPUT U$
1412 IF U$ = "Y" THEN 1499
1414 IF U$ = "N" THEN 1499
1416 PRINT
1418 PRINT "INVALID RESPONSE"
1420 GOTO 1406
1499 RETURN
9999 END
```

```
PROGRAM 5-1

COMPUTE THE MEAN AND
STANDARD DEVIATION FOR
ONE OR MORE SAMPLES.

NUMBER OF OBSERVATIONS? 5

VALUE FOR
OBS 1 ? 12
OBS 2 ? 11
OBS 3 ? 19
OBS 4 ? 14
OBS 5 ? 15

MEAN              14.2
STD DEV           3.11448

TRY ANOTHER SET OF DATA (Y/N)? N

END OF PROGRAM
```

Fig. 5-1. Sample results from Program 5-1.

Statistical Summaries of Simulation Results

Simulation experiments can generate enormous amounts of data. One of the tasks of the simulation model is to summarize the results in a usable form, giving the summary measures and probabilities needed for analysis.

Program 5-2 generates exponentially distributed values and computes the summary measures consisting of the mean and the standard deviation. Figure 5-2 shows the results.

Program 5-2

```
100 REM *******************************
102 REM *    5-2                      *
104 REM *******************************
106 REM  AUTHOR
108 REM      COPYRIGHT 1982
110 REM      BY LAWRENCE MCNITT.
112 REM  PURPOSE
114 REM      MEAN AND STANDARD DEVIATION
116 REM      FOR A SIMULATED SAMPLE.
118 REM  SYSTEM
```

```
120 REM      UNIVERSAL SUBSET
122 REM      OF BASIC.
200 REM **********************************
202 REM *    ORGANIZATION             *
204 REM **********************************
206 REM   900   MAIN ROUTINE
208 REM         1000   INITIAL MESSAGE
210 REM         1100   INPUT
212 REM         1200   PROCESS
214 REM         1300   OUTPUT
216 REM         1400   FINAL MESSAGE
300 REM **********************************
302 REM *    VARIABLES                *
304 REM **********************************
306 REM    X(200)   VALUES
308 REM    U$   USER RESPONSE
310 REM    N    NUMBER OF VALUES
312 REM    I    INDEX
314 REM    T1   SUM
315 REM    T2   SUM OF SQUARES
316 REM    M    ARITHMETIC MEAN
318 REM    S    STANDARD DEVIATION
320 REM    E    EXPECTED VALUE FOR EXPONENTIAL
900 REM **********************************
902 REM *    MAIN ROUTINE             *
904 REM **********************************
906 DIM X(200)
908 REM INITIAL MESSAGE
910 GOSUB 1006
912 REM INPUT
914 GOSUB 1106
916 REM PROCESS
918 GOSUB 1206
920 REM OUTPUT
922 GOSUB 1306
924 REM FINAL MESSAGE
926 GOSUB 1406
928 IF U$ = "Y" THEN 914
930 PRINT
932 PRINT "END OF PROGRAM"
999 STOP
1000 REM **********************************
1002 REM *    INITIAL MESSAGE          *
1004 REM **********************************
1006 PRINT
1008 PRINT
```

```
1010 PRINT
1012 PRINT "PROGRAM 5-2"
1014 PRINT
1016 PRINT "COMPUTE THE MEAN AND"
1018 PRINT "STANDARD DEVIATION FOR"
1020 PRINT "SIMULATED SAMPLES."
1099 RETURN
1100 REM *****************************
1102 REM *    INPUT                  *
1104 REM *****************************
1106 PRINT
1108 PRINT "NUMBER OF OBSERVATIONS";
1110 INPUT N
1112 PRINT
1114 PRINT "MEAN FOR EXPONENTIAL DISTRIBUTION";
1116 INPUT E
1118 FOR I = 1 TO N
1120    LET X(I) = -E * LOG(RND(0))
1122 NEXT I
1199 RETURN
1200 REM *****************************
1202 REM *    PROCESS                *
1204 REM *****************************
1206 LET T1 = 0
1208 LET T2 = 0
1210 FOR I = 1 TO N
1212    LET T1 = T1 + X(I)
1214    LET T2 = T2 + X(I) * X(I)
1216 NEXT I
1218 LET M = T1 / N
1220 LET S = SQR((T2 - T1 * T1 / N) / (N - 1))
1299 RETURN
1300 REM *****************************
1302 REM *    OUTPUT                 *
1304 REM *****************************
1306 PRINT
1308 PRINT "MEAN",M
1310 PRINT "STD DEV",S
1399 RETURN
1400 REM *****************************
1402 REM *    FINAL MESSAGE          *
1404 REM *****************************
1406 PRINT
1408 PRINT "TRY ANOTHER SET OF DATA (Y/N)";
1410 INPUT U$
1412 IF U$ = "Y" THEN 1499
```

```
1414 IF U$ = "N" THEN 1499
1416 PRINT
1418 PRINT "INVALID RESPONSE"
1420 GOTO 1406
1499 RETURN
9999 END
```

Exercise 5-1

1. Write a program generating normally distributed values. Calculate the mean and standard deviation for the simulated sample.

RUN SIZE AND THE STANDARD ERROR

If the simulation experiment includes random elements, there will be some variability from run to run with the same settings for the external variables and decision variables. This means that more than one replication at each setting may be necessary.

Comparing the results of several replications is easier if the program computes the summary measures needed for statistical analysis. The larger the number of replications, the more closely the average result predicts the true expected value for the population.

A *sampling distribution* is the probability distribution of a sample statistic, which is a summary measure describing a sample. A *population parameter* is a summary measure describing a population. The sampling distribution of the mean is the probability distribution of the sample means for all possible samples of a fixed size selected from the population. As the sample size increases the sampling distribution of the mean becomes more closely grouped around the true population mean.

The standard error is the standard deviation among the values obtained from samples of fixed size taken from the population. The standard error of the mean is the standard deviation among the sample means for samples of a fixed size taken from the population. Assuming random sampling, the expression

$$S / SQR(N)$$

gives the standard error of the mean for samples of

```
PROGRAM 5-2

COMPUTE THE MEAN AND
STANDARD DEVIATION FOR
SIMULATED SAMPLES.

NUMBER OF OBSERVATIONS? 100

MEAN FOR EXPONENTIAL DISTRIBUTION? 5

MEAN              5.3478
STD DEV           6.07003

TRY ANOTHER SET OF DATA (Y/N)? N

END OF PROGRAM
```

Fig. 5-2. Sample results from Program 5-2.

size N drawn from a population having a standard deviation of S.

The standard error (measure of spread) of the sample means is inversely proportional to the square root of the sample size. The standard error is a measure of the accuracy of the sample mean as an estimate of the population mean. Quadrupling the sample size will cut the interval describing the error of estimation in half.

A given model may include replicating the experiment many times and summarizing the results. The length of the simulation (number of periods) becomes a parameter of the simulation run. Including the summary of many replications aids in the evaluation of simulation models.

Choice of a good run size is important. Too small a run will result in such a large variation in the output that the results will be unreliable and difficult to interpret. Too large a run size will waste computer time. This is an important issue for complex models. To aid the analyst in choosing the run size, the simulation program may calculate both the mean and the standard deviation for the measure of interest.

An initial pilot run of the model with a small number of replications provides a measure of the variability among the replications. Given the desired accuracy of the prediction and the formula for the standard error of the estimate, the analyst can easily determine the run size needed to obtain the necessary degree of accuracy.

Program 5-3 uses a formula with a random component simulating demand with order quantity and price as decision variables. Figure 5-3 shows the results.

The standard error of an estimate is a standard deviation. The standard error is usually normally distributed for all but the smallest sample sizes. For

Program 5-3

```
100 REM *******************************
102 REM *    5-3                       *
104 REM *******************************
106 REM   AUTHOR
108 REM       COPYRIGHT 1982
110 REM       BY LAWRENCE MCNITT.
112 REM   PURPOSE
114 REM       EVALUATE ORDER QUANTITY
116 REM       AND PRICE POLICY.
118 REM   SYSTEM
120 REM       UNIVERSAL SUBSET
122 REM       OF BASIC.
200 REM *******************************
202 REM *    ORGANIZATION              *
204 REM *******************************
206 REM   900   MAIN ROUTINE
208 REM         1000   INITIAL MESSAGE
210 REM         1100   DECISION RULE
212 REM         1200   PROCESS
214 REM                2000   DEMAND
216 REM         1300   OUTPUT
218 REM         1400   FINAL MESSAGE
300 REM *******************************
302 REM *    VARIABLES                 *
```

```
304 REM *********************************
306 REM    U$   USER RESPONSE
318 REM    N    NUMBER OF PERIODS
320 REM    I    COUNTER
322 REM    Q    ORDER QUANTITY
324 REM    P    PRICE
326 REM    D    DEMAND
328 REM    U    UNITS SOLD
330 REM    L    UNITS LOST
332 REM    C    COST PER UNIT ORDERED
334 REM    G    GROSS PROFIT
336 REM    T1   SUM OF PROFITS
338 REM    T2   SUM OF SQUARES
340 REM    M    MEAN
342 REM    S1   STANDARD DEVIATION
344 REM    S2   STANDARD ERROR
900 REM *********************************
902 REM *    MAIN ROUTINE               *
904 REM *********************************
906 REM INITIAL MESSAGE
908 GOSUB 1006
910 REM DECISION RULE
912 GOSUB 1106
914 REM PROCESS
916 GOSUB 1206
918 REM OUTPUT
920 GOSUB 1306
922 REM FINAL MESSAGE
924 GOSUB 1406
926 IF U$ = "Y" THEN 912
928 PRINT
930 PRINT "END OF PROGRAM"
999 STOP
1000 REM ******************************
1002 REM *    INITIAL MESSAGE          *
1004 REM ******************************
1006 PRINT
1008 PRINT
1010 PRINT
1012 PRINT "PROGRAM P5-3"
1014 PRINT
1016 PRINT "EVALUATE ORDER QUANTITY"
1018 PRINT "AND PRICE DECISIONS."
1020 LET C = .05
1022 PRINT
1024 PRINT "COST PER UNIT",C
```

```
1026 PRINT
1028 PRINT "EXPECTED DEMAND FOR"
1030 PRINT "SELLING PRICE OF .20 IS 400."
1099 RETURN
1100 REM *******************************
1102 REM *    DECISION RULE            *
1104 REM *******************************
1106 PRINT
1108 PRINT "ORDER QUANTITY";
1110 INPUT Q
1112 PRINT
1114 PRINT "UNIT PRICE";
1116 INPUT P
1118 PRINT
1120 PRINT "NUMBER OF PERIODS";
1122 INPUT N
1199 RETURN
1200 REM *******************************
1202 REM *    PROCESS                  *
1204 REM *******************************
1206 LET T1 = 0
1208 LET T2 = 0
1210 FOR I = 1 TO N
1212     REM DEMAND
1214     GOSUB 2006
1216     LET S = D
1218     IF D <= Q THEN 1222
1220     LET S = Q
1222     LET G = P * S - C * Q
1224     LET T1 = T1 + G
1226     LET T2 = T2 + G * G
1228 NEXT I
1299 RETURN
1300 REM *******************************
1302 REM *    OUTPUT                   *
1304 REM *******************************
1306 LET M = T1 / N
1308 LET S1 = SQR((T2 - T1 * T1 / N) / (N - 1))
1310 LET S2 = S1 / SQR(N)
1312 PRINT
1314 PRINT "AVERAGE PROFIT",M
1316 PRINT "STD DEV",S1
1318 PRINT "STD ERROR",S2
1399 RETURN
1400 REM *******************************
1402 REM *    FINAL MESSAGE            *
```

```
1404 REM *******************************
1406 PRINT
1408 PRINT "TRY ANOTHER SIMULATION RUN (Y/N)";
1410 INPUT U$
1412 IF U$ = "Y" THEN 1499
1414 IF U$ = "N" THEN 1499
1416 PRINT
1418 PRINT "INVALID RESPONSE"
1420 GOTO 1406
1499 RETURN
2000 REM *******************************
2002 REM *     DEMAND                   *
2004 REM *******************************
2006 LET D = 400 * (.20 / P) [ 2
2008 LET D = D * (.9 + .2 * RND(0))
2010 LET D = INT(.5 + D)
2099 RETURN
9999 END
```

the normal distribution, about 68 percent of the values fall within one standard deviation of the mean and 95 percent fall within two standard deviations of the mean.

Applying this rule to sample means and the standard error of the mean suggests that about 95 percent of the sample means will fall within two standard errors of the true population mean. Thus the standard error is a measure of the accuracy of the sample mean for estimating the population mean.

Exercise 5-2

1. From the example in this section determine the

```
PROGRAM 5-3

EVALUATE ORDER QUANTITY          UNIT PRICE? .20

AND PRICE DECISIONS.             NUMBER OF PERIODS? 4

COST PER UNIT     .05            AVERAGE PROFIT    58.85
                                 STD DEV           6.56528
EXPECTED DEMAND FOR              STD ERROR         3.28264
SELLING PRICE OF .20 IS 430
                              _____
TRY ANOTHER SIMULATION (Y/N)? Y

ORDER QUANTITY? 430              AVERAGE PROFIT    59.125
                                 STD DEV           3.91369
UNIT PRICE? .20                  STD ERROR         .978421

NUMBER OF PERIODS? 16
```

```
TRY ANOTHER SIMULATION RUN (Y/N)? Y

ORDER QUANTITY? 430            AVERAGE PROFIT    59.4281
                              STD DEV           4.75957
UNIT PRICE? .20               STD ERROR         .594947

NUMBER OF PERIODS? 64

TRY ANOTHER SIMULATION RUN (Y/N)? Y

ORDER QUANTITY? 430            AVERAGE PROFIT    58.5408
                              STD DEV           4.45859
UNIT PRICE? .20               STD ERROR         .281986

NUMBER OF PERIODS? 250

TRY ANOTHER SIMULATION RUN (Y/N)? Y

ORDER QUANTITY? 430            AVERAGE PROFIT    58.4056
                              STD DEV           4.34049
UNIT PRICE? .20               STD ERROR         .137258

NUMBER OF PERIODS? 1000

TRY ANOTHER SIMULATION RUN (Y/N)? N

END OF PROGRAM
```

Fig. 5-3. Sample results from Program 5-3.

run size needed to be 95 percent confident that the sample mean will be within .45 of the population mean.

REPLICATIONS

Increasing the run size is one method of reducing the variability of the summary measures. The dynamic behavior of some models rules against this method. Another method is to rerun the model several times using a given run size. The variability in results among the reruns is an estimate of the standard error of underlying population for the run size.

Rather than use a run size of 100 iterations, an analyst may make 4 runs of 25 iterations each. The overall effect is the same, but the analyst has the additional estimate of the standard error and can visualize the variability among the sample means.

Program 5-3 can be used to create the output from four runs of 25 iterations each. The results are shown in Fig. 5-4.

Summary of Simulation Results

The simulation results are then processed by standard library programs for statistical analysis. Program 5-1 gives the summary shown in Fig. 5-5.

Exercise 5-3

1. Use Program 5-3 to simulate four runs of one hundred iterations each. Compute the mean and the standard deviation of the sample means.

```
EVALUATE ORDER QUANTITY
AND PRICE DECISIONS.

COST PER UNIT? .05              UNIT PRICE? .20

EXPECTED DEMAND FOR            NUMBER OF PERIODS? 25
SELLING PRICE OF .20 IS 400.
                               AVERAGE PROFIT    59.06
ORDER QUANTITY? 430            STD DEV           5.07836
                               STD ERROR         1.01567

TRY ANOTHER SIMULATION RUN (Y/N)? Y

ORDER QUANTITY? 430            AVERAGE PROFIT    57.988
                               STD DEV           4.1404
UNIT PRICE? .20               STD ERROR         .82808

NUMBER OF PERIODS? 25
TRY ANOTHER SIMULATION RUN (Y/N)? Y

ORDER QUANTITY? 430            AVERAGE PROFIT    59.548
                               STD DEV           4.21952
UNIT PRICE? .20               STD ERROR         .839904

NUMBER OF PERIODS? 25

TRY ANOTHER SIMULATION RUN (Y/N)? Y

ORDER QUANTITY? 430            AVERAGE PROFIT    58.732
                               STD DEV           4.7511
UNIT PRICE? .20               STD ERROR         .950219

NUMBER OF PERIODS? 25


TRY ANOTHER SIMULATION RUN (Y/N)? N

END OF PROGRAM
```

Fig. 5-4. Further results from Program 5-3.

REGRESSION ANALYSIS

The purpose of *regression analysis* is to determine the functional relationship between two variables. It seeks to predict the value of the dependent variable Y as a function of the independent variable X.

Linear regression seeks to estimate the Y-intercept, a, and the slope, b, needed to predict Y

```
COMPUTE THE MEAN AND
STANDARD DEVIATION FOR
ONE OR MORE SAMPLES.

NUMBER OF OBSERVATIONS? 4

VALUE FOR
OBS 1 ? 59.06
OBS 2 ? 59.548
OBS 3 ? 57.988
OBS 4 ? 58.732

MEAN                58.832
STD DEV             .65476

TRY ANOTHER SET OF DATA
 (Y/N)? N

END OF PROGRAM
```

Fig. 5-5. Further results from Program 5-3.

using an equation of the form

$$Y = a + bX.$$

Multiple regression seeks to determine the functional relationship between a dependent variable Y and two or more independent variables X1, X2, ... Multiple linear regression seeks to fit a function of the form

$$Y = b0 + b1X1 + b2X2 ... + bkXk.$$

The *standard error* is a measure of goodness of fit using the same units as the dependent variable Y. It is interpreted as are other standard errors. About 95 percent of the observed values will fall within two standard errors of the regression line if the errors are random and normally distributed.

The *correlation coefficient* is a unitless measure of goodness of fit scaled between −1 and 1 for simple regression involving one independent variable. The square of the correlation coefficient gives the fraction of the variability of the dependent variable explained by its association with the independent variable.

Tests of hypotheses exist for the slope and the overall regression equation. The F statistic from the F distribution is most commonly applied. F tables from standard statistics textbooks give critical limits for rejecting the hypothesis that the correlation coefficient is zero; that is, that the variables are unrelated.

The primary use of regression analysis is in determining equations for the simulation model using historical data. The primary limitation in using regression analysis for evaluating results of simulation experiments is that the results may not be linear with respect to the values of the decision variables.

Extrapolating regression results beyond the limits actually tested is hazardous and should be avoided. For example, if regression analysis includes values in the temperature range between 40 degrees and 90 degrees Fahrenheit, you should not use the model to predict results for temperatures not in this range.

If the fit seems to be linear, then regression analysis is useful for interpolating between tested values of the decision variable. If the temperatures of 40, 50, 60, 70, 80, and 90 are included in the analysis and the fit seems to be linear, interpolating the results using other temperatures, such as 65 and 72, within the tested range is valid.

The following data results from using Program 5-3 for several order quantities at a fixed price of .20 and a run size of 100:

Average price	Order quantity
57.244	390
57.468	390
57.034	400
58.248	400
58.54	410
58.036	410
59.04	420
59.094	420

Program 5-4 fits an equation estimating the average profit as a function of order quantity for the

Program 5-4

```
100 REM ********************************
102 REM *    5-4                       *
104 REM ********************************
106 REM   AUTHOR
108 REM       COPYRIGHT 1982
110 REM       BY LAWRENCE MCNITT.
112 REM   PURPOSE
114 REM       SIMPLE LINEAR REGRESSION.
116 REM   SYSTEM
118 REM       UNIVERSAL SUBSET
120 REM       OF BASIC.
200 REM ********************************
202 REM *    ORGANIZATION              *
204 REM ********************************
206 REM   900   MAIN ROUTINE
208 REM         1000   INITIAL MESSAGE
210 REM         1100   INPUT
212 REM         1200   PROCESS
214 REM         1300   OUTPUT
216 REM         1400   FINAL MESSAGE
300 REM ********************************
302 REM *    VARIABLES                 *
304 REM ********************************
306 REM   Y(200)    DEPENDENT VARIABLE
308 REM   X(200)    INDEPENDENT VARIABLE
310 REM   U$  USER RESPONSE
312 REM   N   NUMBER OF OBSERVATIONS
314 REM   I   INDEX
316 REM   T1  SUM FOR Y
318 REM   T2  SUM FOR X
320 REM   W1  SUM OF SQUARES FOR Y
322 REM   W2  SUM OF SQUARES FOR X
324 REM   W3  SUM OF CROSS PRODUCTS
326 REM   V1  VARIATION FOR Y
328 REM   V2  VARIATION FOR X
330 REM   V3  COVARIATION
332 REM   A   Y-INTERCEPT
334 REM   B   SLOPE
336 REM   R   CORRELATION
338 REM   S   STANDARD ERROR OF ESTIMATE
900 REM ********************************
902 REM *    MAIN ROUTINE              *
904 REM ********************************
906 DIM Y(200),X(200)
```

```
908 REM INITIAL MESSAGE
910 GOSUB 1006
912 REM INPUT
914 GOSUB 1106
916 REM PROCESS
918 GOSUB 1206
920 REM OUTPUT
922 GOSUB 1306
924 REM FINAL MESSAGE
926 GOSUB 1406
928 IF U$ = "Y" THEN 914
930 PRINT
932 PRINT "END OF PROGRAM"
999 STOP
1000 REM ******************************
1002 REM *    INITIAL MESSAGE       *
1004 REM ******************************
1006 PRINT
1008 PRINT
1010 PRINT
1012 PRINT "PROGRAM 5-4"
1014 PRINT
1016 PRINT "SIMPLE LINEAR REGRESSION"
1018 PRINT "ANALYSIS GIVING Y-INTERCEPT,"
1020 PRINT "SLOPE, CORRELATION, AND"
1022 PRINT "STANDARD ERROR OF ESTIMATE."
1099 RETURN
1100 REM ******************************
1102 REM *    INPUT                 *
1104 REM ******************************
1106 PRINT
1108 PRINT "NUMBER OF OBSERVATIONS";
1110 INPUT N
1112 PRINT
1114 PRINT "VALUES Y,X FOR"
1116 FOR I = 1 TO N
1118    PRINT "OBS";I;
1120    INPUT Y(I),X(I)
1122 NEXT I
1199 RETURN
1200 REM ******************************
1202 REM *    PROCESS               *
1204 REM ******************************
1206 LET T1 = 0
1208 LET T2 = 0
1210 LET W1 = 0
```

```
1212 LET W2 = O
1214 LET W3 = O
1216 FOR I = 1 TO N
1218    LET T1 = T1 + Y(I)
1220    LET T2 = T2 + X(I)
1222    LET W1 = W1 + Y(I) * Y(I)
1224    LET W2 = W2 + X(I) * X(I)
1226    LET W3 = W3 + Y(I) * X(I)
1228 NEXT I
1230 LET V1 = W1 - T1 * T1 / N
1232 LET V2 = W2 - T2 * T2 / N
1234 LET V3 = W3 - T1 * T2 / N
1236 LET B = V3 / V2
1238 LET A = T1 / N - B * T2 / N
1240 LET S = SQR((W1 - A * T1 - B * W3) / (N - 2))
1242 LET R = V3 / SQR(V1 * V2)
1244 LET F = (R * R) / ((1 - R * R) / (N - 2))
1299 RETURN
1300 REM ****************************
1302 REM *    OUTPUT                *
1304 REM ****************************
1306 PRINT
1308 PRINT "Y-INTERCEPT",A
1310 PRINT "SLOPE",B
1312 PRINT
1314 PRINT "STD ERROR",S
1316 PRINT "CORRELATION",R
1318 PRINT "F RATIO",F
1399 RETURN
1400 REM ****************************
1402 REM *    FINAL MESSAGE         *
1404 REM ****************************
1406 PRINT
1408 PRINT "TRY ANOTHER SET OF DATA (Y/N)";
1410 INPUT U$
1412 IF U$ = "Y" THEN 1499
1414 IF U$ = "N" THEN 1499
1416 PRINT
1418 PRINT "INVALID RESPONSE"
1420 GOTO 1406
1499 RETURN
9999 END
```

unit price of .20 within the limits of 390 to 420 for the order quantity. Figure 5-6 shows the results.

The computed F ratio of 49.2721 is much larger than the critical F ratio of 6.61 having a level of significance of .05 with 1 degree of freedom for the numerator and $n-2=6$ degrees of freedom for

```
PROGRAM 5-4

SIMPLE LINEAR REGRESSION
ANALYSIS GIVING Y-INTERCEPT,
SLOPE, CORRELATION, AND
STANDARD ERROR OF ESTIMATE.

NUMBER OF OBSERVATIONS? 8

VALUES Y,X FOR
OBS 1 ? 57.244,390
OBS 2 ? 57.468,390
OBS 3 ? 58.034,400
OBS 4 ? 58.248,400
OBS 5 ? 58.540,410
OBS 6 ? 58.036,410
OBS 7 ? 59.040,420
OBS 8 ? 59.094,420

Y-INTERCEPT        36.8303
SLOPE              .0527969

STD ERROR          .237308
CORRELATION        .944164
F RATIO            49.2721

TRY ANOTHER SET OF DATA
  (Y/N)? N

END OF PROGRAM
```

Fig. 5-6. Sample results from Program 5-4

the denominator. The regression equation

$$Y = 36.8 + .0528X$$

is highly significant. To test for linearity, plot the pairs of values Y, X with X on the horizontal axis and Y on the vertical axis. If the values appear to be randomly distributed around an imaginary straight line, linear regression is appropriate.

Exercise 5-4

1. Extend the experiment of this section to include order quantities of 370, 380, nd 430. Does a linear fit still seem appropriate? Use Program 5-4 with the combined results. Compare the new standard error and correlation coefficient with those given in the text.

ANALYSIS OF VARIANCE

The purpose of the *analysis of variance* is to test hypotheses about the equality of population means. The measurable quantity of interest is called the *response variable*. There may be two or more factors of interest that have an influence on the response variable. Two-way analysis of variance has two factors. Three way analysis of variance has three factors that may influence the response variable.

A factor is divided into distinct levels. Each observations falls into one level of a given factor. Consider a two-way analysis of variance having sex as one factor and choice of a soft drink as a second factor. The levels for sex are male and female. The levels for soft drink are the brands included in the study.

Remember that the response variable is the main variable of interest. The purpose of analysis of variance is to test whether the factors have an effect on the response variable. The response variable corresponds to the dependent variable of regression analysis.

A *main effect* results when the means among the levels of a factor are significantly different. An *interaction effect* results if the pattern of means for one factor differs with respect to the levels of the other factor.

Analysis of variance is one of the main techniques used in the careful evaluation of simulation experiment results. The analyst replicates (reruns) the experiment for each of several model settings. Analysis of variance tests whether the averages among the settings are significantly different.

Here is an example using Program 5-3 as in the previous sections. In this case the purpose is to test whether there is a difference in average profit among the settings .20 and .19 for unit prices and 410, 430, and 450 for order quantities. There are

156

two replications for each setting and a sample size of 100 periods for each replication.

The average profit levels are given below in the order required by Program 5-3.

Price		.20	
Quantity	410	430	450
Average	58.858	58.342	57.026
Profit	58.834	59.108	57.128

Price		.19	
Quantity	410	430	450
Average	57.286	59.1341	60.7086
Profit	57.2518	59.3355	60.0664

Program 5-5 performs a two-way analysis of variance with replications. The data must be placed in data statements in the same order as given in the table. The first three numbers are the number of rows (price), the number of columns (order quantity), and the number of replications per cell. Figure 5-7 shows the results using the data statements in the program.

The degrees of freedom for the denominator (row of the F table from a statistics textbook) are six. The F ratio for the row effect has one degree of freedom for the numerator (column of the F table). The F ratios for the column effect and the interaction effect both have two degrees of freedom. The

Program 5-5

```
100 REM *******************************
102 REM *    5-5                       *
104 REM *******************************
106 REM   AUTHOR
108 REM       COPYRIGHT 1982
110 REM       BY LAWRENCE MCNITT.
112 REM   PURPOSE
114 REM       TWO-WAY ANALYSIS
116 REM       OF VARIANCE.
118 REM   SYSTEM
120 REM       UNIVERSAL SUBSET
122 REM       OF BASIC.
200 REM *******************************
202 REM *    ORGANIZATION              *
204 REM *******************************
206 REM   900   MAIN ROUTINE
208 REM         1000   INITIAL MESSAGE
210 REM         1100   INITIALIZE
212 REM         1200   ACCUMULATE
214 REM         1300   CALCULATE
216 REM         1400   ANOVA OUTPUT
218 REM         1500   SUMMARY MEASURES
300 REM *******************************
302 REM *    VARIABLES                 *
304 REM *******************************
306 REM   T(5,5)   TABLE OF SUMS
308 REM   S(5,5)   TABLE OF SUMS OF SQUARES
310 REM   R(5,2)   ROW SUMS AND SUMS OF SQUARES
```

```
312 REM    C(5,2)  COLUMN SUMS AND SUMS OF SQUARES
314 REM    U$  USER RESPONSE
316 REM    R1  NUMBER OF ROWS
318 REM    C1  NUMBER OF COLUMNS
320 REM    N   NUMBER OF REPLICATIONS PER CELL
322 REM    I   INDEX
324 REM    J   INDEX
326 REM    K   INDEX
327 REM    X   CURRENT VALUE
328 REM    M   NUMBER OF OBSERVATIONS FOR GROUP
330 REM    A1  AVERAGE FOR GROUP
332 REM    G1  SUM FOR GROUP
334 REM    G2  SUM OF SQUARES FOR GROUP
336 REM    A1  MEAN FOR GROUP
338 REM    V1  STANDARD DEVIATION FOR GROUP
340 REM    T1  OVERALL SUM
342 REM    T2  OVERALL SUM OF SQUARES
344 REM    T3  SUM OF SQUARES OF ROW TOTALS
346 REM    T4  SUM OF SQUARES OF COLUMN TOTALS
348 REM    T5  SUM OF SQUARES OF CELL TOTALS
349 REM    A   ADJUSTMENT FOR SUMS OF SQUARES
350 REM    S1  ROW SUM OF SQUARES
352 REM    S2  COLUMN SUM OF SQUARES
354 REM    S3  INTERACTION SUM OF SQUARES
356 REM    S4  ERROR SUM OF SQUARES
358 REM    S5  TOTAL SUM OF SQUARES
360 REM    D1  ROW DEGREES OF FREEDOM
362 REM    D2  COLUMN DEGREES OF FREEDOM
364 REM    D3  INTERACTION DEGREES OF FREEDOM
366 REM    D4  ERROR DEGREES OF FREEDOM
368 REM    M1  ROW MEAN SQUARE
370 REM    M2  COLUMN MEAN SQUARE
372 REM    M3  INTERACTION MEAN SQUARE
374 REM    M4  ERROR MEAN SQUARE
376 REM    F1  ROW F RATIO
378 REM    F2  COLUMN F RATIO
380 REM    F3  INTERACTION F RATIO
900 REM ******************************
902 REM *    MAIN ROUTINE            *
904 REM ******************************
906 DIM T(5,5),S(5,5),R(5,2),C(5,2)
908 REM INITIAL MESSAGE
910 GOSUB 1006
912 REM INITIALIZE
914 GOSUB 1106
916 REM ACCUMULATE
```

```
 918 GOSUB 1206
 920 REM CALCULATE
 922 GOSUB 1306
 924 REM OUTPUT
 926 GOSUB 1406
 928 REM FINAL MESSAGE
 930 GOSUB 1506
 932 PRINT
 934 PRINT "END OF PROGRAM"
 999 STOP
1000 REM ******************************
1002 REM *    INITIAL MESSAGE         *
1004 REM ******************************
1006 PRINT
1008 PRINT
1010 PRINT
1012 PRINT "PROGRAM 5-5"
1014 PRINT
1016 PRINT "TWO-WAY ANALYSIS OF VARIANCE"
1018 PRINT "WITH MORE THAN ONE OBSERVATION"
1020 PRINT "PER CELL.
1099 RETURN
1100 REM ******************************
1102 REM *    INITIALIZE              *
1104 REM ******************************
1106 READ R1,C1,N
1108 FOR I = 1 TO R1
1110    FOR J = 1 TO C1
1112       LET T(I,J) = 0
1114       LET S(I,J) = 0
1116    NEXT J
1118 NEXT I
1199 RETURN
1200 REM ******************************
1202 REM *    ACCUMULATE              *
1204 REM ******************************
1206 FOR K = 1 TO N
1208    FOR I = 1 TO R1
1210       FOR J = 1 TO C1
1212          READ X
1214          LET T(I,J) = T(I,J) + X
1216          LET S(I,J) = S(I,J) + X * X
1218       NEXT J
1220    NEXT I
1222 NEXT K
1224 FOR I = 1 TO R1
```

```
1226    LET G1 = 0
1228    LET G2 = 0
1230    FOR J = 1 TO C1
1232       LET G1 = G1 + T(I,J)
1234       LET G2 = G2 + S(I,J)
1236    NEXT J
1238    LET R(I,1) = G1
1240    LET R(I,2) = G2
1242 NEXT I
1244 FOR J = 1 TO C1
1246    LET G1 = 0
1248    LET G2 = 0
1250    FOR I = 1 TO R1
1252       LET G1 = G1 + T(I,J)
1254       LET G2 = G2 + S(I,J)
1256    NEXT I
1258    LET C(J,1) = G1
1260    LET C(J,2) = G2
1262 NEXT J
1264 LET T1 = 0
1266 LET T2 = 0
1268 FOR I = 1 TO R1
1270    LET T1 = T1 + R(I,1)
1272    LET T2 = T2 + R(I,2)
1274 NEXT I
1299 RETURN
1300 REM *******************************
1302 REM *    CALCULATE                 *
1304 REM *******************************
1306 LET M = R1 * C1 * N
1308 LET A = T1 * T1 / M
1310 LET S5 = T2 - A
1312 LET T3 = 0
1314 FOR I = 1 TO R1
1316    LET G1 = R(I,1)
1318    LET T3 = T3 + G1 * G1
1320 NEXT I
1322 LET S1 = T3 / (C1 * N) - A
1324 LET T4 = 0
1326 FOR J = 1 TO C1
1328    LET G1 = C(J,1)
1330    LET T4 = T4 + G1 * G1
1332 NEXT J
1334 LET S2 = T4 / (R1 * N) - A
1336 LET T5 = 0
1338 FOR I = 1 TO R1
```

```
1340    FOR J = 1 TO C1
1342       LET G1 = T(I,J)
1344        LET T5 = T5 + G1 * G1
1346     NEXT J
1348 NEXT I
1350 LET S3 = T5 / N - A - S1 - S2
1352 LET S4 = S5 - S1 - S2 - S3
1356 LET D1 = R1 - 1
1358 LET D2 = C1 - 1
1360 LET D3 = (R1 - 1) * (C1 - 1)
1362 LET D4 = R1 * C1 * (N - 1)
1364 LET M1 = S1 / D1
1366 LET M2 = S2 / D2
1368 LET M3 = S3 / D3
1370 LET M4 = S4 / D4
1372 LET F1 = M1 / M4
1374 LET F2 = M2 / M4
1376 LET F3 = M3 / M4
1399 RETURN
1400 REM *******************************
1402 REM *    ANOVA OUTPUT             *
1404 REM *******************************
1406 PRINT
1408 PRINT "ANOVA SUMMARY"
1410 PRINT
1412 PRINT "SOURCE OF","F RATIO","DEGREES OF"
1414 PRINT "VARIATION",,"FREEDOM"
1416 PRINT "ROW EFFECT",F1,D1
1418 PRINT "COL EFFECT",F2,D2
1420 PRINT "INTERACTION",F3,D3
1422 PRINT
1424 PRINT "ERROR"
1426 PRINT "DEGREES OF FREEDOM",D4
1428 PRINT "MEAN SQUARE      ",M4
1499 RETURN
1500 REM *******************************
1502 REM *    SUMMARY MEASURES         *
1504 REM *******************************
1506 PRINT
1508 PRINT "DISPLAY SUMMARY MEASURES (Y/N)";
1510 INPUT U$
1512 IF U$ = "Y" THEN 1522
1514 IF U$ = "N" THEN 1599
1516 PRINT
1518 PRINT "INVALID RESPONSE"
1520 GOTO 1506
```

```
1522 PRINT
1524 PRINT "CELL MEANS"
1526 FOR I = 1 TO R1
1528     PRINT
1530     FOR J = 1 TO C1
1532         LET A1 = T(I,J) / N
1534         PRINT A1,
1536     NEXT J
1538     PRINT
1540 NEXT I
1542 PRINT
1544 PRINT "CELL STANDARD DEVIATIONS"
1546 FOR I = 1 TO R1
1548     PRINT
1550     FOR J = 1 TO C1
1552         LET G1 = T(I,J)
1554         LET G2 = S(I,J)
1556         LET V1 = SQR((G2 - G1 * G1 / N) / (N - 1))
1558         PRINT V1,
1560     NEXT J
1562     PRINT
1564 NEXT I
1566 PRINT
1568 PRINT "TYPE ANYTHING TO CONTINUE";
1570 INPUT U$
1572 PRINT
1574 PRINT "ROW","MEAN"
1576 FOR I = 1 TO R1
1578     LET A1 = R(I,1) / (C1 * N)
1580     PRINT I,A1
1582 NEXT I
1584 PRINT
1586 PRINT "COLUMN","MEAN"
1588 FOR J = 1 TO C1
1590     LET A1 = C(J,1) / (R1 * N)
1592     PRINT J,A1
1594 NEXT J
1599 RETURN
8000 REM ******************************
8002 REM *    NUMBER OF ROWS              *
8004 REM *    NUMBER OF COLUMNS           *
8006 REM *    NUMBER OF REPLICATIONS      *
8008 REM *          PER CELL              *
8010 REM *    OBSERVATIONS FOR            *
8012 REM *          REPLICATION 1         *
8014 REM *    OBSERVATIONS FOR            *
```

```
8016 REM *        REPLICATION 2        *
8018 REM *     THROUGH                 *
8020 REM *     OBSERVATIONS FOR        *
8022 REM *        REPLICATION N        *
8024 REM *****************************
9000 DATA 2,3,3
9001 DATA 34,39,43,52,56,55
9002 DATA 37,42,39,47,58,60
9003 DATA 42,40,42,53,54,59
9999 END

9000 DATA 2,3,2
9001 DATA 58.858,58.342,57.026,57.286,59.1341,60.7086
9002 DATA 58.834,59.108,57.128,57.2518,59.3355,60.0664
```

critical F ratios are 5.99 and 13.75 for the .05 and .01 levels for row effect. The critical F ratios are 5.14 and 10.92 for the column and interaction effects. All effects are significant at the .05 level. The row and interaction effects are significant at the .01 level. The interaction effects seem to predominate. This shows that price and order quantity are highly interrelated with respect to average profit.

Exercise 5-5

1. Continue the simulation experiment using the analysis of variance program to aid in the search for the best combination of price and order quantity.

EVOLUTIONARY OPERATION

Models aren't always simple. They may contain dozens of decision variables. Trying to juggle all of them at the same time is impossible, even with the aid of the computer. Each decision variable constitutes one dimension of the decision problem. A problem having four decision variables has four dimensions. Many of the decision variables may be interrelated. Analysis of multidimensional decision problems requires some way of evaluating interaction effects.

The term *curse of dimensionality* comes from the field of dynamic programming, but it is just as appropriate to simulation. It refers to the complex-ity resulting from problems having many decision variables.

Evolutionary operation is a method developed for fine tuning an ongoing physical production process that contains many decision variables that control quality. When starting up a new process, the engineers will often build a pilot plant. Experience with the pilot plant forms the basis for the initial settings for the production facility.

Over a period of days, months, and years improvements will be made in the settings. These improvements may come from hunches on the part of operators or from statistical analysis of the output. The problem is one of fine tuning the ongoing process. The evolutionary operation procedure involves making small adjustments in two or three settings at a time. Analysis of variance is the vehicle for analyzing the results. To keep things simple, each of the factors contains only two or three levels. The settings are replicated until the analysis of variance test is significant.

If the new settings (factor levels) are too close to the old settings, the difference won't be apparent until many replications have been completed. When this happens, the size of the adjustment (differences in settings) must be increased, so that differences will become apparent. If the adjustments are too large, potential improvements will be overlooked or the process will go out of control and produce defective products.

```
PROGRAM 5-5

TWO-WAY ANALYSIS OF VARIANCE
WITH MORE THAN ONE OBSERVATION
PER CELL.

ANOVA SUMMARY

SOURCE OF          F RATIO          DEGREES OF
VARIATION                           FREEDOM
ROW EFFECT         19.0667          1
COL EFFECT         10.3556          2
INTERACTION        68.4444          2


ERROR
DEGREES OF FREEDOM                  6
MEAN SQUARE                         .0878906

DISPLAY SUMMARY MEASURES (Y/N)? Y

CELL MEANS

 58.846            58.725           57.077

 57.2689           59.2348          60.3875

CELL STANDARD DEVIATIONS

 0                 .541717          .0732878

 .0220971          .14149           .45447

TYPE ANYTHING TO CONTINUE?

ROW               MEAN
 1                 58.216
 2                 58.9637

COLUMN            MEAN
 1                 58.0575
 2                 58.9799
 3                 58.7323

END OF PROGRAM
```

Fig. 5-7. Sample results from Program 5-5.

When no more improvement is possible, keep the optimum settings for those decision variables that have been tested and work with another set of variables. The analyst should choose the variables based on his understanding of the process.

The concept of evolutionary operation applies to simulation modeling and to the fine tuning of an ongoing production process. The big difference is that the simulation analyst is not as concerned about making the differences in the sizes of the adjustments too large since no physical process is involved. At the worst, he only has to rerun the model.

As an example, the problem involving finding the order quantity and the price that maximize the average profit for the model contained in Listing 5-3 will again be used. The following summarizes the profits after one replication for the prices of .20 and .19 and the order quantities of 400 and 450:

Price	Order quantity	
	400	450
.20	57.37	57.036
.19	55.9981	60.1405

The following summarizes the profits after the second replication:

Price	Order quantities	
	400	450
.20	58.06	57.032
.19	56	60.4141

Program 5-5 does a two-way analysis of variance. Using it with the data from these two replications results in F ratios of 15.2658 for the row effect, 84.2025 for the column effect (order quantity), and 158.911 for the interaction effect. The following gives the cell means:

Price	Order quantity	
	400	450
.20	57.708	57.034
.19	55.9991	60.2773

Inspection of this table suggests that an order quantity of 450 together with a price of .19 gives the best average profit.

The obvious choice is to increase order quantity while cutting price, but the adjustments may be so large that the optimum setting is overlooked. Another serious problem comes from the interaction between order quantity and price. They must be set together.

The next stage may consist of comparing order quantities of 450 and 500 together with prices of .19 and .18. From stage to stage, the adjustments move together toward the best setting.

Exercise 5-6

1. Use the method of evolutionary operation with its fine tuning to work toward the best combination of order quantity and price.

Chapter 6

Industrial Processes

Computer simulation is an excellent means of modeling industrial processes. Information gathering is one of the most important uses of the computer in process control. The computer can monitor several variables, recording and analyzing their values. The computer can also model this information gathering and analysis process. It can model product quality for the evaluation of quality control plans. In addition, the computer can model complex waiting line situations involving random arrivals, and can handle servicing requirements including the scheduling jobs to machines.

MONITORING AND INFORMATION GATHERING

Sensors measure the characteristics of a process. Information gathering consists of recording the sensor values at intervals for later analysis. The same mechanism applies to simulation models with one important difference. The sensing and recording mechanism is much easier to build into the computer simulation model.

One problem inherent in complex models is the random fluctuation of readings from period to period. The real need is for average readings or trends. Some way is needed to smooth out the random fluctuations.

One method of smoothing random fluctuations is to compute a moving average. A centered moving average includes observations on both sides of the center. This applies to the analysis of historical data. Another method is to take the most recent values for the moving average. Any moving average requires saving the most recently observed values. To keep the list current requires storage and housekeeping.

Exponential smoothing involves maintaining a weighted mean based on the previous mean plus the most recent value. Exponential smoothing does not require maintaining the most recent values in memory. Only the previous mean and the new observation are needed. This eliminates the complex housekeeping needed to maintain the list of recent values necessary for a moving average. Exponential smoothing is easy to incorporate into computer analysis.

The smoothing coefficient determines the degree of smoothing. The formula

$$M(i+1) = A * X(i+1) + (1 - A) * M(i)$$

computes the new mean for the (i+1)th term as the weighted average between the old mean for the ith term and the new observation for the (i+1)th term.

The coefficient of smoothing is a fraction between 0 and 1. A coefficient close to zero gives a high degree of smoothing. The results are similar to having a large sample size. A coefficient close to 1 results in a small degree of smoothing similar to using a small sample.

If the process is stable with rare changes in average level, a coefficient close to zero provides a stable, accurate estimate of the process mean. If the process is volatile with frequent changes in process mean, a coefficient close to zero will be slow to detect significant changes.

In statistical analysis, the *deviation* of a value about the mean is the amount by which the individual value differs from the mean of all such values. The *variance* of a set of data is the average squared deviation. The *standard deviation* is the square root of the variance. Using the exponential smoothing mechanism, the smoothed average squared deviation of the observed values around their respective smoothed means is an estimate of the underlying variance of the process.

The sum of 12 random numbers generated using the RND function is about normally distributed. Program 6-1 illustrates exponential smoothing by estimating the mean and standard deviation for a normally distributed random variable. Figure 6-1 shows the results.

Program 6-1

```
100 REM ******************************
102 REM *    6-1                     *
104 REM ******************************
106 REM   AUTHOR
108 REM        COPYRIGHT 1982
110 REM        BY LAWRENCE MCNITT.
112 REM   PURPOSE
114 REM        EXPONENTIAL SMOOTHING.
116 REM   SYSTEM
118 REM        UNIVERSAL SUBSET
120 REM        OF BASIC.
200 REM ******************************
202 REM *    ORGANIZATION            *
204 REM ******************************
206 REM   900    MAIN ROUTINE
208 REM        1000    INITIAL MESSAGE
210 REM        1100    PARAMETERS
212 REM        1200    PROCESS
214 REM             2000    GENERATE
216 REM        1300    FINAL MESSAGE
300 REM ******************************
302 REM *    VARIABLES               *
304 REM ******************************
306 REM   U$   USER RESPONSE
308 REM   M1   POPULATION MEAN
```

```
310 REM    S1   POPULATION STANDARD DEVIATION
312 REM    N    NUMBER OF VALUES
314 REM    I    COUNTER
316 REM    J    COUNTER
318 REM    R    RANDOM NUMBER
320 REM    Z    STANDARD SCORE
322 REM    M2   SMOOTHED MEAN
324 REM    V2   SMOOTHED VARIANCE
326 REM    S2   SMOOTHED STANDARD DEVIATION
328 REM    X    CURRENT VALUE
900 REM ******************************
902 REM *    MAIN ROUTINE             *
904 REM ******************************
906 REM INITIAL MESSAGE
908 GOSUB 1006
910 REM PARAMETERS
912 GOSUB 1106
914 REM PROCESS
916 GOSUB 1206
918 REM FINAL MESSAGE
920 GOSUB 1306
922 IF U$ = "Y" THEN 912
924 PRINT
926 PRINT "END OF PROGRAM"
999 STOP
1000 REM ******************************
1002 REM *    INITIAL MESSAGE          *
1004 REM ******************************
1006 PRINT
1008 PRINT
1010 PRINT
1012 PRINT "PROGRAM 6-1"
1014 PRINT
1016 PRINT "USE EXPONENTIAL SMOOTHING"
1018 PRINT "TO ESTIMATE THE MEAN AND"
1020 PRINT "STANDARD DEVIATION OF A"
1022 PRINT "SERIES OF RANDOM VALUES."
1099 RETURN
1100 REM ******************************
1102 REM *    PARAMETERS               *
1104 REM ******************************
1106 PRINT
1108 PRINT "GENERATE NORMALLY DISTRIBUTED VALUES"
1110 PRINT
1112 PRINT "POPULATION"
1114 PRINT "MEAN    ";
```

```
1116 INPUT M1
1118 PRINT "STD DEV";
1120 INPUT S1
1122 PRINT
1124 PRINT "NUMBER OF VALUES";
1126 INPUT N
1128 PRINT
1130 PRINT "SMOOTHING CONSTANT";
1132 INPUT A
1134 IF ABS(A - .5) < .5 THEN 1142
1136 PRINT
1138 PRINT "MUST BE FRACTION BETWEEN 0 AND 1"
1140 GOTO 1128
1142 PRINT
1144 PRINT "INITIAL ESTIMATE FOR"
1146 PRINT "MEAN     ";
1148 INPUT M2
1150 PRINT "STD DEV";
1152 INPUT S2
1154 LET V2 = S2 * S2
1199 RETURN
1200 REM ******************************
1202 REM *     PROCESS                *
1204 REM ******************************
1206 PRINT
1208 PRINT "VALUE","MEAN","STD DEV"
1210 FOR I = 1 TO N
1212    REM GENERATE
1214    GOSUB 2006
1216    LET M2 = A * X + (1 - A) * M2
1218    LET V2 = A * (X - M2) [ 2 + (1 - A) * V2
1220    LET S2 = SQR(V2)
1222    PRINT X,M2,S2
1224 NEXT I
1299 RETURN
1300 REM ******************************
1302 REM *    FINAL MESSAGE           *
1304 REM ******************************
1306 PRINT
1308 PRINT "TRY ANOTHER SET OF VALUES (Y/N)";
1310 INPUT U$
1312 IF U$ = "Y" THEN 1399
1314 IF U$ = "N" THEN 1399
1316 PRINT
1318 PRINT "INVALID RESPONSE"
1320 GOTO 1306
```

```
1399 RETURN
2000 REM ***********************************
2002 REM *     GENERATE                    *
2004 REM ***********************************
2006 LET Z = -6
2008 FOR J = 1 TO 12
2010     LET Z = Z + RND(0)
2012 NEXT J
2014 LET X = M1 + Z * S1
2099 RETURN
9999 END
```

Exercise 6-1

1. Try various smoothing coefficients and longer run sizes to observe the effect on the stability of the smoothed estimate.
2. Increase the process mean by forty units every twenty periods for one hundred periods. Observe the behavior of the estimate for smoothing coefficients of .1, .2, and .4.

QUALITY CONTROL

Mass production techniques require interchangeable parts. Individual parts must meet specified limits or the assembled product will not meet performance goals. Each part must meet limits set for qualities such as dimensions, weight, strength, and appearance. This quality may be a measurable quantity such as weight or length, or it may be a qualitative aspect such as good or defective.

Engineers design parts with tolerance limits. Those parts falling within the tolerance limits should perform well in the assembled product. Physical production facilities, when adjusted and operated correctly, should produce products that fall within design specifications.

Problems that affect the quality level will arise. Machines may need adjustment. Operators may use incorrect procedures. Statistical quality control procedures involve monitoring the output of an ongoing process. If the level of quality deteriorates beyond critical limits, the signal is given for a review of the production procedure and of the machine settings.

There are many costs to consider when establishing a quality control plan. Costs result from shutting down a machine or an assembly line for inspection or adjustment. There are costs involved in the sampling process itself reflecting the size of the sample and the frequency of sampling. There are still other costs resulting from the below normal quality level of the output.

The quality level often changes during the course of production. Program 6-2 incorporates some of these cost factors in the economic analysis of statistical quality control plans. Figure 6-2 shows the results.

Exercise 6-2

1. Continue working with the example in this section to determine the optimum sample size and the critical limit for batches of 100.

FEEDBACK AND CONTROL

Feedback occurs when the output of a system also becomes the input of that same system at a later stage. The lagged variables of econometric models use the feedback mechanism. In process control applications, readings from sensing instruments are fed back into the model.

Automatic control is an important concept in modern engineering. It is a giant step beyond the simple monitoring of measurable quantities. Thermostats provide simple control over home heating systems. Automatic pilots provide much more sophisticated control over complex aircraft.

The system may undergo shocks, called

170

```
PROGRAM 6-1

USE EXPONENTIAL SMOOTHING
TO ESTIMATE THE MEAN AND
STANDARD DEVIATION OF A
SERIES OF RANDOM VALUES.

GENERATE NORMALLY DISTRIBUTED VALUES

POPULATION
MEAN    ? 100
STD DEV? 20

NUMBER OF VALUES? 10

SMOOTHING CONSTANT? .2

INITIAL ESTIMATE FOR
MEAN    ? 105
STD DEV? 25

VALUE              MEAN              STD DEV
 123.114            108.623           23.2809
 79.7398            102.846           23.2461
 56.9252            93.6621           26.4995
 103.855            95.7007           23.9808
 116.199            99.8003           22.6682
 137.359            107.312           24.3236
 79.7237            101.794           23.89
 85.9151            98.6185           22.1102
 90.0396            96.9027           20.0128
 98.938             97.3098           17.9148

TRY ANOTHER SET OF VALUES (Y/N)? N

END OF PROGRAM
```

Fig. 6-1. Sample results from Program 6-1.

stimuli, at unpredictable times. Someone opens the door, thus lowering the temperature in the house and requiring a reaction from the thermostat. An aircraft encounters an air pocket requiring a reaction by the automatic pilot. The control mechanism must be able to respond to shocks.

Performance goals are part of the design of the automatic system. The goal of the thermostatically controlled system is to provide a steady temperature within a small range. The goal of the automatic pilot is to maintain a steady course, altitude, and speed.

Program 6-2

```
100 REM ********************************
102 REM *    6-2                       *
104 REM ********************************
106 REM   AUTHOR
108 REM      COPYRIGHT 1982
110 REM        BY LAWRENCE MCNITT.
112 REM   PURPOSE
114 REM      QUALITY CONTROL
116 REM        POLICY SIMULATION.
118 REM   SYSTEM
120 REM      UNIVERSAL SUBSET
122 REM        OF BASIC.
200 REM ********************************
202 REM *    ORGANIZATION              *
204 REM ********************************
206 REM   900  MAIN ROUTINE
208 REM          1000   INITIAL MESSAGE
210 REM          1100   PARAMETERS
212 REM          1200   PROCESS
214 REM               2000   BATCH
216 REM          1300   OUTPUT
218 REM          1400   FINAL MESSAGE
300 REM ********************************
302 REM *    VARIABLES                 *
304 REM ********************************
306 REM    U$  USER RESPONSE
308 REM    M   NUMBER OF BATCHES
310 REM    N   SIZE OF EACH BATCH
312 REM    I   COUNTER
314 REM    J   COUNTER
316 REM    P   PROCESS FRACTION DEFECTIVE
318 REM    C1  COST OF ADJUSTING MACHINE
320 REM    C2  COST PER SAMPLE ITEM IN SAMPLE
322 REM    C3  COST PER DEFECTIVE ITEM
324 REM    N1  SAMPLE SIZE
326 REM    R1  NUMBER OF DEFECTIVES IN BATCH
328 REM    R2  NUMBER OF DEFECTIVES IN SAMPLE
330 REM    R3  CRITICAL NUMBER OF DEFECTIVES FOR ADJUSTING
332 REM    T1  TOTAL COST OF ADJUSTING MACHINE
334 REM    T2  TOTAL COST OF SAMPLING
336 REM    T3  TOTAL COST OF DEFECTIVES
338 REM    T   TOTAL COST OF QUALITY CONTROL PLAN
340 REM    P1  PROCESS FRACTION DEFECTIVE AFTER ADJUST
900 REM ********************************
```

```
902 REM *    MAIN ROUTINE           *
904 REM *******************************
906 REM INITIAL MESSAGE
908 GOSUB 1006
910 REM PARAMETERS
912 GOSUB 1106
914 REM PROCESS
916 GOSUB 1206
918 REM OUTPUT
920 GOSUB 1306
922 REM FINAL MESSAGE
924 GOSUB 1406
926 IF U$ = "Y" THEN 916
928 PRINT
930 PRINT "END OF PROGRAM"
999 STOP
1000 REM *******************************
1002 REM *    INITIAL MESSAGE          *
1004 REM *******************************
1006 PRINT
1008 PRINT
1010 PRINT
1012 PRINT "6-2"
1014 PRINT
1016 PRINT "EVALUATE QUALITY CONTROL"
1018 PRINT "DECISION RULES ASSUMING"
1020 PRINT "A RANDOM WALK OF THE"
1022 PRINT "PROCESS FRACTION DEFECTIVE."
1099 RETURN
1100 REM *******************************
1102 REM *    PARAMETERS               *
1104 REM *******************************
1106 PRINT
1108 PRINT "COST PER DEFECTIVE ITEM";
1110 INPUT C3
1112 PRINT "COST PER SAMPLE ITEM    ";
1114 INPUT C2
1116 PRINT "COST PER ADJUSTMENT      ";
1118 INPUT C1
1120 PRINT
1122 PRINT "PROCESS FRACTION DEFECTIVE"
1124 PRINT "AFTER MACHINE ADJUSTMENT";
1126 INPUT P1
1199 RETURN
1200 REM *******************************
1202 REM *    PROCESS                  *
```

```
1204 REM ******************************
1206 PRINT
1208 PRINT "BATCH SIZE";
1210 INPUT N
1212 PRINT
1214 PRINT "NUMBER OF BATCHES";
1216 INPUT M
1218 PRINT
1220 PRINT "SAMPLE SIZE";
1222 INPUT N1
1224 PRINT
1226 PRINT "CRITICAL NUMBER OF DEFECTIVES"
1228 PRINT "FORCING MACHINE ADJUSTMENT";
1230 INPUT R3
1232 LET P = P1
1234 LET T1 = 0
1236 LET T2 = 0
1238 LET T3 = 0
1242 FOR I = 1 TO M
1244     REM BATCH
1246     GOSUB 2006
1248     IF R2 < R3 THEN 1252
1249     LET P = P1
1250     LET T1 = T1 + C1
1252     LET T2 = T2 + C2 * N1
1254     LET T3 = T3 + C3 * R1
1256 NEXT I
1258 LET T = T1 + T2 + T3
1299 RETURN
1300 REM ******************************
1302 REM *    OUTPUT                   *
1304 REM ******************************
1306 PRINT
1308 PRINT ,"TOTAL COST","AVERAGE COST PER BATCH"
1310 PRINT "ADJUSTING",T1,T1/M
1312 PRINT "SAMPLING",T2,T2/M
1314 PRINT "DEFECTIVES",T3,T3/M
1316 PRINT "TOTAL",T,T/M
1399 RETURN
1400 REM ******************************
1402 REM *    FINAL MESSAGE            *
1404 REM ******************************
1406 PRINT
1408 PRINT "TRY ANOTHER DECISION RULE (Y/N)";
1410 INPUT U$
1412 IF U$ = "Y" THEN 1499
```

```
1414 IF U$ = "N" THEN 1499
1416 PRINT
1418 PRINT "INVALID RESPONSE"
1420 GOTO 1406
1499 RETURN
2000 REM *******************************
2002 REM *    BATCH                    *
2004 REM *******************************
2006 LET R1 = 0
2008 FOR J = 1 TO N
2010    IF RND(0) > P THEN 2014
2012    LET R1 = R1 + 1
2014    IF J <> N1 THEN 2018
2016    LET R2 = R1
2018 NEXT J
2020 LET P = P + .2 * P * RND(0)
2099 RETURN
9999 END
```

```
PROGRAM 6-2

EVALUATE QUALITY CONTROL
DECISION RULES ASSUMING
A RANDOM WALK OF THE
PROCESS FRACTION DEFECTIVE.

COST PER DEFECTIVE ITEM? 5
COST PER SAMPLE ITEM    ? .75
COST PER ADJUSTMENT     ? 100

PROCESS FRACTION DEFECTIVE
AFTER ADJUSTMENT? .1

BATCH SIZE? 100

NUMBER OF BATCHES? 10

SAMPLE SIZE? 10

CRITICAL NUMBER OF DEFECTIVES
FORCING MACHINE ADJUSTMENT? 3

                TOTAL COST      AVERAGE COST PER BATCH
ADJUSTING        200              20
```

```
SAMPLING            75              7.5
DEFECTIVES          560             56
TOTAL               835             83.5

TRY ANOTHER DECISION RULE (Y/N)? Y

BATCH SIZE? 100

NUMBER OF BATCHES? 10

SAMPLE SIZE? 20

CRITICAL NUMBER OF DEFECTIVES
FORCING MACHINE ADJUSTMENT? 4

                    TOTAL COST      AVERAGE COST PER BATCH
ADJUSTING           100             10
SAMPLING            150             15
DEFECTIVES          560             56
TOTAL               810             81

TRY ANOTHER DECISION RULE (Y/N)? N

END OF PROGRAM
```

Fig. 6-2. Sample results from Program 6-2.

Unless carefully engineered, the system may amplify certain shocks. The system may over correct resulting in wider deviations from the goal, which result in more severe responses. This results in destroying the system or making it become inherently unstable.

One of the aims of control is to dampen transient shocks and to smooth out the effects of random changes in the environment. Smoothing is an important tool for this purpose. The response may be to make up some portion of the difference between the current status of the system and the desired status (goal).

Overcontrol results from control policies which amplify shocks to the system. Another form of overcontrol comes from performance goals that are too tightly specified. A thermostat that regulates room temperature to within a quarter of a degree will have the heating unit turning on and off too often. A thermostat that doesn't maintain a close enough range in room temperature causes discomfort for those in the room. Under control is undesirable, too.

Principles of automatic control are not limited to the engineering and design of physical systems such as thermostats and automatic pilots. They also apply to policies involving human decision making. One of these areas involves inventory ordering policies.

The model for Program 6-3 employs some of the principles of automatic control. The goal is to maintain adequate inventories to meet future needs. Customer orders are received and shipments are made a few days later. Shipments from suppliers arrive some time after they are ordered.

The desired inventory level is based on the average demand in recent periods. The order quantity is chosen to bring the actual inventory level closer to the desired inventory level. Since over-control is a serious problem, the order quantity is designed to overcome some fraction of the difference between actual and desired inventory levels. The question concerns what fraction to use.

Program 6-3 simulates the inventory policy consisting of setting the desired inventory level sufficient to meet the demand for six periods similar to the average of the last three. Figure 6-3 shows the results.

Program 6-3

```
100 REM ******************************
102 REM *    6-3                      *
104 REM ******************************
106 REM   AUTHOR
108 REM        COPYRIGHT 1982
110 REM        BY LAWRENCE MCNITT.
112 REM   PURPOSE
114 REM        INVENTORY ORDERING POLICIES
116 REM        WITH FEEDBACK AND CONTROL.
118 REM   SYSTEM
120 REM        UNIVERSAL SUBSET
122 REM        OF BASIC
200 REM ******************************
202 REM *    ORGANIZATION             *
204 REM ******************************
206 REM   900   MAIN ROUTINE
208 REM         1000   INITIAL MESSAGE
210 REM         1100   PARAMETERS
212 REM         1200   PROCESS
214 REM         1300   FINAL MESSAGE
300 REM ******************************
302 REM *    VARIABLES                *
304 REM ******************************
306 REM   U$   USER RESPONSE
308 REM   D1   CURRENT DEMAND LEVEL
310 REM   D2   DEMAND FOR LAST PERIOD
312 REM   D3   DEMAND TWO PERIODS AGO
314 REM   S    SHIPMENTS SENT TO CUSTOMERS
316 REM   R    SHIPMENTS RECEIVED FROM WHOLESALERS
318 REM   C    CUSTOMER ORDERS NOT YET FILLED
320 REM   A    ACTUAL INVENTORY LEVEL
322 REM   L    DESIRED INVENTORY LEVEL
324 REM   Q1   QUANTITY ORDER FOR CURRENT PERIOD
326 REM   Q2   QUANTITY ORDERED LAST PERIOD
328 REM   Q3   QUANTITY ORDERED TWO PERIODS AGO
330 REM   N    NUMBER OF PERIODS
332 REM   I    COUNTER
334 REM   K    COEFFICIENT FOR ADJUSTING ORDER QUANTITY
```

```
900 REM **********************************
902 REM *    MAIN ROUTINE               *
904 REM **********************************
906 REM INITIAL MESSAGE
908 GOSUB 1006
910 REM PARAMETERS
912 GOSUB 1106
914 REM PROCESS
916 GOSUB 1206
918 REM FINAL MESSAGE
920 GOSUB 1306
922 IF U$ = "Y" THEN 912
924 PRINT
926 PRINT "END OF PROGRAM"
999 STOP
1000 REM **********************************
1002 REM *    INITIAL MESSAGE            *
1004 REM **********************************
1006 PRINT
1008 PRINT
1010 PRINT
1012 PRINT "PROGRAM 6-3"
1014 PRINT
1016 PRINT "SIMULATE AN INVENTORY ORDERING"
1018 PRINT "POLICY THAT ADJUSTS ORDER QUANTITY"
1020 PRINT "USING FEEDBACK AND CONTROL."
1099 RETURN
1100 REM **********************************
1102 REM *    PARAMETERS                 *
1104 REM **********************************
1106 PRINT
1108 PRINT "INITIAL DEMAND LEVEL PER PERIOD";
1110 INPUT D1
1112 LET D2 = D1
1114 LET D3 = D1
1116 LET L = 6 * D1
1117 LET A = L
1118 LET Q1 = D1
1120 LET Q2 = D1
1122 LET Q3 = D1
1124 PRINT
1126 PRINT "NUMBER OF PERIODS";
1128 INPUT N
1130 PRINT
1132 PRINT "COEFFICIENT ADJUSTING ORDER QUANTITY"
1134 PRINT "FOR DIFFERENCE BETWEEN ACTUAL AND"
```

```
1136 PRINT "DESIRED INVENTORY LEVELS (USUALLY"
1138 PRINT "BETWEEN 0 AND 1).";
1140 INPUT K
1199 RETURN
1200 REM ******************************
1202 REM *     PROCESS                *
1204 REM ******************************
1206 PRINT
1208 PRINT "DEMAND","SHIPMENTS","SHIPMENTS","QUANTITY"
1210 PRINT ,"DELIVERED","RECEIVED","ORDERED"
1212 FOR I = 1 TO N
1214     LET S = D2
1216     LET R = Q3
1218     LET D3 = D2
1220     LET D2 = D1
1222     LET D1 = D1 * (.95 + .1 * RND(0))
1224     LET C = C + D1 - S
1226     LET A = A + R - S
1228     LET L = 6 * (D1 + D2 + D3) / 3
1230     LET Q3 = Q2
1232     LET Q2 = Q1
1234     LET Q1 = D1 + K * (L - A)
1236     PRINT D1,S,R,Q1
1238 NEXT I
1299 RETURN
1300 REM ******************************
1302 REM *     FINAL MESSAGE          *
1304 REM ******************************
1306 PRINT
1308 PRINT "TRY ANOTHER SIMULATION RUN (Y/N)";
1310 INPUT U$
1312 IF U$ = "Y" THEN 1399
1314 IF U$ = "N" THEN 1399
1316 PRINT
1318 PRINT "INVALID RESPONSE"
1320 GOTO 1306
1399 RETURN
9999 END
```

Exercise 6-3

1. Compare the effect of the coefficient for adjusting the inventory level on the resulting order
quantity. Are there coefficients that provide
dampening?

WAITING LINES

Waiting lines (queues) are common in many
situations. Customers form queues at supermarket
checkout counters. Jobs form queues waiting for
processing in a job-shop production environment. A

```
PROGRAM 6-3

SIMULATE AN INVENTORY ORDERING
POLICY THAT ADJUSTS ORDER QUANTITY
USING FEEDBACK AND CONTROL.

INITIAL DEMAND LEVEL FOR PERIOD? 300

NUMBER OF PERIODS? 10

COEFFICIENT ADJUSTING ORDER QUANTITY
FOR DIFFERENCE BETWEEN ACTUAL AND
DESIRED INVENTORY LEVELS (USUALLY
BETWEEN O AND 1).? .5

DEMAND          SHIPMENTS       SHIPMENTS       QUANTITY
                DELIVERED       RECEIVED        ORDERED
  307.798         300             300             315.597
  321.759         300             300             351.316
  306.433         307.798         300             346.323
  318.996         321.759         315.597         373.164
  328.626         306.433         351.316         367.22
  312.793         318.996         346.323         344.084
  314.892         328.626         373.164         319.81
  318.816         312.793         367.22          286.71
  324.362         314.892         344.084         289.228
  316.968         318.816         319.81          283.414

TRY ANOTHER SIMULATION RUN (Y/N)? N

END OF PROGRAM
```

Fig. 6-3. Sample results from Program 6-3.

backlog of unfinished jobs form at a repair facility. Arrivals may come in independently or in groups. The service time may be constant or random.

If arrivals are truly randomly distributed with each arrival independent of the others, the exponential or negative exponential distribution may describe the distribution of times between arrivals. The only parameter needed to specify the distribution is the mean time between arrivals. This distribution is appropriate for many models involving waiting-line systems.

Service times may also be exponentially distributed. The average service time is the parameter identifying the specific distribution of service times. Service times are less likely to be exponentially distributed than arrival times. However, for some models exponential service times are appropriate.

Models having both exponentially distributed arrival times and exponentially distributed service times are the easiest to solve analytically. Analytic solutions have been derived for arrivals and service patterns following other common distributions as well as exponential distributions.

The Poisson and exponential distributions are directly related. They both result from the same underlying Poisson process. The exponential distribution is described by its mean. There may be an average of 30 seconds between telephone calls arriving at a switchboard. The Poisson distribution gives the probabilities for the number of successes in a given trial space when the expected number of successes is known. The switchboard has an average of two telephone calls per minute. An average of 30 seconds between calls is the same as an average of .5 minutes between calls. The reciprocal

$$2 = 1 / .5$$

gives the average number of telephone calls per minute. Thus, the reciprocal of the exponential mean gives the Poisson mean, and the reciprocal of the Poisson mean gives the exponential mean. For one mean to be the reciprocal of the other mean, both means must involve the same units measuring the time interval.

If the Poisson process defines both arrivals and servicing, the waiting line problem parameters include the two means. Either the Poisson means or the exponential means are possible.

Measures of interest for a service facility and its associated queue include the utilization rate, idle time rate, average number in the queue, average number in the system, average time in the queue, and average time in the system. Costs of interest include the cost of customer waiting and the cost of the service facility.

An infinite queue will theoretically form if the rate of arrivals exceeds the capacity of the service facility. The Poisson means give the expected number of arrivals and the expected capacity of the service facility. Together, they define the intensity of the Poisson processes involved. If the expected number of arrivals per time unit exceeds the expected service capacity per time unit, an infinite queue will begin forming. Analytic models assume that the arrival rate is less than the service capacity rate so that an infinite queue does not form.

For Poisson arrivals and servicing, the formula

$$R = A / S$$

gives the utilization rate of the service facility. The utilization rate is the fraction of the total time that the service facility is busy. The expression $1-R$ gives the fraction of time that the facility is idle.

If customers arrive at the rate of 8 per hour and the service facility can handle 10 per hour, then

$$R = A / S = .8$$

gives the utilization rate. The facility will be busy 80 percent of the time and idle 20 percent of the time.

Program 6-4 gives analytic solutions including cost estimates for a waiting line problem involving one service center and one queue, and Poisson arrivals and servicing. Figure 6-4 shows the results.

Multiple Stations

The simple model is a single channel single station model. More complex models include multiple stations. The multiple stations may include a

Program 6-4

```
100 REM ******************************
102 REM *    6-4                     *
104 REM ******************************
106 REM   AUTHOR
108 REM      COPYRIGHT 1982
110 REM      BY LAWRENCE MCNITT.
112 REM   PURPOSE
```

```
114 REM       SINGLE CHANNEL SINGLE
116 REM       STATION QUEUE ANALYSIS.
118 REM   SYSTEM
120 REM       UNIVERSAL SUBSET
122 REM       OF BASIC.
200 REM ********************************
202 REM *    ORGANIZATION             *
204 REM ********************************
206 REM   900    MAIN ROUTINE
208 REM          1000    INITIAL MESSAGE
210 REM          1100    PARAMETERS
212 REM          1200    PROCESS
214 REM          1300    SUMMARY
216 REM          1400    DISTRIBUTION
218 REM          1500    FINAL MESSAGE
300 REM **********************************
302 REM *    VARIABLES                  *
304 REM **********************************
306 REM    U$   USER RESPONSE
308 REM    A    ARRIVAL RATE
310 REM    S    SERVICE RATE
312 REM    R    UTILIZATION RATE
314 REM    D    FRACTION IDLE TIME
316 REM    P    PROBABILITY FOR NUMBER IN SYSTEM
318 REM    P1   CUMULATIVE PROBABILITY
320 REM    L1   EXPECTED NUMBER IN SYSTEM
322 REM    L2   EXPECTED NUMBER IN QUEUE
324 REM    W1   EXPECTED TIME IN THE SYSTEM
326 REM    W2   EXPECTED TIME IN THE QUEUE
328 REM    N    NUMBER OF CUSTOMERS IN THE SYSTEM
330 REM    K    UPPER LIMIT FOR PROBABILITY DISTRIBUTION
332 REM    C1   WAITING COST PER CUSTOMER PER UNIT OF TIME
334 REM    C2   SERVICE FACILITY COST PER UNIT OF TIME
336 REM    T1   TOTAL WAITING COST PER UNIT OF TIME
338 REM    T2   TOTAL SERVICE COST PER UNIT OF TIME
340 REM    T3   TOTAL SYSTEM COST PER UNIT OF TIME
900 REM ********************************
902 REM *    MAIN ROUTINE               *
904 REM ********************************
906 REM INITIAL MESSAGE
908 GOSUB 1006
910 REM PARAMETERS
912 GOSUB 1106
914 REM PROCESS
916 GOSUB 1206
918 REM SUMMARY
```

```
920  GOSUB 1306
922  REM DISTIBUTION
924  GOSUB 1406
926  REM FINAL MESSAGE
928  GOSUB 1506
930  IF U$ = "Y" THEN 912
932  PRINT
934  PRINT "END OF PROGRAM"
999  STOP
1000 REM ****************************
1002 REM *    INITIAL MESSAGE        *
1004 REM ****************************
1006 PRINT
1008 PRINT
1010 PRINT
1012 PRINT "PROGRAM 6-4"
1014 PRINT
1016 PRINT "SINGLE CHANNEL, SINGLE STATION"
1018 PRINT "QUEUE ANALYSIS WITH POISSON"
1020 PRINT "ARRIVAL AND SERVICE RATES"
1022 PRINT "(EXPONENTIAL ARRIVAL AND"
1024 PRINT "SERVICE TIMES)."
1099 RETURN
1100 REM ****************************
1102 REM *    PARAMETERS             *
1104 REM ****************************
1106 PRINT
1108 PRINT "ARRIVAL RATE";
1110 INPUT A
1112 PRINT "SERVICE RATE";
1114 INPUT S
1116 IF A < S THEN 1126
1118 PRINT
1120 PRINT "ARRIVAL RATE MUST BE"
1122 PRINT "LESS THAN SERVICE RATE"
1124 GOTO 1106
1126 PRINT
1128 PRINT "COST PER UNIT OF TIME FOR"
1130 PRINT "CUSTOMER WAITING";
1132 INPUT C1
1134 PRINT "SERVICE FACILITY";
1136 INPUT C2
1199 RETURN
1200 REM ****************************
1202 REM *    PROCESS                *
1204 REM ****************************
```

```
1206 LET R = A / S
1208 LET D = 1 - R
1210 LET L1 = R / (1 - R)
1212 LET L2 = L1 * R
1214 LET W1 = 1 / (S - A)
1216 LET W2 = W1 * R
1218 LET T1 = C1 * L1
1220 LET T2 = C2
1222 LET T3 = T1 + T2
1299 RETURN
1300 REM ******************************
1302 REM *    SUMMARY                 *
1304 REM ******************************
1306 PRINT
1308 PRINT "UTILIZATION RATE",R
1310 PRINT "IDLE TIME RATE",,D
1312 PRINT
1314 PRINT "EXPECTED NUMBER IN SYSTEM",L1
1316 PRINT "EXPECTED NUMBER IN QUEUE",L2
1318 PRINT
1320 PRINT "EXPECTED TIME IN THE SYSTEM",W1
1322 PRINT "EXPECTED TIME IN THE QUEUE",W2
1324 PRINT
1326 PRINT "SYSTEM COSTS PER UNIT OF TIME"
1328 PRINT "CUSTOMER WAITING",T1
1330 PRINT "SERVICE FACILITY",T2
1332 PRINT "TOTAL",,T3
1399 RETURN
1400 REM ******************************
1402 REM *    DISTRIBUTION            *
1404 REM ******************************
1406 PRINT
1408 PRINT "DISPLAY PROBABILITY DISTRIBUTION (Y/N)";
1410 INPUT U$
1412 IF U$ = "Y" THEN 1422
1414 IF U$ = "N" THEN 1499
1416 PRINT
1418 PRINT "INVALID RESPONSE"
1420 GOTO 1406
1422 PRINT
1424 PRINT "PROBABILITY DISTRIBUTION FOR"
1426 PRINT "NUMBER IN THE SYSTEM"
1428 PRINT
1430 PRINT "UPPER LIMIT FOR PROBABILITY DISTRIBUTION";
1432 INPUT K
1434 PRINT
```

```
1436 PRINT "NUMBER","EXACT","CUMULATIVE"
1438 PRINT ,"PROBABILITY","PROBABILITY"
1440 LET P = D
1442 LET P1 = 0
1444 FOR N = 0 TO K
1446    IF N = 0 THEN 1450
1448    LET P = P * R
1450    LET P1 = P1 + P
1452    PRINT N,P,P1
1454 NEXT N
1499 RETURN
1500 REM ******************************
1302 REM *     FINAL MESSAGE          *
1304 REM ******************************
1306 PRINT
1308 PRINT "TRY ANOTHER SIMULATION RUN (Y/N)";
1310 INPUT U$
1312 IF U$ = "Y" THEN 1399
1314 IF U$ = "N" THEN 1399
1316 PRINT
1318 PRINT "INVALID RESPONSE"
1320 GOTO 1306
1399 RETURN
1502 REM *     FINAL MESSAGE          *
1504 REM ******************************
1506 PRINT
1508 PRINT "TRY ANOTHER SET OF DATA (Y/N)";
1510 INPUT U$
1512 IF U$ = "Y" THEN 1599
1514 IF U$ = "N" THEN 1599
1516 PRINT
1518 PRINT "INVALID RESPONSE"
1520 GOTO 1506
1599 RETURN
9999 END
```

PROGRAM 6-4

SINGLE CHANNEL,SINGLE STATION
QUEUE ANALYSIS WITH POISSON
ARRIVAL AND SERVICE RATES
(EXPONENTIAL ARRIVAL AND
SERVICE TIMES).

```
ARRIVAL RATE? 2
SERVICE RATE? 3

COST PER UNIT OF TIME FOR
CUSTOMER WAITING? 6
SERVICE FACILITY? 15


UTILIZATION RATE              .666667
IDLE TIME RATE               .333333


EXPECTED NUMBER IN SYSTEM     2
EXPECTED NUMBER IN QUEUE      1.33333


EXPECTED TIME IN THE SYSTEM   1
EXPECTED TIME IN THE QUEUE    .666667


SYSTEM COSTS PER UNIT OF TIME
CUSTOMER WAITING              12
SERVICE FACILITY             15
TOTAL                        27


DISPLAY PROBABILITY DISTRIBUTION (Y/N)? Y


PROBABILITY DISTRIBUTION FOR
NUMBER IN THE SYSTEM


UPPER LIMIT FOR PROBABILITY DISTRIBUTION? 5


NUMBER          EXACT           CUMULATIVE
                PROBABILITY     PROBABILITY
  0             .333333         .333333
  1             .222222         .555556
  2             .148148         .703704
  3             .0987654        .802469
  4             .0658436        .868313
  5             .0438958        .912209


TRY ANOTHER SET OF DATA (Y/N)? N

END OF PROGRAM
```

Fig. 6-4. Sample results from Program 6-4.

series of stations each with its own queue. The stations may be in parallel fed from one queue or in parallel each with its own queue. Large systems consist of a complex network of stations and queues with policies controlling the movement of jobs from station to station.

These complex networks require simulation methods for analysis. Certain models involving stations of a similar type have analytic solutions. These stations are commonly in the form of a set of parallel identical stations. These stations can represent several checkout stations at a supermarket or several identical machines in a production job-shop operation.

Program 6-5 gives analytic solutions to the situation involving several service facilities operating in parallel with one queue and Poisson arrival and service rates. Figure 6-5 shows the results.

Waiting Line Simulation

The models assuming Poisson arrivals and servicing are the simplest to solve analytically. They do not always reflect the actual situation, however. Analytic solutions exist for certain specified distributions for arrivals and servicing, but they cannot handle all situations. This is especially true for those situations that allow dependen-

Program 6-5

```
100 REM *********************************
102 REM *     6-5                        *
104 REM *********************************
106 REM   AUTHOR
108 REM        COPYRIGHT 1982
110 REM        BY LAWRENCE MCNITT.
112 REM   PURPOSE
114 REM        MULTIPLE STATION, SINGLE
116 REM        PHASE QUEUE ANALYSIS.
118 REM   SYSTEM
120 REM        UNIVERSAL SUBSET
122 REM        OF BASIC.
200 REM **********************************
202 REM *    ORGANIZATION                *
204 REM **********************************
206 REM   900   MAIN ROUTINE
208 REM         1000   INITIAL MESSAGE
210 REM         1100   PARAMETERS
212 REM         1200   PROCESS
214 REM         1300   SUMMARY
216 REM         1400   DISTRIBUTION
218 REM         1500   FINAL MESSAGE
300 REM **********************************
302 REM *    VARIABLES                   *
304 REM **********************************
306 REM   U$    USER RESPONSE
308 REM   A     ARRIVAL RATE
310 REM   S     SERVICE RATE
312 REM   M     NUMBER OF STATIONS
314 REM   R     UTILIZATION PARAMETER
316 REM   P     PROBABILITY FOR NUMBER IN SYSTEM
318 REM   P1    CUMULATIVE PROBABILITY
```

```
320 REM    L1   EXPECTED NUMBER IN THE SYSTEM
322 REM    L2   EXPECTED NUMBER IN THE QUEUE
324 REM    W1   EXPECTED TIME IN THE SYSTEM
326 REM    W2   EXPECTED TIME IN THE QUEUE
328 REM    N    NUMBER OF CUSTOMERS IN THE SYSTEM
330 REM    K    UPPER LIMIT FOR PROBABILITY DISTRIBUTION
332 REM    C1   WAITING COST PER CUSTOMER PER UNIT OF TIME
334 REM    C2   SERVICE FACILITY COST PER UNIT OF TIME
336 REM    T1   TOTAL WAITING COST PER UNIT OF TIME
338 REM    T2   TOTAL SERVICE COST PER UNIT OF TIME
340 REM    T3   TOTAL SYSTEM COST PER UNIT OF TIME
900 REM ********************************
902 REM *    MAIN ROUTINE             *
904 REM ********************************
906 REM INITIAL MESSAGE
908 GOSUB 1006
910 REM PARAMETERS
912 GOSUB 1106
914 REM PROCESS
916 GOSUB 1206
918 REM SUMMARY
920 GOSUB 1306
922 REM DISTRIBUTION
924 GOSUB 1406
926 REM FINAL MESSAGE
928 GOSUB 1506
930 IF U$ = "Y" THEN 912
932 PRINT
934 PRINT "END OF PROGRAM"
999 STOP
1000 REM ****************************
1002 REM *    INITIAL MESSAGE        *
1004 REM ****************************
1006 PRINT
1008 PRINT
1010 PRINT
1012 PRINT "PROGRAM 6-5"
1014 PRINT
1016 PRINT "MULTIPLE STATION,SINGLE CHANNEL"
1018 PRINT "QUEUE ANALYSIS WITH POISSON"
1020 PRINT "ARRIVAL AND SERVICE RATES."
1099 RETURN
1100 REM ******************************
1102 REM *    PARAMETERS               *
1104 REM ******************************
1106 PRINT
```

```
1108 PRINT "ARRIVAL RATE              ";
1110 INPUT A
1112 PRINT "SERVICE RATE PER STATION ";
1114 INPUT S
1116 PRINT "NUMBER OF STATIONS       ";
1118 INPUT M
1120 IF A < M*S THEN 1130
1122 PRINT
1124 PRINT "SERVICE RATE TIMES NUMBER OF STATIONS"
1126 PRINT "UNABLE TO MEET DEMAND.   TRY AGAIN."
1128 GOTO 1106
1130 PRINT
1132 PRINT "COST PER UNIT OF TIME FOR"
1134 PRINT "CUSTOMER WAITING      ";
1136 INPUT C1
1138 PRINT "ONE SERVICE STATION   ";
1140 INPUT C2
1199 RETURN
1200 REM ********************************
1202 REM *    PROCESS                   *
1204 REM ********************************
1206 LET R = A / (M * S)
1208 LET P1 = 1
1210 LET P = 1
1212 FOR N = 1 TO M-1
1214    LET P1 = P1 * M * R / N
1216    LET P = P + P1
1218 NEXT N
1220 LET P = P + P1 * M * R / (M * (1 - R))
1222 LET P = 1 / P
1224 LET P1 = P1 * M * R * R / (M * (1 - R) [ 2)
1226 LET L2 = P1 * P
1228 LET W2 = L2 / A
1230 LET W1 = W2 + 1 / S
1232 LET L1 = A * W1
1234 LET T1 = C1 * L1
1236 LET T2 = C2 * M
1238 LET T3 = T1 + T2
1299 RETURN
1300 REM ********************************
1302 REM *    SUMMARY                   *
1304 REM ********************************
1306 PRINT
1314 PRINT "EXPECTED NUMBER IN THE SYSTEM",L1
1316 PRINT "EXPECTED NUMBER IN THE QUEUE",L2
1318 PRINT
```

```
1320 PRINT "EXPECTED TIME IN THE SYSTEM",W1
1322 PRINT "EXPECTED TIME IN THE QUEUE",W2
1324 PRINT
1326 PRINT "SYSTEM COSTS PER UNIT OF TIME"
1328 PRINT "CUSTOMER WAITING",T1
1330 PRINT "SERVICE FACILITY",T2
1332 PRINT "TOTAL",,T3
1399 RETURN
1400 REM ****************************
1402 REM *    DISTRIBUTION          *
1404 REM ****************************
1406 PRINT
1408 PRINT "DISPLAY PROBABILITY DISTRIBUTION (Y/N)";
1410 INPUT U$
1412 IF U$ = "Y" THEN 1422
1414 IF U$ = "N" THEN 1499
1416 PRINT
1418 PRINT "INVALID RESPONSE"
1420 GOTO 1406
1422 PRINT
1424 PRINT "PROBABILITY DISTRIBUTION FOR"
1426 PRINT "NUMBER IN THE SYSTEM"
1428 PRINT
1430 PRINT "UPPER LIMIT FOR PROBABILITY DISTRIBUTION";
1432 INPUT K
1434 PRINT
1436 PRINT "NUMBER","EXACT","CUMULATIVE"
1438 PRINT ,"PROBABILITY","PROBABILITY"
1440 LET P1 = P
1442 PRINT 0,P,P1
1444 FOR N = 1 TO K
1446    IF N > M THEN 1452
1448    LET P = P * M * R / N
1450    GOTO 1454
1452    LET P = P * R
1454    LET P1 = P1 + P
1456    PRINT N,P,P1
1458 NEXT N
1499 RETURN
1500 REM ****************************
1502 REM *    FINAL MESSAGE         *
1504 REM ****************************
1506 PRINT
1508 PRINT "TRY ANOTHER SET OF DATA (Y/N)";
1510 INPUT U$
1512 IF U$ = "Y" THEN 1599
```

```
1514 IF U$ = "N" THEN 1599
1516 PRINT
1518 PRINT "INVALID RESPONSE"
1520 GOTO 1506
1599 RETURN
9999 END
```

PROGRAM 6-5

MULTIPLE STATION, SINGLE CHANNEL
QUEUE ANALYSIS WITH POISSON
ARRIVAL AND SERVICE RATES.

ARRIVAL RATE   ? 20
SERVICE RATE PER STATION ? 6
NUMBER OF STATIONS   ? 4

COST PER UNIT OF TIME FOR
CUSTOMER WAITING   ? 6
ONE SERVICE STATION ? 15

EXPECTED NUMBER IN THE SYSTEM   6.62194
EXPECTED NUMBER IN THE QUEUE   3.28861

EXPECTED TIME IN THE SYSTEM   .331097
EXPECTED TIME IN THE QUEUE   .16443

SYSTEM COSTS PER UNIT OF TIME
CUSTOMER WAITING   39.7316
SERVICE FACILITY   60
TOTAL   99.7317

DISPLAY PROBABILITY DISTRIBUTION (Y/N)? Y

PROBABILITY DISTRIBUTION FOR
NUMBER IN THE SYSTEM

UPPER LIMIT FOR PROBABILITY DISTRIBUTION? 7

NUMBER	EXACT PROBABILITY	CUMULATIVE PROBABILITY
0	.0213102	.0213102
1	.071034	.0923441
2	.11839	.210734

```
3                    .131544           .342278
4                    .10962            .451899
5                    .0913502          .543249
6                    .0761252          .619374
7                    .0634377          .682812


TRY ANOTHER SET OF DATA (Y/N)? N

END OF PROGRAM
```

Fig. 6-5. Sample results from Program 6-5.

cies among arrivals or for those that do not apply the FIFO (first come first served) rule to the waiting line.

Program 6-6 illustrates the concept of queue simulation assuming the simplest Poisson pattern for arrivals and servicing. Figure 6-6 shows the results.

Exercise 6-4

1. Customers arrive at a service facility at the rate of 6 per hour. Assign a cost of $9.00 per hour for the time the customer spends in the system. The decision is to choose one of three machines for the service facility. The cost of operating machine A is $15.00 per hour and its capacity is 8 customers per hour. Machine B has an operating cost of $25.00 per hour and a capacity of 10 customers per hour. Machine C costs $35.00 per hour and has a capacity of 14 customers per hour. Which machine gives the least total cost per hour?

2. Customers arrive at a facility at the rate of 50 per hour. An individual service station can handle an average of 8 customers per hour. Each service

Program 6-6

```
100 REM **********************************
102 REM *    6-6                         *
104 REM **********************************
106 REM   AUTHOR
108 REM        COPYRIGHT 1982
110 REM        BY LAWRENCE MCNITT.
112 REM   PURPOSE
114 REM        SIMULATE SINGLE STATION,
116 REM        SINGLE CHANNEL QUEUE.
118 REM   SYSTEM
120 REM        UNIVERSAL SUBSET
122 REM        OF BASIC.
200 REM **********************************
202 REM *    ORGANIZATION                *
204 REM **********************************
206 REM   900   MAIN ROUTINE
208 REM         1000   INITIAL MESSAGE
210 REM         1100   PARAMETERS
212 REM         1200   PROCESS
```

```
214 REM                    2000   ARRIVAL
216 REM                    2100   SERVICE
218 REM           1300   OUTPUT
220 REM           1400   FINAL MESSAGE
300 REM ******************************
302 REM *    VARIABLES                *
304 REM ******************************
306 REM    U$   USER RESPONSE
308 REM    N    NUMBER OF ITEMS TO SIMULATE
310 REM    I    COUNTER
312 REM    A1   TIME INTERVAL TO NEXT ARRIVAL
314 REM    A2   TIME OF NEXT ARRIVAL
316 REM    S1   SERVICE TIME FOR CURRENT ITEM
318 REM    S2   TIME SERVICE IS COMPLETED
320 REM    W    WAIT TIME FOR ITEM
322 REM    T1   TOTAL SERVICE TIME
324 REM    T2   TOTAL WAIT TIME
326 REM    M1   POPULATION MEAN ARRIVAL TIMES
328 REM    M2   POPULATION MEAN SERVICE TIMES
900 REM ******************************
902 REM *    MAIN ROUTINE               *
904 REM ******************************
906 REM INITIAL MESSAGE
908 GOSUB 1006
910 REM PARAMETERS
912 GOSUB 1106
914 REM PROCESS
916 GOSUB 1206
918 REM OUTPUT
920 GOSUB 1306
922 REM FINAL MESSAGE
924 GOSUB 1406
926 IF U$ = "Y" THEN 912
928 PRINT
930 PRINT "END OF PROGRAM"
999 STOP
1000 REM ******************************
1002 REM *    INITIAL MESSAGE           *
1004 REM ******************************
1006 PRINT
1008 PRINT
1010 PRINT
1012 PRINT "PROGRAM 6-6"
1014 PRINT
1016 PRINT "SIMULATE SINGLE CHANNEL,SINGLE STATION"
1018 PRINT "QUEUE WITH EXPONENTIALLY DISTRIBUTED"
```

```
1020 PRINT "ARRIVAL AND SERVICE TIMES."
1099 RETURN
1100 REM ******************************
1102 REM *    PARAMETERS              *
1104 REM ******************************
1106 PRINT
1108 PRINT "AVERAGE TIME BETWEEN ARRIVALS";
1110 INPUT M1
1112 PRINT
1114 PRINT "AVERAGE SERVICE TIME";
1116 INPUT M2
1118 PRINT
1120 PRINT "NUMBER OF ARRIVALS TO SIMULATE";
1122 INPUT N
1199 RETURN
1200 REM ******************************
1202 REM *    PROCESS                 *
1204 REM ******************************
1206 LET A2 = 0
1208 LET S2 = 0
1210 LET T1 = 0
1212 LET T2 = 0
1214 FOR I = 1 TO N
1216     REM ARRIVAL
1218     GOSUB 2006
1220     REM SERVICE
1222     GOSUB 2106
1224     LET A2 = A2 + A1
1226     LET W = 0
1228     IF A2 > S2 THEN 1232
1230     LET W = S2 - A2
1232     LET T1 = T1 + S1
1234     LET T2 = T2 + W
1236     LET S2 = A2 + W + S1
1238 NEXT I
1299 RETURN
1300 REM ******************************
1302 REM *    OUTPUT                  *
1304 REM ******************************
1306 PRINT
1308 PRINT "AVERAGE TIME BETWEEN ARRIVALS";A2/N
1310 PRINT "AVERAGE SERVICE TIME          ";T1/N
1312 PRINT
1314 PRINT "UTILIZATION RATE              ";T1/S2
1316 PRINT "IDLE TIME RATE                ";1-T1/S2
1318 PRINT
```

```
1320 PRINT "AVERAGE WAIT TIME PER ITEM     ";T2/N
1322 PRINT "AVERAGE TIME IN SYSTEM        ";(T1+T2)/N
1399 RETURN
1400 REM *****************************
1402 REM *    FINAL MESSAGE          *
1404 REM *****************************
1406 PRINT
1408 PRINT "TRY ANOTHER SIMULATION RUN (Y/N)";
1410 INPUT U$
1412 IF U$ = "Y" THEN 1499
1414 IF U$ = "N" THEN 1499
1416 PRINT
1418 PRINT "INVALID RESPONSE"
1420 GOTO 1406
1499 RETURN
2000 REM *****************************
2002 REM *    ARRIVAL                *
2004 REM *****************************
2006 LET A1 = -M1 * LOG(RND(0))
2099 RETURN
2100 REM *****************************
2102 REM *    SERVICE                *
2104 REM *****************************
2106 LET S1 = -M2 * LOG(RND(0))
2199 RETURN
9999 END
```

station has an operating cost of $15.00 per hour. Assign a cost of $9.00 per hour for the time the customer spends in the system. There must be at least 7 service stations to provide the total capacity sufficient to meet the demand. Compare total costs for 7, 8, 9, . . . service stations and identify the number of stations that minimizes the total cost.

ASSEMBLY LINE BALANCING AND JOB-SHOP SCHEDULING

Assembly line balancing and job-shop scheduling are important problems in physical production. Solution techniques include those of trial and error employed in the analysis of simulation models.

Assembly Line Balancing

The purpose of assembly line balancing is to assign tasks to work stations in such a manner that requirements are equitably balanced among the work stations. Ideally, each work station has the same amount of work. Furthermore, the throughput is such that there is little, if any, idle time among the work stations.

Another part of the analysis is selecting the number of work stations needed to meet production goals. In the extreme, one work station could do everything. The time of assembly would be the sum of all the task times. Dividing the tasks equitably among two work stations could almost double the throughput. Using three work stations could almost triple the throughput.

There are many possible assignments of tasks to work stations. The simulation approach is to assign them randomly. The total assembly time gives the measure of performance. Only those assignments that decrease the total completion time over previous assignments are considered further.

```
PROGRAM P6-6

SIMULATE SINGLE CHANNEL,SINGLE STATION
QUEUE WITH EXPONENTIALLY DISTRIBUTED
ARRIVAL AND SERVICE TIMES.

AVERAGE TIME BETWEEN ARRIVALS? 8

AVERAGE SERVICE TIME? 6

NUMBER OF ARRIVALS TO SIMULATE? 200

AVERAGE TIME BETWEEN ARRIVALS    8.04221
AVERAGE SERVICE TIME             5.82881

UTILIZATION RATE                 .723748
IDLE TIME RATE                   .276252

AVERAGE WAIT TIME PER ITEM       11.4053

AVERAGE TIME IN SYSTEM           17.2341

TRY ANOTHER SIMULATION RUN (Y/N)? N

END OF PROGRAM
```

Fig. 6-6. Sample results from Program 6-6.

The idle time for a work station is the difference between the time taken for the tasks assigned to that work station and the maximum of the times of the tasks assigned to any work station. No further improvement is possible when all work stations have no idle time. If none of the work stations have any idle time, further improvement will require additional work stations. Because of the discreteness of the task times, it may not be possible to fully utilize all work stations.

The tasks typically have a precedence ordering. Some tasks have to be completed before others begin. However, some sets of tasks can proceed in parallel. A network similar to that used in CPM (critical path method) or PERT (program evaluation and review technique) shows precedence ordering. The nodes of the network represent milestones during the assembly process. The branches represent tasks. Each branch has a predecessor and a successor node.

To make the computer analysis easier, the convention that the milestones (task completion points) should be numbered in ascending numerical order is used. Each branch leads from a lower numbered to a higher numbered node.

Program 6-7 does a trial and error search to determine the assignment of tasks to work stations that minimizes the total idle time and the total time of assembly. Figure 6-7 shows the results.

Job-Shop Scheduling

Job-shop scheduling is a complex task requiring human skill and intuition. The computer can aid in this task. Tasks are not assigned in the lock-step fashion of the assembly line. The orders may be for custom products or for products of a diverse nature.

Program 6-7

```
100 REM ********************************
102 REM *    6-7                        *
104 REM ********************************
106 REM   AUTHOR
108 REM      COPYRIGHT 1982
110 REM        BY LAWRENCE MCNITT.
112 REM   PURPOSE
114 REM        ASSEMBLY LINE BALANCING.
116 REM   SYSTEM
118 REM        UNIVERSAL SUBSET
120 REM        OF BASIC.
200 REM ********************************
202 REM *    ORGANIZATION               *
204 REM ********************************
206 REM   900    MAIN ROUTINE
208 REM          1000   INITIAL MESSAGE
210 REM          1100   GET TASKS
212 REM          1200   PROCESS
214 REM                 2000   GET PARAMETERS
216 REM                 2100   INITIALIZE
218 REM                 2200   ASSIGNABLE TASKS
220 REM                 2300   CULLED TASKS
222 REM                 2400   CHOOSE TASK
224 REM                 2500   CHECK RESULT
226 REM                 2600   DISPLAY RESULT
228 REM          1300   FINAL MESSAGE
300 REM ********************************
302 REM *    VARIABLES                  *
304 REM ********************************
306 REM   T(50,5)   TASK INFORMATION: FROM, TO,
308 REM             TIME, STATION, ASSIGNABLE
310 REM   N$(50)    TASK NAMES
312 REM   M(20)     MILESTONES ACHIEVED
314 REM   W(20)     TIMES FOR WORK STATIONS
316 REM   A(50)     LIST OF ASSIGNABLE TASKS
318 REM   U$   USER RESPONSE
320 REM   N1   NUMBER OF TASKS
322 REM   N2   NUMBER OF MILESTONES
324 REM   N3   NUMBER OF WORK STATIONS
326 REM   N4   NUMBER OF TASKS TO CHOOSE FROM
328 REM   I    INDEX
330 REM   J    INDEX
332 REM   K    INDEX
334 REM   I1   INDEX
```

```
336 REM    J1    INDEX
338 REM    C1    CYCLE TIME, MAXIMUM TIME PER WORK STATION
340 REM    S1    TIME PER SHIFT
342 REM    M2    MAXIMUM TIME FOR CURRENT WORK STATIONS
344 REM    T1    TIME FOR CURRENT WORK STATION
346 REM    T2    TOTAL TIME FOR ALL WORK STATIONS
348 REM    D     TOTAL IDLE TIME
350 REM    D1    IDLE TIME FOR CURRENT WORK STATION
900 REM ******************************
902 REM *    MAIN ROUTINE            *
904 REM ******************************
906 DIM N$(50),T(50,5),M(20),W(20),A(50)
908 REM INITIAL MESSAGE
910 GOSUB 1006
914 REM GET TASKS
916 GOSUB 1106
918 REM PROCESS
920 GOSUB 1208
922 REM FINAL MESSAGE
924 GOSUB 1306
926 IF U$ = "Y" THEN 914
928 PRINT
930 PRINT "END OF PROGRAM"
999 STOP
1000 REM ******************************
1002 REM *    INITIAL MESSAGE          *
1004 REM ******************************
1006 PRINT
1008 PRINT
1010 PRINT
1012 PRINT "SCH1"
1014 PRINT
1016 PRINT "ASSIGN TASKS TO ASSEMBLY LINE"
1018 PRINT "WORK STATIONS TO MINIMIZE"
1020 PRINT "TOTAL IDLE TIME USING RANDOMIZED"
1022 PRINT "SEARCH PROCEDURE."
1099 RETURN
1100 REM ******************************
1102 REM *    GET TASKS                *
1104 REM ******************************
1106 PRINT
1108 PRINT "NUMBER OF TASKS";
1110 INPUT N1
1112 PRINT
1114 PRINT "DATA FOR"
1116 FOR I = 1 TO N1
```

```
1118    PRINT
1120    PRINT "TASK";I
1122    PRINT "NAME OF TASK";
1124    INPUT N$(I)
1126    PRINT "FROM NODE    ";
1128    INPUT T(I,1)
1130    PRINT "TO NODE      ";
1132    INPUT T(I,2)
1134    PRINT "TASK TIME    ";
1136    INPUT T(I,3)
1138 NEXT I
1140 LET N2 = 0
1142 FOR I = 1 TO N1
1144    IF T(I,2) <= N2 THEN 1148
1146    LET N2 = T(I,2)
1148 NEXT I
1199 RETURN
1200 REM *****************************
1202 REM *     PROCESS               *
1204 REM *****************************
1206 REM GET PARAMETERS
1208 GOSUB 2006
1210 REM INITIALIZE
1212 GOSUB 2106
1214 FOR K = 1 TO N3
1216    LET T1 = 0
1218    REM ASSIGNABLE TASKS
1220    GOSUB 2206
1222    REM CULLED TASKS
1224    GOSUB 2306
1226    IF N4 = 0 THEN 1236
1228    REM CHOOSE TASK
1230    GOSUB 2406
1232    IF M(J1) = 1 THEN 1220
1234    GOTO 1224
1236    LET W(K) = T1
1238 NEXT K
1240 REM CHECK RESULT
1242 GOSUB 2506
1244 IF M2 >= C1 THEN 1212
1246 REM DISPLAY RESULT
1248 GOSUB 2606
1250 IF D > 0 THEN 1258
1252 PRINT
1254 PRINT "BEST POSSIBLE ASSIGNMENT"
1256 GOTO 1274
```

```
1258 PRINT
1260 PRINT "CONTINUE SEARCH (Y/N)";
1262 INPUT U$
1264 IF U$ = "Y" THEN 1212
1266 IF U$ = "N" THEN 1274
1268 PRINT
1270 PRINT "INVALID RESPONSE"
1272 GOTO 1258
1274 PRINT
1276 PRINT "TRY OTHER WORK STATIONS (Y/N)";
1278 INPUT U$
1280 IF U$ = "Y" THEN 1208
1282 IF U$ = "N" THEN 1299
1284 PRINT
1286 PRINT "INVALID RESPONSE"
1288 GOTO 1274
1299 RETURN
1300 REM *****************************
1302 REM *    FINAL MESSAGE          *
1304 REM *****************************
1306 PRINT
1308 PRINT "TRY ANOTHER SET OF DATA (Y/N)";
1310 INPUT U$
1312 IF U$ = "Y" THEN 1399
1314 IF U$ = "N" THEN 1399
1316 PRINT
1318 PRINT "INVALID RESPONSE"
1320 GOTO 1306
1399 RETURN
2000 REM *****************************
2002 REM *    GET PARAMETERS         *
2004 REM *****************************
2006 PRINT
2008 PRINT "NUMBER OF WORK STATIONS";
2010 INPUT N3
2012 PRINT
2014 PRINT "MAXIMUM TIME PER WORK STATION";
2016 INPUT C1
2018 PRINT
2020 PRINT "TIME PER SHIFT";
2022 INPUT S1
2099 RETURN
2100 REM *****************************
2102 REM *    INITIALIZE             *
2104 REM *****************************
2106 FOR I = 1 TO N1
```

```
2108    LET T(I,4) = O
2110    LET T(I,5) = O
2112 NEXT I
2114 FOR I = 1 TO N2
2116    LET M(I) = O
2118 NEXT I
2120 LET M(1) = 1
2122 LET J1 = 1
2199 RETURN
2200 REM *******************************
2202 REM *    ASSIGNABLE TASKS         *
2204 REM *******************************
2206 FOR I = 1 TO N1
2208    IF T(I,4) > O THEN 2214
2210    LET I1 = T(I,1)
2212    LET T(I,5) = M(I1).
2214 NEXT I
2299 RETURN
2300 REM *******************************
2302 REM *    CULLED TASKS             *
2304 REM *******************************
2306 LET N4 = O
2308 FOR I = 1 TO N1
2310    IF T(I,5) = O THEN 2320
2312    IF K = N3 THEN 2316
2314    IF T(I,3)+T1 >= C1 THEN 2320
2316    LET N4 = N4 + 1
2318    LET A(N4) = I
2320 NEXT I
2322 RETURN
2400 REM *******************************
2402 REM *    CHOOSE TASK              *
2404 REM *******************************
2406 IF K < N3 THEN 2412
2408 LET R = 1
2410 GOTO 2414
2412 LET R = 1 + INT(N4 * RND(O))
2414 LET I = A(R)
2416 LET T(I,4) = K
2418 LET T(I,5) = O
2420 LET T1 = T1 + T(I,3)
2422 LET J1 = T(I,2)
2424 LET M(J1) = 1
2426 FOR I = 1 TO N1
2428    IF T(I,2) <> J1 THEN 2442
2430    IF T(I,4) > O THEN 2438
```

```
2432    LET M(J1) = 0
2434    LET I = N1
2436    GOTO 2442
2438    LET I1 = T(I,1)
2440    LET M(J1) = M(J1) * M(I1)
2442 NEXT I
2499 RETURN
2500 REM ******************************
2502 REM *    CHECK RESULT            *
2504 REM ******************************
2506 LET T2 = 0
2508 LET M2 = 0
2510 FOR K = 1 TO N3
2512    LET T2 = T2 + W(K)
2514    IF W(K) <= M2 THEN 2518
2516    LET M2 = W(K)
2518 NEXT K
2599 RETURN
2600 REM ******************************
2602 REM *    DISPLAY RESULT          *
2604 REM ******************************
2606 LET C1 = M2
2608 LET D = N3 * M2 - T2
2610 PRINT
2612 PRINT "CYCLE TIME",C1
2614 PRINT "IDLE TIME",D
2616 PRINT "UNITS PER SHIFT",S1/C1
2618 FOR K = 1 TO N3
2620    PRINT
2622    PRINT "WORK STATION",K
2624    LET D1 = M2 - W(K)
2626    PRINT "IDLE TIME",D1
2628    PRINT "TASKS",
2630    FOR I = 1 TO N1
2632       IF T(I,4) <> K THEN 2636
2634       PRINT " ";N$(I);
2636    NEXT I
2638    PRINT
2640 NEXT K
2699 RETURN
9999 END
```

The shop may contain general purpose and special purpose machines. Each job will need the attention of certain machines in a specific order. The job may pass from one machine to another machine and then back to the first machine.

Typically, each task is done as a batch. A cus-

```
ASSIGN TASKS TO ASSEMBLY LINE       CYCLE TIME        26
WORK STATIONS TO MINIMIZE           IDLE TIME         19
TOTAL IDLE TIME USING RANDOMIZED    UNITS PER SHIFT   18.4615
SEARCH PROCEDURE.
                                    WORK STATION      1
NUMBER OF TASKS? 5                  IDLE TIME         0
                                    TASKS             A B C D
DATA FOR
                                    WORK STATION       2
TASK 1                              IDLE TIME         19
NAME OF TASK? A                     TASKS             E
FROM NODE     ? 1
TO NODE       ? 2                   CONTINUE SEARCH (Y/N)? Y
TASK TIME     ? 8
                                    CYCLE TIME        21
TASK 2                              IDLE TIME         9
NAME OF TASK? B                     UNITS PER SHIFT   22.857
FROM NODE     ? 1
TO NODE       ? 3                   WORK STATION      1
TASK TIME     ? 10                  IDLE TIME         0
                                    TASKS             A B D
TASK 3
NAME OF TASK? C                     WORK STATION      2
FROM NODE     ? 2                   IDLE TIME         9
TO NODE       ? 4                   TASKS             C E
TASK TIME     ? 5
                                    CONTINUE SEARCH (Y/N)? Y
TASK 4
NAME OF TASK? D                     CYCLE TIME        18
FROM NODE     ? 2                   IDLE TIME         3
TO NODE       ? 3                   UNITS PER SHIFT   26.667
TASK TIME     ? 3
                                    WORK STATION      1
TASK 5                              IDLE TIME         0
NAME OF TASK? E                     TASKS             A B
FROM NODE     ? 3
TO NODE       ? 4                   WORK STATION      2
TASK TIME     ? 7                   IDLE TIME         3
                                    TASKS             C D E
NUMBER OF WORK STATIONS? 2
                                    CONTINUE SEARCH (Y/N)? Y
MAXIMUM TIME PER WORK STATION? 30
                                    CYCLE TIME        17
TIME PER SHIFT? 480                 IDLE TIME         1
                                    UNITS PER SHIFT   28.2353
```

```
WORK STATION      1          WORK STATION      3
IDLE TIME         1          IDLE TIME         8
TASKS             A C D      TASKS             E

WORK STATION      2          CONTINUE SEARCH (Y/N)? Y
IDLE TIME         0
TASKS             B E        CYCLE TIME        12
                            IDLE TIME         3
CONTINUE SEARCH (Y/N)? N     UNITS PER SHIFT   40

TRY OTHER WORK STATIONS (Y/N)? Y
                            WORK STATION      1
                            IDLE TIME         1
NUMBER OF WORK STATIONS? 3   TASKS             A D

MAXIMUM TIME PER
  WORK STATION? 16           WORK STATION      2
                            IDLE TIME         2
CYCLE TIME        15         TASKS             B
IDLE TIME         12
UNITS PER SHIFT   32         WORK STATION      3
                            IDLE TIME         0
WORK STATION      1          TASKS             C E
IDLE TIME         4
TASKS             A D        CONTINUE SEARCH (Y/N)? N

WORK STATION      2          TRY OTHER WORK STATIONS
IDLE TIME         0            (Y/N)? N
TASKS             B C
                            END OF PROGRAM
```

Fig. 6-7. Sample results from Program 6-7.

tomer orders a specified number of units of a product. The batch moves from machine to machine during the processing steps. During the processing of the batch on one machine, that machine cannot be processing other jobs. Neither can that job be in process on another machine. Record keeping within the job-shop environment consists of tracking the flow of work through the shop.

Each machine center has its own queue of jobs waiting for processing. Statistics are maintained in terms of the utilization rate of each machine. This is the same as a complex waiting line situation, which describes the job-shop environment perfectly. Queue lengths are also of interest.

There are different types of jobs. The jobs differ in terms of which machines are used, what order they are used in, and how long each is used. For a given mix of job types and frequencies, statistics of interest include machine utilization and job completion times.

The most common rule for selecting the next task from the queue is to select the one that has been there longest. This is the FIFO (first in first out) rule. Other queue disciplines include LIFO (last in first out), SPT (shortest processing time), and deadline (earliest due date) rules. These are the best known rules for choosing tasks in the job-shop environment.

The purpose of the simulation is to measure the effect of decision rules, mix of jobs, and frequency of job orders on machine utilization and job completion times. A lightly loaded job shop will have excellent job completion times but poor machine utilization. During times of peak demand, the job shop will be heavily loaded with jobs in progress. Machine utilization will be heavy, but job

completion times become critical. Measures of performance under heavy utilization are of greatest interest.

Program 6-8 illustrates methods for evaluating the job-shop environment and dispatching rules. Figure 6-8 shows the results.

Program 6-8

```
100 REM ******************************
102 REM *    6-8                     *
104 REM ******************************
106 REM   AUTHOR
108 REM       COPYRIGHT 1982
110 REM        BY LAWRENCE MCNITT.
112 REM   PURPOSE
114 REM        JOB-SHOP SCHEDULING.
116 REM   SYSTEM
118 REM       UNIVERSAL SUBSET
120 REM       OF BASIC.
200 REM ******************************
202 REM *    ORGANIZATION            *
204 REM ******************************
206 REM   900   MAIN ROUTINE
208 REM         1000   INITIAL MESSAGE
210 REM         1100   GET JOB DATA
212 REM         1200   CLEAR EVERYTHING
214 REM         1300   PROCESS
216 REM                2000   GET PARAMETERS
218 REM                2100   CLEAR STATISTICS
220 REM                2200   SIMULATE
222 REM                       3000   GENERATE ORDER
224 REM                       3100   FINISH TASKS
226 REM                       3200   SELECT TASKS
228 REM                              4000   SEARCH
230 REM                2300   DISPLAY RESULT
232 REM         1400   FINAL MESSAGE
300 REM ******************************
302 REM *    VARIABLES               *
304 REM ******************************
306 REM   C(100,5)   CUSTOMER ORDER LIST GIVING
308 REM              JOB SEQUENCE NUMBER
310 REM              INITIATION TIME
312 REM              DUE TIME
314 REM              JOB TYPE
316 REM              CURRENT TASK NUMBER
```

```
318 REM    Q(10,40)   JOB POINTERS FOR QUEUES
320 REM    M(10,10)   JOB TASK POINTERS
322 REM    H(10,10)   JOB HOUR REQUIREMENTS
324 REM    T(10,5)    JOB TYPE STATISTICS
326 REM               NUMBER INITIATED
328 REM               NUMBER COMPLETED
330 REM               NUMBER LATE
332 REM               SUM OF TIMES
334 REM               SUM OF SQUARES
336 REM    W(10,5)    MACHINE, WORK STATION STATISTICS
338 REM               JOB POINTER
340 REM               NUMBER OF JOBS IN QUEUE
342 REM               TOTAL IDLE TIME SO FAR
344 REM               SUM OF NUMBER IN QUEUE
346 REM               TIME TO FINISH CURRENT TASK
348 REM    P(11)      CUMULATIVE PROBABILITIES
350 REM    N(10)      NUMBER OF TASKS BY JOB TYPE
352 REM    U$  USER RESPONSE
354 REM    N1  NUMBER OF MACHINES
356 REM    N2  NUMBER OF JOB TYPES
358 REM    N3  NUMBER OF HOURS TO SIMULATE
360 REM    N4  NUMBER IN QUEUE
362 REM    N5  NUMBER OF TASKS
364 REM    A   MEAN
366 REM    S   STANDARD DEVIATION
368 REM    S1  SUM
370 REM    R   RANDOM NUMBER
372 REM    U1  UTILIZATION RATE
374 REM    P1  PRIORITY SCHEME FOR SELECTING TASKS
376 REM    J1  JOB TYPE
378 REM    J2  POINTER TO CUSTOMER ORDER
380 REM    J3  JOB SEQUENCE NUMBER
382 REM    J4  INDEX TO TASK
384 REM    D1  MULTIPLIER FOR DUE DATE
386 REM    D2  TIME FOR JOB OR TASK
388 REM    D3  TIME FOR JOB OR TASK
390 REM    T1  CURRENT CLOCK TIME
392 REM    T2  BEGINNING CLOCK TIME
394 REM    T3  ENDING CLOCK TIME
396 REM    I,I1,I2,I3   INDEX
900 REM ********************************
902 REM *    MAIN ROUTINE               *
904 REM ********************************
906 DIM C(100,5),T(10,5),W(10,5),Q(10,40)
908 DIM M(10,10),H(10,10),P(11)
910 REM INITIAL MESSAGE
```

```
912 GOSUB 1006
916 REM GET JOB DATA
918 GOSUB 1106
920 REM CLEAR EVERYTHING
922 GOSUB 1206
924 REM PROCESS
926 GOSUB 1308
928 REM FINAL MESSAGE
930 GOSUB 1406
932 IF U$ = "Y" THEN 918
934 PRINT
936 PRINT "END OF PROGRAM"
999 STOP
1000 REM ******************************
1002 REM *    INITIAL MESSAGE         *
1004 REM ******************************
1006 PRINT
1008 PRINT
1010 PRINT
1012 PRINT "PROGRAM 6-8"
1014 PRINT
1016 PRINT "EVALUATE JOB-SHOP SCHEDULING"
1018 PRINT "RULES SIMULATING RANDOM ORDERS"
1020 PRINT "FROM A SPECIFIED JOB MIX."
1099 RETURN
1100 REM ******************************
1102 REM *    GET DATA                *
1104 REM ******************************
1106 PRINT
1108 PRINT "NUMBER OF MACHINES";
1110 INPUT N1
1112 PRINT
1114 PRINT "NUMBER OF JOB TYPES";
1116 INPUT N2
1118 PRINT
1120 PRINT "PROBABILITY THAT NO ORDER"
1122 PRINT "IS RECEIVED DURING GIVEN HOUR";
1124 INPUT P(1)
1126 PRINT
1128 PRINT "INFORMATION ABOUT JOB TYPES"
1130 FOR J1 = 1 TO N2
1132     PRINT
1134     PRINT "JOB TYPE";J1
1136     PRINT "PROBABILITY     ";
1138     INPUT P(J1+1)
1140     PRINT "NUMBER OF TASKS";
```

```
1142    INPUT N5
1143    LET N(J1) = N5
1144    PRINT "INFORMATION FOR"
1146    FOR I = 1 TO N5
1148       PRINT "TASK";I
1150       PRINT "   MACHINE";
1152       INPUT M(J1,I)
1154       PRINT "   HOURS   ";
1156       INPUT H(J1,I)
1158    NEXT I
1160 NEXT J1
1162 LET S1 = 0
1164 FOR I = 1 TO N2+1
1166    LET S1 = S1 + P(I)
1168    LET P(I) = S1
1170 NEXT I
1172 IF ABS(S1 - 1) < .000001 THEN 1199
1174 PRINT
1176 PRINT "PROBABILITIES DO NOT TOTAL 1.0"
1178 PRINT "ENTER THEM AGAIN"
1180 PRINT
1182 PRINT "PROBABILITY OF"
1184 PRINT "NO ORDER";
1186 INPUT P(1)
1188 FOR I = 1 TO N2
1190    PRINT "JOB TYPE";I;
1192    INPUT P(I+1)
1194 NEXT I
1196 GOTO 1162
1199 RETURN
1200 REM ******************************
1202 REM *    CLEAR EVERYTHING        *
1204 REM ******************************
1206 FOR I = 1 TO 100
1208    LET C(I,1) = -999
1210 NEXT I
1212 FOR I = 1 TO N2
1214    LET W(I,1) = 0
1216    LET W(I,2) = 0
1218 NEXT I
1220 LET T2 = 1
1222 LET J3 = 0
1299 RETURN
1300 REM ******************************
1302 REM *    PROCESS                 *
1304 REM ******************************
```

```
1306 REM GET PARAMETERS
1308 GOSUB 2006
1310 REM CLEAR STATISTICS
1312 GOSUB 2106
1318 REM SIMULATE
1320 GOSUB 2206
1322 REM DISPLAY RESULTS
1324 GOSUB 2306
1326 PRINT
1328 PRINT "TRY ANOTHER SIMULATION RUN"
1330 PRINT "USING THIS JOB MIX (Y/N)";
1332 INPUT U$
1334 IF U$ = "Y" THEN 1308
1336 IF U$ = "N" THEN 1399
1338 PRINT
1340 PRINT "INVALID RESPONSE"
1342 GOTO 1326
1399 RETURN
1400 REM ****************************
1402 REM *    FINAL MESSAGE         *
1404 REM ****************************
1406 PRINT
1408 PRINT "TRY ANOTHER JOB MIX (Y/N)";
1410 INPUT U$
1412 IF U$ = "Y" THEN 1499
1414 IF U$ = "N" THEN 1499
1416 PRINT
1418 PRINT "INVALID RESPONSE"
1420 GOTO 1406
1499 RETURN
2000 REM ****************************
2002 REM *    GET PARAMETERS        *
2004 REM ****************************
2006 PRINT
2008 PRINT "DUE DATE MULTIPLIER";
2010 INPUT D1
2012 PRINT
2014 PRINT "NUMBER OF HOURS TO SIMULATE";
2016 INPUT N3
2018 PRINT
2020 PRINT "TASK SELECTION CRITERION"
2022 PRINT "    1    FIFO      FIRST IN FIRST OUT"
2024 PRINT "    2    LIFO      LAST IN FIRST OUT"
2026 PRINT "    3    SPT       SHORTEST PROCESSING TIME"
2028 PRINT "    4    DEADLINE  EARLIEST DUE DATE"
2030 PRINT
```

```
2032 PRINT "NUMBER OF DESIRED CRITERION";
2034 INPUT P1
2036 IF P1 = 1 THEN 2099
2038 IF P1 = 2 THEN 2099
2040 IF P1 = 3 THEN 2099
2042 IF P1 = 4 THEN 2099
2044 PRINT
2046 PRINT "INVALID RESPONSE"
2048 GOTO 2018
2054     LET D2 = D2 + H(J1,1)
2099 RETURN
2100 REM ****************************
2102 REM *    CLEAR STATISTICS        *
2104 REM ****************************
2106 FOR I = 1 TO N2
2108     FOR J = 1 TO 5
2110         LET T(I,J) = 0
2112     NEXT J
2114 NEXT I
2116 FOR I = 1 TO N1
2118     LET W(I,3) = 0
2120     LET W(I,4) = 0
2122 NEXT I
2199 RETURN
2200 REM ****************************
2202 REM *    SIMULATE               *
2204 REM ****************************
2206 LET T3 = T2 + N3 - 1
2208 FOR T1 = T2 TO T3
2210     REM GENERATE ORDER
2212     GOSUB 3006
2214     REM FINISH TASKS
2216     GOSUB 3106
2218     REM SELECT TASKS
2220     GOSUB 3206
2222 NEXT T1
2224 LET T2 = T2 + N3
2299 RETURN
2300 REM ****************************
2302 REM *    DISPLAY RESULTS        *
2304 REM ****************************
2306 PRINT
2308 PRINT "DISPLAY JOB TYPE SUMMARY (Y/N)";
2310 INPUT U$
2312 IF U$ = "Y" THEN 2322
2314 IF U$ = "N" THEN 2348
```

```
2316 PRINT
2318 PRINT "INVALID RESPONSE"
2320 GOTO 2306
2322 PRINT
2324 PRINT "JOB",,"TIME IN SYSTEM"
2326 PRINT "TYPE INIT COMP LATE","MEAN","STD DEV"
2328 FOR J1 = 1 TO N2
2330    PRINT J1;TAB(4);T(J1,1);
2331    PRINT TAB(9);T(J1,2);TAB(14);T(J1,3);
2332    IF T(J1,2) < 2 THEN 2344
2334    LET A = T(J1,4) / T(J1,2)
2336    LET S = (T(J1,5)-T(J1,4)*T(J1,4)/T(J1,2))/T(J1,2)
2338    LET S = SQR(S)
2340    PRINT TAB(33);A,S
2342    GOTO 2346
2344    PRINT
2346 NEXT J1
2348 PRINT
2350 PRINT "DISPLAY MACHINE SUMMARY (Y/N)";
2352 INPUT U$
2354 IF U$ = "Y" THEN 2364
2356 IF U$ = "N" THEN 2399
2358 PRINT
2360 PRINT "INVALID RESPONSE"
2362 GOTO 2348
2364 PRINT
2366 PRINT "MACHINE","FRACTION","NUMBER IN QUEUE"
2368 PRINT ,"UTILIZED","AVERAGE","FINAL"
2370 FOR I = 1 TO N1
2372    LET U1 = (N3 - W(I,3)) / N3
2374    LET A = W(I,4) / N3
2376    PRINT I,U1,A,W(I,2)
2378 NEXT I
2399 RETURN
3000 REM *******************************
3002 REM *     GENERATE ORDER           *
3004 REM *******************************
3006 LET R = RND(0)
3008 IF R < P(1) THEN 3099
3010 LET J1 = 0
3012 FOR I = 1 TO N2
3014    IF R > P(I+1) THEN 3020
3016    LET J1 = I
3018    LET I = N2
3020 NEXT I
3022 LET J2 = 0
```

```
3024 FOR I = 1 TO 100
3026    IF C(I,1) > 0 THEN 3032
3028    LET J2 = I
3030    LET I = 100
3032 NEXT I
3034 IF J2 > 0 THEN 3042
3036 PRINT
3038 PRINT "EXCEEDED JOB CAPACITY"
3040 STOP
3042 LET J3 = J3 + 1
3044 LET C(J2,1) = J3
3046 LET C(J2,2) = T1
3048 LET N5 = N(J1)
3050 LET D2 = 0
3052 FOR I = 1 TO N5
3054    LET D2 = D2 + H(J1,I)
3056 NEXT I
3058 LET C(J2,3) = T1 + D1 * D2
3060 LET C(J2,4) = J1
3062 LET C(J2,5) = 1
3064 LET I1 = M(J1,1)
3066 LET N4 = W(I1,2) + 1
3068 LET Q(I1,N4) = J2
3070 LET W(I1,2) = N4
3072 LET T(J1,1) = T(J1,1) + 1
3099 RETURN
3100 REM ******************************
3102 REM *    FINISH TASKS            *
3104 REM ******************************
3106 FOR I1 = 1 TO N1
3108    IF W(I1,1) = 0 THEN 3154
3110    IF T1 < W(I1,5) THEN 3154
3112    LET J2 = W(I1,1)
3114    LET W(I1,1) = 0
3116    LET J1 = C(J2,4)
3118    LET J4 = C(J2,5)
3120    IF J4 < N(J1) THEN 3142
3122    REM TERMINATE JOB ORDER
3124    LET T(J1,2) = T(J1,2) + 1
3126    IF T1 <= C(J2,3) THEN 3130
3128    LET T(J1,3) = T(J1,3) + 1
3130    LET D2 = T1 - C(J2,2)
3132    LET T(J1,4) = T(J1,4) + D2
3134    LET T(J1,5) = T(J1,5) + D2 * D2
3136    LET C(J2,1) = -999
3138    GOTO 3154
```

```
3140    REM ADVANCE TO NEXT MACHINE
3142    LET J4 = J4 + 1
3144    LET C(J2,5) = J4
3146    LET I2 = M(J1,J4)
3148    LET N4 = W(I2,2) + 1
3150    LET Q(I2,N4) = J2
3152    LET W(I2,2) = N4
3154 NEXT I1
3199 RETURN
3200 REM ****************************
3202 REM *    SELECT TASKS           *
3204 REM ****************************
3206 FOR I1 = 1 TO N1
3208    IF W(I1,1) > 0 THEN 3232
3210    LET N4 = W(I1,2)
3212    IF N4 = 0 THEN 3228
3214    IF N4 = 1 THEN 3220
3216    REM SEARCH
3218    GOSUB 4006
3220    LET J2 = Q(I1,N4)
3222    LET W(I1,1) = J2
3224    LET W(I1,2) = N4 - 1
3226    LET W(I1,5) = T1 + H(C(J2,4),C(J2,5))
3228    IF W(I1,1) > 0 THEN 3232
3230    LET W(I1,3) = W(I1,3) + 1
3232    LET W(I1,4) = W(I1,4) + W(I1,2)
3234 NEXT I1
3299 RETURN
4000 REM ****************************
4002 REM *    SEARCH                 *
4004 REM ****************************
4006 ON P1 GOTO 4010,4099,4024,4052
4008 REM FIFO
4010 LET Z = Q(I1,1)
4012 FOR I3 = 1 TO N4-1
4014    LET Q(I1,I3) = Q(I1,I3+1)
4016 NEXT I3
4018 LET Q(I1,N4) = Z
4020 GOTO 4099
4022 REM SPT
4024 LET J2 = Q(I1,1)
4025 LET I4 = 1
4026 LET D2 = H(C(J2,4),C(J2,5))
4028 FOR I3 = 2 TO N4
4030    LET J4 = Q(I1,I3)
4032    LET D3 = H(C(J4,4),C(J4,5))
```

```
4034    IF D3 >= D2 THEN 4040
4036    LET I4 = I3
4038    LET D2 = D3
4040 NEXT I3
4042 LET Z = Q(I1,I4)
4044 LET Q(I1,I4) = Q(I1,N4)
4046 LET Q(I1,N4) = Z
4048 GOTO 4099
4050 REM DEADLINE
4052 LET J2 = Q(I1,1)
4054 LET I4 = 1
4056 LET D2 = C(J2,3)
4058 FOR I3 = 2 TO N4
4060    LET D3 = C(Q(I1,I3),3)
4062    IF D3 >= D2 THEN 4068
4064    LET I4 = I3
4066    LET D2 = D3
4068 NEXT I3
4070 LET Z = Q(I1,I4)
4072 LET Q(I1,I4) = Q(I1,N4)
4074 LET Q(I1,N4) = Z
4099 RETURN
9999 END
```

```
EVALUATE JOB-SHOP SCHEDULING
RULES SIMULATING RANDOM ORDERS
FROM A SPECIFIED JOB MIX.

NUMBER OF MACHINES? 2

NUMBER OF JOB TYPES? 2

PROBABILITY THAT NO ORDER
IS RECEIVED DURING GIVEN HOUR? .8

INFORMATION ABOUT JOB TYPES

JOB TYPE 1
PROBABILITY    ? .1
NUMBER OF TASKS? 2
INFORMATION FOR
TASK 1
   MACHINE? 1
   HOURS  ? 5
```

```
TASK 2
    MACHINE? 2
    HOURS   ? 6

JOB TYPE 2
PROBABILITY      ? .1
NUMBER OF TASKS? 2
INFORMATION FOR
TASK 1
    MACHINE? 2
    HOURS   ? 3
TASK 2
    MACHINE? 1
    HOURS   ? 3

DUE DATE MULTIPLIER? 1.5

NUMBER OF HOURS TO SIMULATE? 50

TASK SELECTION CRITERION
    1    FIFO       FIRST IN FIRST OUT
    2    LIFO       LAST IN FIRST OUT
    3    SPT        SHORTEST PROCESSING TIME
    4    DEADLINE   EARLIEST DUE DATE

NUMBER OF DESIRED CRITERION? 2

DISPLAY JOB TYPE SUMMARY (Y/N)? Y

JOB                            TIME IN SYSTEM
TYPE INIT COMP LATE            MEAN              STD DEV
  1    7    6    3             16.3333           2.56038
  2    5    3    2             20.6667           15.7973

DISPLAY MACHINE SUMMARY (Y/N)? Y

MACHINE           FRACTION        NUMBER IN QUEUE
                  UTILIZED        AVERAGE       FINAL
  1                 .9            1.32          0
  2                 .98           1.4           1

TRY ANOTHER SIMULATION RUN
USING THIS JOB MIX (Y/N)? N

TRY ANOTHER JOB MIX (Y/N)? N

END OF PROGRAM
```

Fig. 6-8. Sample results from Program 6-8.

Under the best circumstances, a given job will be completed within the time given by the sum of the task times for that job. In practice, one or more of the machines will be busy. The multiplier for the due date determines the due date needed for the scheduled deadline. The multiplier must be larger than 1. A multiplier of 1.5 means that the due time for the job is fifty percent more than the minimum job completion time. Even this large a multiplier is practical only for lightly loaded systems.

Exercise 6-5

1. Develop a much more complex model requiring assembly line balancing. Use Program 6-7 with your model. Include many more tasks and allow for a large number of work stations.

2. Develop a much more complex job mix and machine mix for the job-shop scheduling problem. Evaluate the decision rules using Program 6-8. Include many more machines and run the simulation for longer time periods.

Chapter 7

Inventory Systems

Inventories act as buffers between the use and sale of products and their supply channels. Holding large inventories is costly. Not having products available when needed is also costly. The cost of placing and receiving orders is significant. This chapter covers both analytic and simulation methods for analyzing simple inventory situations.

EOQ MODELS

One of the early quantitative models in business was the simple economic order quantity (EOQ) model for inventory policy analysis. It is a highly idealized model, but it provides an objective basis for making decisions and gives insight into cost interactions. Demand occurs at a constant rate. There is no lead time, no risk of stockouts, and no need for extra inventory to cover emergencies. Ordered items arrive just when needed.

The formula

$$Q = SQR(2 * P * D / H)$$

gives the order quantity, Q, as a function of cost per order, P, and annual per-unit holding cost, H. The demand is D units per year. This order quantity minimizes the total annual inventory costs.

The order quantity, Q, together with an annual demand of D units results in D/Q orders per year with the expression

$$P * D / Q$$

giving the annual ordering cost. The maximum inventory level is Q. The minimum inventory of 0 is reached just as the next shipment arrives. Since demand is at a constant rate of D per year, the average inventory level is Q/2. The expression

$$H * Q / 2$$

gives the annual holding cost. Combining the two inventory costs gives

$$T = P * D / Q + H * Q / 2$$

as the total annual inventory cost. Solving this expression for the value of Q that minimizes the sum of the two inventory costs results in the EOQ formula.

Program 7-1 asks for the demand and cost parameters and then solves for the economic order quantity. Figure 7-1 shows the results.

Program 7-1

```
100 REM *****************************
102 REM *    7-1                     *
104 REM *****************************
106 REM   AUTHOR
108 REM       COPYRIGHT 1982
110 REM       BY LAWRENCE MCNITT.
112 REM   PURPOSE
114 REM       DETERMINE ECONOMIC
116 REM       ORDER QUANTITY.
118 REM   SYSTEM
120 REM       UNIVERSAL SUBSET
122 REM       OF BASIC.
200 REM *****************************
202 REM *    ORGANIZATION            *
204 REM *****************************
206 REM   900   MAIN ROUTINE
208 REM         1000   INITIAL MESSAGE
210 REM         1100   PARAMETERS
212 REM         1200   PROCESS
214 REM         1300   FINAL MESSAGE
300 REM *****************************
302 REM *    VARIABLES               *
304 REM *****************************
306 REM   U$   USER RESPONSE
308 REM   C1   COST PER ORDER
310 REM   C2   HOLDING COST PER UNIT PER YEAR
312 REM   D    UNITS DEMANDED PER YEAR
314 REM   Q    ORDER QUANTITY
316 REM   T1   ANNUAL ORDERING COSTS
318 REM   T2   ANNUAL HOLDING COST
320 REM   T    TOTAL ANNUAL INVENTORY COST
322 REM   Q1   ORDER QUANTITY FOR SENSITIVITY ANALYSIS
900 REM *****************************
902 REM *    MAIN ROUTINE            *
904 REM *****************************
906 REM INITIAL MESSAGE
908 GOSUB 1006
910 REM PARAMETERS
912 GOSUB 1106
914 REM PROCESS
```

```
916 GOSUB 1206
918 REM FINAL MESSAGE
920 GOSUB 1306
922 IF U$ = "Y" THEN 912
924 PRINT
926 PRINT "END OF PROGRAM"
999 STOP
1000 REM ******************************
1002 REM *    INITIAL MESSAGE        *
1004 REM ******************************
1006 PRINT
1008 PRINT
1010 PRINT
1012 PRINT "PROGRAM 7-1"
1014 PRINT
1016 PRINT "INVENTORY ANALYSIS TO DETERMINE"
1018 PRINT "THE ECONOMIC ORDER QUANTITY"
1020 PRINT "ASSUMING CONSTANT DEMAND AND"
1022 PRINT "NO LEAD TIME."
1099 RETURN
1100 REM ******************************
1102 REM *    PARAMETERS             *
1104 REM ******************************
1106 PRINT
1108 PRINT "COST PER ORDER PLACED         ";
1110 INPUT C1
1112 PRINT "ANNUAL PER-UNIT HOLDING COST ";
1114 INPUT C2
1116 PRINT "UNITS DEMANDED PER YEAR       ";
1118 INPUT D
1199 RETURN
1200 REM ******************************
1202 REM *    PROCESS                *
1204 REM ******************************
1206 LET Q = INT(.5 + SQR(2 * C1 * D / C2))
1208 PRINT
1210 PRINT "ORDER","ANNUAL INVENTORY COSTS"
1212 PRINT "QUANTITY","ORDERING","HOLDING","TOTAL"
1214 FOR Q1 = Q-1 TO Q+1
1216     LET T1 = C1 * D / Q1
1218     LET T2 = C2 * Q1 / 2
1220     LET T = T1 + T2
1222     PRINT Q1,T1,T2,T
1224 NEXT Q1
1299 RETURN
1300 REM ******************************
```

```
1302 REM *    FINAL MESSAGE            *
1304 REM *****************************
1306 PRINT
1308 PRINT "TRY ANOTHER SET OF DATA (Y/N)";
1310 INPUT U$
1312 IF U$ = "Y" THEN 1399
1314 IF U$ = "N" THEN 1399
1316 PRINT
1318 PRINT "INVALID RESPONSE"
1320 GOTO 1306
1399 RETURN
9999 END
```

Sensitivity

How sensitive is the inventory cost to deviations in the order quantity? Because of packaging for shipment, it may not be possible to order the exact number specified by the model. It is best to explore the area around the optimum. What are the results of choosing other order quantities?

Program 7-2 computes the ordering cost, the holding cost, and the total cost for a set of order quantities. Figure 7-2 shows the results.

Exercises 7-1

1. Determine the economic order quantity assuming an annual demand for 4000 units, an ordering cost of $50.00 per order, and a per-unit annual holding cost of $15.00. Do a sensitivity analysis of order quantities in the area of the optimum.

STOCHASTIC DEMAND AND STOCKOUTS

Stockouts occur when the immediate demand for a product exceeds the inventory level. The cus-

```
PROGRAM P7-1

INVENTORY ANALYSIS TO DETERMINE
THE ECONOMIC ORDER QUANTITY
ASSUMING CONSTANT DEMAND AND
NO LEAD TIME.

COST PER ORDER PLACED          ? 30
ANNUAL PER-UNIT HOLDING COST   ? 5
UNITS DEMANDED PER YEAR        ? 200

ORDER            ANNUAL INVENTORY COSTS
QUANTITY         ORDERING        HOLDING         TOTAL
  48             125             120             245
  49             122.449         122.5           244.949
  50             120             125             245

TRY ANOTHER SET OF DATA (Y/N)? N
```

Fig. 7-1. Sample results from Program 7-1.

Program 7-2

```
100 REM *******************************
102 REM *     7-2                      *
104 REM *******************************
106 REM   AUTHOR
108 REM      COPYRIGHT 1982
110 REM      BY LAWRENCE MCNITT.
112 REM   PURPOSE
114 REM      COMPARE INVENTORY
116 REM      ORDER QUANTITIES.
118 REM   SYSTEM
120 REM      UNIVERSAL SUBSET
122 REM      OF BASIC.
200 REM *******************************
202 REM *    ORGANIZATION              *
204 REM *******************************
206 REM   900   MAIN ROUTINE
208 REM         1000   INITIAL MESSAGE
210 REM         1100   PARAMETERS
212 REM         1200   PROCESS
214 REM         1300   FINAL MESSAGE
300 REM *******************************
302 REM *    VARIABLES                 *
304 REM *******************************
306 REM    U$   USER RESPONSE
308 REM    C1   COST PER ORDER
310 REM    C2   HOLDING COST PER UNIT PER YEAR
312 REM    D    UNITS DEMANDED PER YEAR
314 REM    Q    ORDER QUANTITY
316 REM    Q1   LOWEST QUANTITY
318 REM    Q2   LARGEST QUANTITY
320 REM    Q3   STEP SIZE FOR QUANTITY
322 REM    T1   ANNUAL ORDERING COST
324 REM    T2   ANNUAL HOLDING COST
326 REM    T    TOTAL ANNUAL INVENTORY COST
900 REM *******************************
902 REM *    MAIN ROUTINE              *
904 REM *******************************
906 REM INITIAL MESSAGE
908 GOSUB 1006
910 REM PARAMETERS
912 GOSUB 1106
914 REM PROCESS
916 GOSUB 1206
918 REM FINAL MESSAGE
```

```
920 GOSUB 1306
922 IF U$ = "Y" THEN 912
924 PRINT
926 PRINT "END OF PROGRAM"
999 STOP
1000 REM ******************************
1002 REM *    INITIAL MESSAGE         *
1004 REM ******************************
1006 PRINT
1008 PRINT
1010 PRINT
1012 PRINT "PROGRAM 7-2"
1014 PRINT
1016 PRINT "COMPARE A SET OF INVENTORY ORDER"
1018 PRINT "QUANTITIES GIVING THE ANNUAL"
1020 PRINT "ORDERING COSTS, HOLDING COSTS,"
1022 PRINT "AND TOTAL INVENTORY COSTS."
1099 RETURN
1100 REM ******************************
1102 REM *    PARAMETERS              *
1104 REM ******************************
1106 PRINT
1108 PRINT "COST PER ORDER PLACED          ";
1110 INPUT C1
1112 PRINT "ANNUAL PER-UNIT HOLDING COST   ";
1114 INPUT C2
1116 PRINT "UNITS DEMANDED PER YEAR        ";
1118 INPUT D
1120 PRINT
1122 PRINT "ORDER QUANTITIES TO COMPARE"
1124 PRINT
1126 PRINT "SMALLEST QUANTITY              ";
1128 INPUT Q1
1130 PRINT "LARGEST QUANTITY               ";
1132 INPUT Q2
1134 PRINT "STEP SIZE BETWEEN QUANTITIES   ";
1136 INPUT Q3
1199 RETURN
1200 REM ******************************
1202 REM *    PROCESS                 *
1204 REM ******************************
1206 PRINT
1208 PRINT "ORDER","ANNUAL INVENTORY COSTS"
1210 PRINT "QUANTITY","ORDERING","HOLDING","TOTAL"
1212 FOR Q = Q1 TO Q2 STEP Q3
1214     LET T1 = C1 * D / Q
```

```
1216    LET T2 = C2 * Q / 2
1218    LET T = T1 + T2
1220    PRINT Q,T1,T2,T
1222 NEXT Q
1299 RETURN
1300 REM ******************************
1302 REM *    FINAL MESSAGE           *
1304 REM ******************************
1306 PRINT
1308 PRINT "TRY ANOTHER SET OF DATA (Y/N)";
1310 INPUT U$
1312 IF U$ = "Y" THEN 1399
1314 IF U$ = "N" THEN 1399
1316 PRINT
1318 PRINT "INVALID RESPONSE"
1320 GOTO 1306
1399 RETURN
9999 END
```

```
PROGRAM 7-2

COMPARE A SET OF INVENTORY ORDER
QUANTITIES GIVING THE ANNUAL
ORDERING COSTS, HOLDING COSTS,
AND TOTAL INVENTORY COSTS.

COST PER ORDER PLACED            ? 30
ANNUAL PER-UNIT HOLDING COST     ? 5
UNITS DEMANDED PER YEAR          ? 200

ORDER QUANTITIES TO COMPARE

SMALLEST QUANTITY                ? 40
LARGEST QUANTITY                 ? 60
STEP SIZE BETWEEN QUANTITIES     ? 5
```

ORDER QUANTITY	ANNUAL INVENTORY COSTS ORDERING	HOLDING	TOTAL
40	150	100	250
45	133.333	112.5	245.833
50	120	125	245
55	109.091	137.5	246.591
60	100	150	250

```
TRY ANOTHER SET OF DATA (Y/N)? N

END OF PROGRAM
```

Fig. 7-2. Sample results from Program 7-2.

tomer may agree to a backorder, in which case the order will be filled when the next shipment arrives from the supplier. The customer may seek another source of supply. Too many out-of-stock situations cause the customer to lose confidence.

The customer may be external to the company or he may be an internal user of the inventory. In either case there is a cost for not meeting the demand.

If the demand per period undergoes random fluctuations, stockouts are possible. If there is uncertainty about the lead time between the placing of the order and its arrival, there is a significant risk of stockouts.

The safety stock is the amount of cushion maintained by the inventory policy to cover variability in demand and lead time. There is a direct trade-off between the holding cost of the safety stock and the reduced stockout cost.

The reorder point is the inventory level that triggers an order. The safety stock is the difference between the reorder point and the expected demand that would occur during the lead time. The inventory decision rule covers choosing the reorder point and the order quantity that minimizes total inventory costs.

Program 7-3 simulates demand that is normally distributed using the decision rule that specifies the reorder point and order quantity. Figure 7-3 shows the results.

Exercise 7-2

1. Continue the search for the optimum reorder point and order quantity.

Program 7-3

```
100 REM ********************************
102 REM *    7-3                       *
104 REM ********************************
106 REM   AUTHOR
108 REM       COPYRIGHT 1982
110 REM       BY LAWRENCE MCNITT.
112 REM   PURPOSE
114 REM       INVENTORY SIMULATION WITH
116 REM       NORMALLY DISTRIBUTED DEMAND.
118 REM   SYSTEM
120 REM       UNIVERSAL SUBSET
122 REM       OF BASIC.
200 REM ********************************
202 REM *    ORGANIZATION              *
204 REM ********************************
206 REM   900   MAIN ROUTINE
208 REM         1000   INITIAL MESSAGE
210 REM         1100   PARAMETERS
212 REM         1200   PROCESS
214 REM               2000   DEMAND
216 REM         1300   OUTPUT
218 REM         1400   FINAL MESSAGE
300 REM ********************************
302 REM *    VARIABLES                 *
304 REM ********************************
306 REM   U$   USER RESPONSE
```

```
308 REM     M     POPULATION MEAN DEMAND
310 REM     S     POPULATION STANDARD DEVIATION DEMAND
312 REM     C1    COST PER ORDER
314 REM     C2    HOLDING COST PER UNIT PER PERIOD
316 REM     C3    STOCKOUT COST PER UNIT
318 REM     N     NUMBER OF PERIODS
320 REM     I     COUNTER
322 REM     J     COUNTER
324 REM     Z     STANDARD SCORE FOR NORMAL DISTRIBUTION
326 REM     D     OBSERVED DEMAND
328 REM     R     REORDER POINT
330 REM     Q     ORDER QUANTITY
332 REM     U     UNITS SOLD
334 REM     L     UNITS LOST
336 REM     T1    TOTAL ORDERING COST
338 REM     T2    TOTAL HOLDING COST
340 REM     T3    TOTAL STOCKOUT COST
342 REM     T     TOTAL INVENTORY COST
344 REM     B     BEGINNING INVENTORY LEVEL
346 REM     Q1    QUANTITY ON ORDER
900 REM *****************************
902 REM *    MAIN ROUTINE            *
904 REM *****************************
906 REM INITIAL MESSAGE
908 GOSUB 1006
910 REM PARAMETERS
912 GOSUB 1106
914 REM PROCESS
916 GOSUB 1206
918 REM OUTPUT
920 GOSUB 1306
922 REM FINAL MESSAGE
924 GOSUB 1406
926 IF U$ = "Y" THEN 916
928 PRINT
930 PRINT "END OF PROGRAM"
999 STOP
1000 REM *****************************
1002 REM *    INITIAL MESSAGE         *
1004 REM *****************************
1006 PRINT
1008 PRINT
1010 PRINT
1012 PRINT "PROGRAM 7-3 "
1014 PRINT
1016 PRINT "EVALUATE REORDER POINT"
```

```
1018 PRINT "AND ORDER QUANTITY FOR"
1020 PRINT "INVENTORY HAVING NORMALLY"
1022 PRINT "DISTRIBUTED DEMAND."
1099 RETURN
1100 REM ******************************
1102 REM *    PARAMETERS              *
1104 REM ******************************
1106 PRINT
1108 PRINT "DEMAND PER PERIOD IS"
1110 PRINT "NORMALLY DISTRIBUTED."
1112 PRINT
1114 PRINT "AVERAGE DEMAND";
1116 INPUT M
1118 PRINT "STD DEV DEMAND";
1120 INPUT S
1122 PRINT
1124 PRINT "COST PER ORDER PLACED";
1126 INPUT C1
1128 PRINT
1130 PRINT "HOLDING COST PER UNIT PER PERIOD";
1132 INPUT C2
1134 PRINT
1136 PRINT "STOCKOUT COST PER UNIT";
1138 INPUT C3
1199 RETURN
1200 REM ******************************
1202 REM *    PROCESS                 *
1204 REM ******************************
1206 PRINT
1208 PRINT "REORDER POINT";
1210 INPUT R
1212 PRINT
1214 PRINT "ORDER QUANTITY";
1216 INPUT Q
1218 PRINT
1220 PRINT "NUMBER OF PERIODS";
1222 INPUT N
1224 LET B = Q
1226 LET T1 = 0
1228 LET T2 = 0
1230 LET T3 = 0
1232 FOR I = 1 TO N
1234     REM DEMAND
1236     GOSUB 2006
1238     LET U = D
1240     LET L = 0
```

```
1242    IF D <= B THEN 1250
1244    LET U = B
1246    LET L = D - B
1248    LET T3 = T3 + C3 * L
1250    LET B = B - U + Q1
1251    LET Q1 = 0
1252    LET T2 = T2 + C2 * B
1254    IF B > R THEN 1260
1256    LET Q1 = Q
1258    LET T1 = T1 + C1
1260 NEXT I
1262 LET T = T1 + T2 + T3
1299 RETURN
1300 REM ******************************
1302 REM *    OUTPUT                  *
1304 REM ******************************
1306 PRINT
1308 PRINT ,"TOTAL COST","AVERAGE PER PERIOD"
1310 PRINT "ORDERING",T1,T1/N
1312 PRINT "HOLDING",T2,T2/N
1314 PRINT "STOCKOUT",T3,T3/N
1316 PRINT "TOTAL",T,T/N
1399 RETURN
1400 REM ******************************
1402 REM *    FINAL MESSAGE           *
1404 REM ******************************
1406 PRINT
1408 PRINT "TRY ANOTHER SIMULATION RUN (Y/N)";
1410 INPUT U$
1412 IF U$ = "Y" THEN 1499
1414 IF U$ = "N" THEN 1499
1416 PRINT
1418 PRINT "INVALID RESPONSE"
1420 GOTO 1406
1499 RETURN
2000 REM ******************************
2002 REM *    DEMAND                  *
2004 REM ******************************
2006 LET Z = -6
2008 FOR J = 1 TO 12
2010    LET Z = Z + RND(0)
2012 NEXT J
2014 LET D = M + Z * S
2016 LET D = INT(.5 + D)
2099 RETURN
9999 END
```

```
PROGRAM 7-3
EVALUATE REORDER POINT
AND ORDER QUANTITY FOR
INVENTORY HAVING NORMALLY
DISTRIBUTED DEMAND.

DEMAND PER PERIOD IS
NORMALLY DISTRIBUTED.
AVERAGE DEMAND? 10
STD DEV DEMAND? 2

COST PER ORDER PLACED? 30

HOLDING COST PER UNIT PER PERIOD? .15

STOCKOUT COST PER UNIT? 5

REORDER POINT? 9

ORDER QUANTITY? 50

NUMBER OF PERIODS? 100

                 TOTAL COST      AVERAGE PER PERIOD
ORDERING         540             5.4
HOLDING          405.15          4.0515
STOCKOUT         510             5.1

TRY ANOTHER SIMULATION RUN (Y/N)? Y

REORDER POINT? 11

ORDER QUANTITY? 100

NUMBER OF PERIODS? 100

                 TOTAL COST      AVERAGE PER PERIOD
ORDERING         270             2.7
HOLDING          875.4           8.754
STOCKOUT         165             1.65
TOTAL            1310.4          13.104

TRY ANOTHER SIMULATION RUN (Y/N)? N

END OF PROGRAM
```

Fig. 7-3. Sample results from Program 7-3.

INVENTORY ANALYSIS

Uncertainties in demand and in lead time increase the risk of stockout. Safety stock added to reduce the risk of stockout adds to the holding cost. Increasing the order quantity adds to the holding cost and reduces the frequency of stockouts. Stockouts usually occur at the end of the inventory cycle after the order has been placed but before the shipment arrives.

Many probability distributions are available for describing demand. The normal distribution is the most common. Other specialized distributions exhibiting different properties are possible.

The next three programs illustrate different approaches to evaluating inventory policies assuming uncertain demand and uncertain lead time. In all three, the decision policy determines the reorder point and the order quantity. The probability distributions for demand and lead time are straightforward. The formulas for the ordering cost

and the holding cost are not difficult. The formula for the stockout is more complex.

A method for determining the probability distribution of demand during lead time is needed. Even this isn't difficult if the lead time is fixed. The problem is more complex when both the lead time and the demand per period are random.

One approach is to develop a complete probability tree giving the probabilities for the possible levels of demand during the lead time. This analysis must incorporate all possible lead time intervals and all possible levels of demand per period for each period during the lead time. Enumeration of the complete probability tree is not practical for extremely large problems having many levels of demand per period and many levels of lead time.

Program 7-4 uses the probability tree enumeration approach to determine the probability distribution for demand during lead time. Figure 7-4 shows the results.

Program 7-4

```
100 REM ******************************
102 REM *   7 - 4                    *
104 REM ******************************
106 REM   AUTHOR
108 REM       COPYRIGHT 1982
110 REM       BY LAWRENCE MCNITT.
112 REM   PURPOSE
114 REM       INVENTORY ANALYSIS WITH
116 REM       PROBABILISTIC DEMAND
118 REM       AND LEAD TIMES.
120 REM   SYSTEM
122 REM       UNIVERSAL SUBSET
124 REM       OF BASIC.
200 REM ******************************
202 REM *     ORGANIZATION           *
204 REM ******************************
206 REM   900   MAIN ROUTINE
208 REM         1000   INITIAL MESSAGE
210 REM         1100   GET PROBABILITIES
212 REM         1200   DEMAND DURING LEAD TIME
214 REM         1300   GET COSTS
216 REM         1400   GET DECISIONS
```

```
218 REM          1500   PROCESS
220 REM          1600   FINAL MESSAGE
300 REM ******************************
302 REM *   VARIABLES                *
304 REM ******************************
306 REM    D(50,2)  PROB DIST FOR DEMAND PER PERIOD
308 REM    L(50,2)  PROB DIST FOR LEAD TIME
310 REM    S(500)   PROBS FOR DEMAND DURING LEAD TIME
312 REM    U$  USER RESPONSE
314 REM    I   INDEX
316 REM    J   INDEX
318 REM    J1  INDEX
320 REM    K1  NUMBER OF STATES FOR DEMAND
322 REM    K2  NUMBER OF STATES FOR LEAD TIME
324 REM    K3  LARGEST INDEX FOR DEMAND DURING LEAD TIME
326 REM    E1  EXPECTED DEMAND PER PERIOD
328 REM    E2  EXPECTED LEAD TIME
330 REM    E3  EXPECTED DEMAND DURING LEAD TIME
331 REM    E4  EXPECTED UNITS OF STOCKOUT PER ORDER
332 REM    N2  LENGTH OF LEAD TIME
334 REM    M   NUMBER OF LEAVES IN PROBABILITY TREE
336 REM    Z   UNITS DEMANDED DURING LEAD TIME
338 REM    P   PROBABILITY FOR UNITS DEMANDED
340 REM    J2  INDEX FOR DEMAND
342 REM    M1  NODE NUMBER FOR PROB TREE
344 REM    M2  NODE NUMBER FOR PROB TREE
346 REM    C1  COST PER ORDER
348 REM    C2  ANNUAL PER-UNIT HOLDING COST
350 REM    C3  PER-UNIT STOCKOUT COST
352 REM    N1  NUMBER OF PERIODS PER YEAR
354 REM    Q1  LOWER LIMIT FOR ORDER QUANTITY
356 REM    Q2  UPPER LIMIT FOR ORDER QUANTITY
358 REM    Q3  STEP SIZE FOR ORDER QUANTITY
360 REM    Q   CURRENT ORDER QUANTITY
362 REM    R1  LOWER LIMIT FOR REORDER POINT
364 REM    R2  UPPER LIMIT FOR REORDER POINT
366 REM    R3  STEP SIZE FOR REORDER POINT
368 REM    R   CURRENT REORDER POINT
370 REM    T1  ANNUAL ORDERING COST
372 REM    T2  ANNUAL HOLDING COST
374 REM    T3  ANNUAL STOCKOUT COST
376 REM    T   TOTAL ANNUAL INVENTORY COST
900 REM ******************************
902 REM *   MAIN ROUTINE              *
904 REM ******************************
906 DIM D(50,2),L(50,2),S(500)
```

```
908 REM INITIAL MESSAGE
910 GOSUB 1006
914 REM GET PROBABILITIES
916 GOSUB 1106
918 REM REM DEMAND DURING LEAD TIME
920 GOSUB 1206
922 REM GET COSTS
924 GOSUB 1306
926 REM GET DECISIONS
928 GOSUB 1406
930 REM PROCESS
932 GOSUB 1506
934 REM FINAL MESSAGE
936 GOSUB 1606
938 IF U$ = "1" THEN 928
940 IF U$ = "2" THEN 924
942 IF U$ = "3" THEN 916
944 PRINT
946 PRINT "END OF PROGRAM"
999 STOP
1000 REM ******************************
1002 REM *    INITIAL MESSAGE         *
1004 REM ******************************
1006 PRINT
1008 PRINT
1010 PRINT
1012 PRINT "PROGRAM 7 - 4 "
1014 PRINT
1016 PRINT "INVENTORY ANALYSIS WITH PROBABILISTIC"
1018 PRINT "DEMAND AND LEAD TIMES USING A"
1020 PRINT "PROBABILITY TREE TO DEVELOP THE"
1022 PRINT "PROBABILITY DISTRIBUTION OF"
1024 PRINT "DEMAND DURING LEAD TIME."
1099 RETURN
1100 REM ******************************
1102 REM *    GET PROBABILITIES       *
1104 REM ******************************
1106 PRINT
1108 PRINT "PROBABILITY DISTRIBUTION"
1110 PRINT "FOR DEMAND PER PERIOD"
1112 PRINT
1114 PRINT "NUMBER OF LEVELS OF DEMAND";
1116 INPUT K1
1118 PRINT
1120 PRINT "DEMAND, PROBABILITY FOR"
1122 LET E1 = 0
```

```
1124 FOR I = 1 TO K1
1126    PRINT "STATE";I;
1128    INPUT D(I,1),D(I,2)
1130    LET E1 = E1 + D(I,1) * D(I,2)
1132 NEXT I
1134 PRINT
1136 PRINT "EXPECTED DEMAND PER PERIOD",E1
1138 PRINT
1140 PRINT "PROBABILITY DISTRIBUTION"
1142 PRINT "FOR LEAD TIME"
1144 PRINT
1146 PRINT "NUMBER OF DIFFERENT LEAD TIMES";
1148 INPUT K2
1150 PRINT
1152 PRINT "LEAD TIME, PROBABILITY FOR"
1154 LET E2 = 0
1156 FOR I = 1 TO K2
1158    PRINT "STATE";I;
1160    INPUT L(I,1),L(I,2)
1162    LET E2 = E2 + L(I,1) * L(I,2)
1164 NEXT I
1166 PRINT
1168 PRINT "EXPECTED LEAD TIME",E2
1199 RETURN
1200 REM *******************************
1202 REM *    DEMAND DURING LEAD TIME *
1204 REM *******************************
1206 LET K3 = D(K1,1) [ L(K2,1) + 1
1208 FOR I = 1 TO K3
1210    LET S(I) = 0
1212 NEXT I
1214 FOR I = 1 TO K2
1216    LET N2 = L(I,1)
1218    LET M = K1 * N2
1220    FOR J = 1 TO M
1222       LET M1 = J - 1
1224       LET Z = 0
1226       LET P = L(I,2)
1228       FOR J1 = 1 TO N2
1230          LET M2 = INT(M1 / K1)
1232          LET J2 = M1 - K1 * M2 + 1
1234          LET Z = Z + D(J2,1)
1236          LET P = P * D(J2,2)
1237          LET M1 = M2
1238       NEXT J1
1240       LET S(Z+1) = S(Z+1) + P
```

```
1242    NEXT J
1244 NEXT I
1246 LET E3 = 0
1248 FOR I = 1 TO K3
1250    LET E3 = E3 + (I - 1) * S(I)
1252 NEXT I
1254 PRINT
1256 PRINT "EXPECTED DEMAND DURING LEAD TIME",E3
1299 RETURN
1300 REM *****************************
1302 REM *    GET COSTS               *
1304 REM *****************************
1306 PRINT
1308 PRINT "COST PER ORDER PLACED          ";
1310 INPUT C1
1312 PRINT "ANNUAL PER-UNIT HOLDING COST ";
1314 INPUT C2
1316 PRINT "STOCKOUT COST PER UNIT         ";
1318 INPUT C3
1320 PRINT "NUMBER OF PERIODS PER YEAR   ";
1322 INPUT N1
1399 RETURN
1400 REM *****************************
1402 REM *    GET DECISIONS           *
1404 REM *****************************
1406 PRINT
1408 PRINT "ORDER QUANTITIES OF INTEREST"
1410 PRINT "LOWER LIMIT ";
1412 INPUT Q1
1414 PRINT "UPPER LIMIT ";
1416 INPUT Q2
1418 PRINT "STEP SIZE    ";
1420 INPUT Q3
1422 PRINT
1424 PRINT "REORDER POINTS OF INTEREST"
1426 PRINT "LOWER LIMIT ";
1428 INPUT R1
1430 PRINT "UPPER LIMIT ";
1432 INPUT R2
1434 PRINT "STEP SIZE    ";
1436 INPUT R3
1499 RETURN
1500 REM *****************************
1502 REM *    PROCESS                 *
1504 REM *****************************
1506 PRINT
```

```
1508 PRINT "REORDER","ANNUAL INVENTORY COSTS"
1510 PRINT "POINT/QUANTITY"
1512 PRINT "ORDERING","HOLDING","STOCKOUT","TOTAL"
1514 FOR R = R1 TO R2 STEP R3
1516    LET E4 = 0
1518    FOR I = 1 TO K3
1520       IF R >= I - 1 THEN 1524
1522       LET E4 = E4 + (I - 1 - R) * S(I)
1524    NEXT I
1526    FOR Q = Q1 TO Q2 STEP Q3
1528       LET T1 = C1 * N1 * E1 / Q
1530       LET T2 = C2 * (Q / 2 + R - E3)
1532       LET T3 = C3 * E4 * N1 * E1 / Q
1534       LET T = T1 + T2 + T3
1536       PRINT R;Q
1538       PRINT T1,T2,T3,T
1540    NEXT Q
1542 NEXT R
1599 RETURN
1600 REM ****************************
1602 REM *     FINAL MESSAGE         *
1604 REM ****************************
1606 PRINT
1608 PRINT "MENU OF OPTIONS"
1610 PRINT "    1     TRY NEW REORDER POINTS AND QUANTITIES"
1612 PRINT "    2     TRY ANOTHER SET OF COSTS"
1614 PRINT "    3     TRY OTHER PROBABILITIES"
1616 PRINT "    4     TERMINATE"
1618 PRINT
1620 PRINT "DESIRED OPTION";
1622 INPUT U$
1624 IF U$ = "1" THEN 1699
1626 IF U$ = "2" THEN 1699
1628 IF U$ = "3" THEN 1699
1630 IF U$ = "4" THEN 1699
1632 PRINT
1634 PRINT "INVALID RESPONSE"
1636 GOTO 1606
1699 RETURN
9999 END
```

Exercise 7-3

1. Continue the search for the best combination of reorder point and order quantity using the model of this section.

MONTE CARLO SIMULATION

Enumerating all possible outcomes of a probability tree is not always feasible because there may be too many combinations. Monte Carlo simulation

```
PROGRAM P7-4
INVENTORY ANALYSIS WITH PROBABILISTIC
DEMAND AND LEAD TIMES USING A
PROBABILITY TREE TO DEVELOP THE
PROBABILITY DISTRIBUTION OF
DEMAND DURING LEAD TIME.

PROBABILITY DISTRIBUTION
FOR DEMAND PER PERIOD
NUMBER OF LEVELS OF DEMAND? 3

DEMAND, PROBABILITY FOR
STATE 1 ? 10,.3
STATE 2 ? 11,.5
STATE 3 ? 12,.2

EXPECTED DEMAND PER PERIOD          10.9

PROBABILITY DISTRIBUTION
FOR LEAD TIME

NUMBER OF DIFFERENT LEAD TIMES? 2

LEAD TIME, PROBABILITY FOR
STATE 1 ? 1,.8
STATE 2 ? 2,.2

EXPECTED LEAD TIME                  1.2

EXPECTED DEMAND DURING LEAD TIME                    13.676

COST PER ORDER PLACED          ? 30
ANNUAL PER-UNIT HOLDING COST ? 10
STOCKOUT COST PER UNIT         ? 20
NUMBER OF PERIODS PER YEAR     ? 52

ORDER QUANTITIES OF INTEREST
LOWER LIMIT? 40
UPPER LIMIT? 60
STEP SIZE   ? 10

REORDER POINTS OF INTEREST
LOWER LIMIT? 15
UPPER LIMIT? 15
STEP SIZE   ? 1
```

```
REORDER               ANNUAL INVENTORY COSTS
POINT/QUANTITY
ORDERING            HOLDING         STOCKOUT          TOTAL
 15   40
 425.1              213.24          453.303          1073.64
 15   50
 340.08             263.24          348.242          951.562
 15   60
 283.4              313.24          290.202          886.842
MENU OF OPTIONS
     1    TRY NEW REORDER POINTS AND QUANTITIES
     2    TRY ANOTHER SET OF COSTS
     3    TRY OTHER PROBABILITIES
     4    TERMINATE

NUMBER OF DESIRED OPTION? 4

END OF PROGRAM
```

Fig. 7-4. Sample results from Program 7-4.

is another method for estimating the probability distribution for demand during lead time.

The Monte Carlo approach simulates a large number of lead times and demands during those lead times. The results are summarized to estimate the probability distribution for demand during lead time. Although accurate results require long simulation runs, Monte Carlo simulation provides a practical alternative to enumerating the probability tree. The probability enumeration scheme is better for small problems because it gives exact probabilities rather than estimates taken from simulation runs. For large problems there may be no choice but to use the Monte Carlo simulation approach.

Program 7-5 uses Monte Carlo techniques to estimate the probability distribution for demand during lead time. Figure 7-5 shows the results.

Program 7-5

```
100 REM *********************************
102 REM *    7-5                        *
104 REM *********************************
106 REM   AUTHOR
108 REM        COPYRIGHT 1982
110 REM        BY LAWRENCE MCNITT.
112 REM   PURPOSE
114 REM        INVENTORY ANALYSIS USING MONTE CARLO
116 REM        SIMULATION TO ESTIMATE PROB DIST
118 REM        OF DEMAND DURING LEAD TIME.
120 REM   SYSTEM
122 REM        UNIVERSAL SUBSET
124 REM        OF BASIC.
200 REM *********************************
```

```
202 REM *    ORGANIZATION                    *
204 REM ********************************
206 REM   900   MAIN ROUTINE
208 REM         1000   INITIAL MESSAGE
210 REM         1100   GET PROBABILITIES
212 REM         1200   DEMAND DURING LEAD TIME
214 REM         1300   GET COSTS
216 REM         1400   GET DECISIONS
218 REM         1500   PROCESS
220 REM         1600   FINAL MESSAGE
300 REM ********************************
302 REM *    VARIABLES                      *
304 REM ********************************
306 REM   D(50,2)   PROB DIST FOR DEMAND PER PERIOD
308 REM   L(50,2)   PROB DIST FOR LEAD TIME
310 REM   S(500)    PROBS FOR DEMAND DURING LEAD TIME
312 REM   U$   USER RESPONSE
314 REM   I    INDEX
316 REM   J    INDEX
318 REM   J1   INDEX
320 REM   K1   NUMBER OF STATES FOR DEMAND
322 REM   K2   NUMBER OF STATES FOR LEAD TIME
324 REM   K3   LARGEST INDEX FOR DEMAND DURING LEAD TIME
326 REM   E1   EXPECTED DEMAND PER PERIOD
328 REM   E2   EXPECTED LEAD TIME
330 REM   E3   EXPECTED DEMAND DURING LEAD TIME
332 REM   E4   EXPECTED STOCKOUT PER ORDER
334 REM   I1   INDEX FOR DISTRIBUTION
336 REM   M    LENGTH OF LEAD TIME
338 REM   Z    UNITS DEMANDED DURING LEAD TIME
340 REM   P    PROBABILITY FOR DEMAND DURING LEAD TIME
342 REM   J2   INDEX FOR DEMAND
344 REM   C1   COST PER ORDER
346 REM   C2   ANNUAL PER-UNIT HOLDING COST
348 REM   C3   STOCKOUT COST PER UNIT
350 REM   N1   NUMBER OF PERIODS PER YEAR
352 REM   Q1   LOWER LIMIT FOR ORDER QUANTITY
354 REM   Q2   UPPER LIMIT FOR ORDER QUANTITY
356 REM   Q3   STEP SIZE FOR ORDER QUANTITY
358 REM   Q    ORDER QUANTITY
360 REM   R1   LOWER LIMIT FOR REORDER POINT
362 REM   R2   UPPER LIMIT FOR REORDER POINT
364 REM   R3   STEP SIZE FOR REORDER POINT
366 REM   R    REORDER POINT
368 REM   T1   ANNUAL ORDERING COST
370 REM   T2   ANNUAL HOLDING COST
```

```
372 REM    T3   ANNUAL STOCKOUT COST
374 REM    T    TOTAL ANNUAL INVENTORY COST
900 REM ******************************
902 REM *    MAIN ROUTINE             *
904 REM ******************************
906 DIM D(50,2),L(50,2),S(500)
908 REM INITIAL MESSAGE
910 GOSUB 1006
914 REM GET PROBABILITIES
916 GOSUB 1106
918 REM REM DEMAND DURING LEAD TIME
920 GOSUB 1206
922 REM GET COSTS
924 GOSUB 1306
926 REM GET DECISIONS
928 GOSUB 1406
930 REM PROCESS
932 GOSUB 1506
934 REM FINAL MESSAGE
936 GOSUB 1606
938 IF U$ = "1" THEN 928
940 IF U$ = "2" THEN 924
942 IF U$ = "3" THEN 916
944 PRINT
946 PRINT "END OF PROGRAM"
999 STOP
1000 REM ******************************
1002 REM *    INITIAL MESSAGE         *
1004 REM ******************************
1006 PRINT
1008 PRINT
1010 PRINT
1012 PRINT "PROGRAM 7-5"
1014 PRINT
1016 PRINT "INVENTORY ANALYSIS WITH PROBABILISTIC"
1018 PRINT "DEMAND AND LEAD TIMES USING MONTE"
1020 PRINT "CARLO SIMULATION TO ESTIMATE"
1022 PRINT "THE PROBABILITY DISTRIBUTION OF"
1024 PRINT "DEMAND DURING LEAD TIME."
1099 RETURN
1100 REM ******************************
1102 REM *    GET PROBABILITIES       *
1104 REM ******************************
1106 PRINT
1108 PRINT "PROBABILITY DISTRIBUTION"
1110 PRINT "FOR DEMAND PER PERIOD"
```

```
1112 PRINT
1114 PRINT "NUMBER OF LEVELS OF DEMAND";
1116 INPUT K1
1118 PRINT
1120 PRINT "DEMAND, PROBABILITY FOR"
1122 LET E1 = 0
1124 FOR I = 1 TO K1
1126     PRINT "STATE";I;
1128     INPUT D(I,1),D(I,2)
1130     LET E1 = E1 + D(I,1) * D(I,2)
1132 NEXT I
1134 PRINT
1136 PRINT "EXPECTED DEMAND PER PERIOD",E1
1138 PRINT
1140 PRINT "PROBABILITY DISTRIBUTION"
1142 PRINT "FOR LEAD TIME"
1144 PRINT
1146 PRINT "NUMBER OF DIFFERENT LEAD TIMES";
1148 INPUT K2
1150 PRINT
1152 PRINT "LEAD TIME, PROBABILITY FOR"
1154 LET E2 = 0
1156 FOR I = 1 TO K2
1158     PRINT "STATE";I;
1160     INPUT L(I,1),L(I,2)
1162     LET E2 = E2 + L(I,1) * L(I,2)
1164 NEXT I
1166 PRINT
1168 PRINT "EXPECTED LEAD TIME",E2
1170 LET P = 0
1172 FOR I = 1 TO K1
1174     LET P = P + D(I,2)
1176     LET D(I,2) = P
1178 NEXT I
1180 LET P = 0
1182 FOR I = 1 TO K2
1184     LET P = P + L(I,2)
1186     LET L(I,2) = P
1188 NEXT I
1199 RETURN
1200 REM ****************************
1202 REM *    DEMAND DURING LEAD TIME *
1204 REM ****************************
1206 PRINT
1208 PRINT "NUMBER OF TRIALS IN MONTE CARLO"
1210 PRINT "SIMULATION FOR DEMAND DURING LEAD TIME";
```

```
1212 INPUT N1
1214 LET K3 = D(K1,1) [ L(K2,1) + 1
1216 FOR I = 1 TO K3
1218    LET S(I) = 0
1220 NEXT I
1222 RANDOM
1224 FOR I = 1 TO N1
1226    LET P = RND(0)
1228    FOR J = 1 TO K2
1230       IF P > L(J,2) THEN 1236
1232       LET I1 = J
1234       LET J = K2
1236    NEXT J
1238    LET M = L(I1,1)
1240    LET Z = 0
1242    FOR J = 1 TO M
1244       LET P = RND(0)
1246       FOR J1 = 1 TO K1
1248          IF P > D(J1,2) THEN 1254
1250          LET J2 = J1
1252          LET J1 = K1
1254       NEXT J1
1256       LET Z = Z + D(J2,1)
1258    NEXT J
1260    LET S(Z+1) = S(Z+1) + 1
1262 NEXT I
1264 LET E3 = 0
1266 FOR I = 1 TO K3
1268    LET S(I) = S(I) / N1
1270    LET E3 = E3 + (I - 1) * S(I)
1272 NEXT I
1274 PRINT
1276 PRINT "EXPECTED DEMAND DURING LEAD TIME",E3
1299 RETURN
1300 REM *****************************
1302 REM *    GET COSTS              *
1304 REM *****************************
1306 PRINT
1308 PRINT "COST PER ORDER PLACED          ";
1310 INPUT C1
1312 PRINT "ANNUAL PER-UNIT HOLDING COST ";
1314 INPUT C2
1316 PRINT "STOCKOUT COST PER UNIT         ";
1318 INPUT C3
1320 PRINT "NUMBER OF PERIODS PER YEAR    ";
1322 INPUT N1
```

```
1399 RETURN
1400 REM *****************************
1402 REM *    GET DECISIONS           *
1404 REM *****************************
1406 PRINT
1408 PRINT "ORDER QUANTITIES OF INTEREST"
1410 PRINT "LOWER LIMIT ";
1412 INPUT Q1
1414 PRINT "UPPER LIMIT ";
1416 INPUT Q2
1418 PRINT "STEP SIZE    ";
1420 INPUT Q3
1422 PRINT
1424 PRINT "REORDER POINTS OF INTEREST"
1426 PRINT "LOWER LIMIT ";
1428 INPUT R1
1430 PRINT "UPPER LIMIT ";
1432 INPUT R2
1434 PRINT "STEP SIZE    ";
1436 INPUT R3
1499 RETURN
1500 REM *****************************
1502 REM *    PROCESS                 *
1504 REM *****************************
1506 PRINT
1508 PRINT "REORDER","ANNUAL INVENTORY COSTS"
1510 PRINT "POINT/QUANTITY"
1512 PRINT "ORDERING","HOLDING","STOCKOUT","TOTAL"
1514 FOR R = R1 TO R2 STEP R3
1516     LET E4 = 0
1518     FOR I = 1 TO K3
1520         IF R >= I - 1 THEN 1524
1522         LET E4 = E4 + (I - 1 - R) * S(I)
1524     NEXT I
1526     FOR Q = Q1 TO Q2 STEP Q3
1528         LET T1 = C1 * N1 * E1 / Q
1530         LET T2 = C2 * (Q / 2 + R - E3)
1532         LET T3 = C3 * E4 * N1 * E1 / Q
1534         LET T = T1 + T2 + T3
1536         PRINT R;Q
1538         PRINT T1,T2,T3,T
1540     NEXT Q
1542 NEXT R
1599 RETURN
1600 REM *****************************
1602 REM *    FINAL MESSAGE           *
```

```
1604 REM *******************************
1606 PRINT
1608 PRINT "MENU OF OPTIONS"
1610 PRINT "   1   TRY NEW REORDER POINTS AND QUANTITIES"
1612 PRINT "   2   TRY ANOTHER SET OF COSTS"
1614 PRINT "   3   TRY OTHER PROBABILITIES"
1616 PRINT "   4   TERMINATE"
1618 PRINT
1620 PRINT "DESIRED OPTION"
1622 INPUT U$
1624 IF U$ = "Y" THEN 1699
1626 IF U$ = "2" THEN 1699
1628 IF U$ = "3" THEN 1699
1630 IF U$ = "4" THEN 1699
1632 PRINT
1634 PRINT "INVALID RESPONSE"
1636 GOTO 1606
1699 RETURN
9999 END
```

PROGRAM 7-5

INVENTORY ANALYSIS WITH PROBABILISTIC
DEMAND AND LEAD TIMES USING MONTE
CARLO SIMULATION TO ESTIMATE
THE PROBABILITY DISTRIBUTION OF
DEMAND DURING LEAD TIME.

PROBABILITY DISTRIBUTION
FOR DEMAND PER PERIOD

NUMBER OF LEVELS OF DEMAND? 3

DEMAND, PROBAILITY FOR
STATE 1 ? 10,.3
STATE 2 ? 11,.5
STATE 3 ? 12,.2

EXPECTED DEMAND PER PERIOD?   10.9

PROBABILITY DISTRIBUTION
FOR LEAD TIME

NUMBER OF DIFFERENT LEAD TIMES? 2

```
LEAD TIME, PROBABILITY FOR
STATE 1 ? 1,.8
STATE 2 ? 2,.2

EXPECTED LEAD TIME                    1.2
NUMBER OF TRIALS IN MONTE CARLO
SIMULATING FOR DEMAND DURING LEAD TIME? 500

EXPECTED DEMAND DURING LEAD TIME              12.98

COST PER ORDER PLACED        ? 30
ANNUAL PER-UNIT HOLDING COST ? 10
STOCKOUT COST PER UNIT       ? 20
NUMBER OF PERIODS PER YEAR   ? 52

ORDER QUANTITIES OF INTEREST
LOWER LIMIT? 40
UPPER LIMIT? 60
STEP SIZE   ? 10

REORDER POINTS OF INTEREST
LOWER LIMIT? 15
UPPER LIMIT? 15
STEP SIZE   ? 1

REORDER            ANNUAL INVENTORY COSTS
POINT/QUANTITY
ORDERING           HOLDING         STOCKOUT        TOTAL
 15   40
 425.1             220.2           370.687         1015.99
 15   50
 340.08            270.2           296.55          906.83
 15   60
 283.4             320.2           247.125         850.725

MENU OF OPTIONS
    1    TRY NEW REORDER POINTS AND QUANTITIES
    2    TRY ANOTHER SET OF COSTS
    3    TRY OTHER PROBABILITIES
    4    TERMINATE

DESIRED OPTION? 4

END OF PROGRAM
```

Fig. 7-5. Sample results from Program 7-5.

Exercise 7-4

1. Use the Monte Carlo simulation method to determine the best reorder point and order quantity combination. Use the probability distributions given in the example in this section.

PERIOD BY PERIOD SIMULATION

Neither the probability tree enumeration scheme nor the Monte Carlo simulation approach works well if the total demand during the lead time is very large. An alternative is to simulate the inventory system on a period-by-period basis. The Monte Carlo simulation approach of the previous section involves only one simulation run estimating the distribution of demand during the lead time.

The period-by-period simulation approach is potentially much more costly, especially for small problems. This is because a separate simulation run is necessary for each decision setting consisting of order quantity and reorder point. Although long simulation runs are costly in terms of computer

Program 7-6

```
100 REM *******************************
102 REM *    7-6                       *
104 REM *******************************
106 REM   AUTHOR
108 REM       COPYRIGHT 1982
110 REM       BY LAWRENCE MCNITT.
112 REM   PURPOSE
114 REM       INVENTORY SIMULATION.
116 REM   SYSTEM
118 REM       UNIVERSAL SUBSET
120 REM       OF BASIC.
200 REM *******************************
202 REM *    ORGANIZATION              *
204 REM *******************************
206 REM   900   MAIN ROUTINE
208 REM         1000   INITIAL MESSAGE
210 REM         1100   GET PROBABILITIES
212 REM         1200   GET COSTS
214 REM         1300   GET DECISIONS
216 REM         1400   SIMULATE
218 REM                2000   UPDATE PIPELINE
220 REM                2100   GENERATE DEMAND
222 REM                2200   PLACE ORDER
224 REM                2300   DISPLAY RESULT
226 REM         1500   FINAL MESSAGE
300 REM *******************************
302 REM *    VARIABLES                 *
304 REM *******************************
306 REM    D(50,2)   PROB DIST FOR DEMAND PER PERIOD
308 REM    L(50,2)   PROB DIST FOR LEAD TIME
310 REM    Y(50)     PIPELINE FOR ORDERS COMING IN
312 REM    U$  USER RESPONSE
```

```
314 REM     I     INDEX
316 REM     I1    INDEX
318 REM     K1    NUMBER OF STATES FOR DEMAND
320 REM     K2    NUMBER OF STATES FOR LEAD TIME
322 REM     K3    MAXIMUM PERIODS FOR LEAD TIME
324 REM     E1    EXPECTED DEMAND PER PERIOD
326 REM     E2    EXPECTED LEAD TIME
328 REM     T1    NUMBER OF ORDERS PLACED
330 REM     T2    TOTAL FOR ALL INVENTORY LEVELS
332 REM     T3    TOTAL UNITS LOST
334 REM     T4    TOTAL UNITS LOST
336 REM     N1    NUMBER OF PERIODS PER YEAR
338 REM     N2    NUMBER OF PERIODS TO SIMULATE
340 REM     Q     ORDER QUANTITY
342 REM     R     REORDER POINT
344 REM     B     BEGINNING INVENTORY
346 REM     P     VALUE OF RANDOM NUMBER
348 REM     Z     DEMAND FOR PERIOD
350 REM     S1    UNITS SOLD FOR PERIOD
352 REM     S2    UNITS LOST FOR PERIOD
354 REM     V     TOTAL UNITS ON HAND AND IN PIPELINE
356 REM     L1    INDEX FOR RANDOMLY SELECTED EVENT
358 REM     T5    ANNUAL ORDERING COST
360 REM     T6    ANNUAL HOLDING COST
362 REM     T7    ANNUAL STOCKOUT COST
364 REM     T     TOTAL ANNUAL INVENTORY COST
900 REM *****************************
902 REM *    MAIN ROUTINE           *
904 REM *****************************
906 DIM L(50,2),D(50,2),Y(50)
908 REM INITIAL MESSAGE
910 GOSUB 1006
914 REM GET PROBABILITIES
916 GOSUB 1106
918 REM GET COSTS
920 GOSUB 1206
922 REM GET DECISIONS
924 GOSUB 1306
926 REM SIMULATE
928 GOSUB 1406
930 REM FINAL MESSAGE
932 GOSUB 1506
934 IF U$ = "1" THEN 924
936 IF U$ = "2" THEN 920
938 IF U$ = "3" THEN 916
940 PRINT
```

```
942 PRINT "END OF PROGRAM"
999 STOP
1000 REM ******************************
1002 REM *    INITIAL MESSAGE        *
1004 REM ******************************
1006 PRINT
1008 PRINT
1010 PRINT
1012 PRINT "PROGRAM 7-6 "
1014 PRINT
1016 PRINT "SIMULATE AN INVENTORY PROBLEM ON A"
1018 PRINT "PERIOD BY PERIOD BASIS SUMMARIZING"
1020 PRINT "AND NORMALIZING THE RESULTS ON AN"
1022 PRINT "ANNUAL BASIS.   DEMAND AND LEAD TIMES"
1024 PRINT "ARE PROBABILISTIC."
1099 RETURN
1100 REM ******************************
1102 REM *    GET PROBABILITIES      *
1104 REM ******************************
1106 PRINT
1108 PRINT "PROBABILITY DISTRIBUTION"
1110 PRINT "FOR DEMAND PER PERIOD"
1112 PRINT
1114 PRINT "NUMBER OF LEVELS OF DEMAND";
1116 INPUT K1
1118 PRINT
1120 PRINT "DEMAND, PROBABILITY FOR"
1122 LET P = 0
1124 LET E1 = 0
1126 FOR I = 1 TO K1
1128     PRINT "STATE";I;
1130     INPUT D(I,1),D(I,2)
1132     LET E1 = E1 + D(I,1) * D(I,2)
1134     LET P = P + D(I,2)
1136     LET D(I,2) = P
1138 NEXT I
1140 PRINT
1142 PRINT "EXPECTED DEMAND PER PERIOD",E1
1144 PRINT
1146 PRINT "PROBABILITY DISTRIBUTION"
1148 PRINT "FOR LEAD TIME"
1150 PRINT
1152 PRINT "NUMBER OF DIFFERENT LEAD TIMES";
1154 INPUT K2
1156 PRINT
1158 PRINT "LEAD TIME, PROBABILITY FOR"
```

```
1160 LET P = 0
1162 LET E2 = 0
1164 FOR I = 1 TO K2
1166    PRINT "STATE";I;
1168     INPUT L(I,1),L(I,2)
1170     LET E2 = E2 + L(I,1) * L(I,2)
1172     LET P = P + L(I,2)
1174     LET L(I,2) = P
1176 NEXT I
1178 PRINT
1180 PRINT "EXPECTED LEAD TIME",E2
1199 RETURN
1200 REM ****************************
1202 REM *    GET COSTS             *
1204 REM ****************************
1206 PRINT
1208 PRINT "COST PER ORDER PLACED         ";
1210 INPUT C1
1212 PRINT "ANNUAL PER-UNIT HOLDING COST ";
1214 INPUT C2
1216 PRINT "STOCKOUT COST PER UNIT       ";
1218 INPUT C3
1220 PRINT "NUMBER OF PERIODS PER YEAR    ";
1222 INPUT N1
1299 RETURN
1300 REM ****************************
1302 REM *    GET DECISIONS         *
1304 REM ****************************
1306 PRINT
1308 PRINT "ORDER QUANTITY                ";
1310 INPUT Q
1312 PRINT "REORDER POINT                 ";
1314 INPUT R
1316 PRINT "BEGINNING INVENTORY           ";
1318 INPUT B
1320 PRINT "NUMBER OF PERIODS TO SIMULATE ";
1322 INPUT N2
1324 FOR I = 1 TO K3
1326    LET Y(I) = 0
1328 NEXT I
1399 RETURN
1400 REM ****************************
1402 REM *    SIMULATE              *
1404 REM ****************************
1406 LET T1 = 0
1408 LET T2 = 0
```

```
1410 LET T3 = 0
1412 LET T4 = 0
1414 LET K3 = L(K2,1)
1416 FOR I2 = 1 TO N2
1418     REM UPDATE PIPELINE
1420     GOSUB 2006
1422     REM GENERATE DEMAND
1424     GOSUB 2106
1426     REM PLACE ORDER
1428     GOSUB 2206
1430     LET T2 = T2 + B
1432     LET T3 = T3 + S2
1434     LET T4 = T4 + S1
1436 NEXT I2
1438 REM DISPLAY RESULT
1440 GOSUB 2306
1499 RETURN
1500 REM ****************************
1502 REM *    FINAL MESSAGE          *
1504 REM ****************************
1506 PRINT
1508 PRINT "MENU OF OPTIONS"
1510 PRINT "   1    TRY ANOTHER SET OF DECISIONS"
1512 PRINT "   2    TRY ANOTHER SET OF COSTS"
1514 PRINT "   3    TRY ANOTHER SET OF PROBABILITIES"
1516 PRINT "   4    TERMINATE"
1518 PRINT
1520 PRINT "NUMBER OF DESIRED OPTION";
1522 INPUT U$
1524 IF U$ = "1" THEN 1599
1526 IF U$ = "2" THEN 1599
1528 IF U$ = "3" THEN 1599
1530 IF U$ = "4" THEN 1599
1532 PRINT
1534 PRINT "INVALID RESPONSE"
1536 GOTO 1506
1599 RETURN
2000 REM ****************************
2002 REM *    UPDATE PIPELINE        *
2004 REM ****************************
2006 LET B = B + Y(1)
2008 FOR I = 1 TO K3-1
2010     LET Y(I) = Y(I+1)
2012 NEXT I
2014 LET Y(K3) = 0
2099 RETURN
```

```
2100 REM ******************************
2102 REM *     GENERATE DEMAND         *
2104 REM ******************************
2106 LET P = RND(0)
2108 FOR I = 1 TO K1
2110    IF P > D(I,2) THEN 2116
2112    LET Z = D(I,1)
2114    LET I = K1
2116 NEXT I
2118 IF Z > B THEN 2126
2120 LET S1 = Z
2122 LET S2 = 0
2124 GOTO 2130
2126 LET S1 = B
2128 LET S2 = Z - B
2130 LET B = B - S1
2199 RETURN
2200 REM ******************************
2202 REM *     PLACE ORDER            *
2204 REM ******************************
2206 LET V = B
2208 FOR I = 1 TO K3
2210    LET V = V + Y(I)
2212 NEXT I
2214 IF V > R THEN 2299
2216 LET P = RND(0)
2218 FOR I = 1 TO K2
2220    IF P > L(I,2) THEN 2226
2222    LET L1 = L(I,1)
2224    LET I = K2
2226 NEXT I
2228 LET T1 = T1 + 1
2230 IF L1 > 0 THEN 2236
2232 LET B = B + Q
2234 GOTO 1299
2236 LET Y(L1) = Y(L1) + Q
2299 RETURN
2300 REM ******************************
2302 REM *     DISPLAY RESULT         *
2304 REM ******************************
2306 PRINT
2308 PRINT "RESULT OF SIMULATION"
2310 PRINT
2312 PRINT "DEMAND",T3+T4
2314 PRINT "UNITS SOLD",T4
2316 PRINT "UNITS LOST",T3
```

```
2318 PRINT "ORDERS",T1
2320 PRINT "AVERAGE INVENTORY LEVEL",T2/N2
2322 LET T5 = (N1 / N2) * C1 * T1
2324 LET T6 = C2 * T2 / N2
2326 LET T7 = (N1 / N2) * C3 * T3
2328 LET T = T5 + T6 + T7
2330 PRINT
2332 PRINT "COSTS ADJUSTED TO ANNUAL BASIS"
2334 PRINT
2336 PRINT "ORDERING",T5
2338 PRINT "HOLDING",T6
2340 PRINT "STOCKOUT",T7
2342 PRINT "TOTAL",T
2344 PRINT
2346 PRINT "TYPE THE VALUE 1 TO CONTINUE";
2348 INPUT U$
2399 RETURN
9999 END
```

PROGRAM 7-6

SIMULATE AN INVENTORY PROBLEM ON A
PERIOD BY PERIOD BASIS SUMMARIZING
AND NORMALIZING THE RESULTS ON AN
ANNUAL BASIS.   DEMAND AND LEAD TIMES
ARE PROBABILISTIC.

PROBABILITY DISTRIBUTION
FOR DEMAND PER PERIOD

NUMBER OF LEVELS OF DEMAND? 3

DEMAND, PROBABILITY FOR
STATE 1 ? 10,.3
STATE 2 ? 11,.5
STATE 3 ? 12,.2

EXPECTED DEMAND PER PERIOD   10.9

PROBABILITY DISTRIBUTION
FOR LEAD TIME

NUMBER OF DIFFERENT LEAD TIMES? 2

```
LEAD TIME, PROBABILITY FOR
STATE 1 ? 1,.8
STATE 2 ? 2,.2

EXPECTED LEAD TIME                    1.2

COST PER ORDER PLACED            ? 30
ANNUAL PER-UNIT HOLDING COST     ? 10
STOCKOUT COST PER UNIT           ? 20
NUMBER OF PERIODS PER YEAR       ? 52

ORDER QUANTITY                   ? 60
REORDER POINT                    ? 12
BEGINNING INVENTORY              ? 60
NUMBER OF PERIODS TO SIMULATE    ? 200

RESULT OF SIMULATION

DEMAND              2175
UNITS SOLD          2132
UNITS LOST          43
ORDERS              35
AVERAGE INVENTORY LEVEL          28.77

COSTS ADJUSTED TO ANNUAL BASIS

ORDERING            273
HOLDING             287.7
STOCKOUT            223.6
TOTAL               784.3

TYPE THE VALUE 1 TO CONTINUE? 1

MENU OF OPTIONS
    1    TRY ANOTHER SET OF DECISIONS
    2    TRY ANOTHER SET OF COSTS
    3    TRY ANOTHER SET OF PROBABILITIES
    4    TERMINATE

NUMBER OF DESIRED OPTION? 4

END OF PROGRAM
```

Fig. 7-6. Sample results from Program 7-6.

time, the introduction of fast yet inexpensive computers makes large scale use of computer simulation feasible.

Program 7-6 uses the period-by-period simulation approach for the same problem situation as the previous programs. Figure 7-6 shows the results.

Exercise 7-5

1. Use the period-by-period simulation to continue searching for the optimum reorder point and order quantity for the example in this section.

Chapter 8
Management Games

Management games are a special type of simulation that involve human interaction during the course of the simulation run. Management games may be educational, entertaining, or both.

A large percentage of the U.S. population is involved with industry and commerce. It is hardly surprising that some entertainment games model these endeavors. Management games of varying complexity are an important part of the educational process in many schools of business.

This chapter introduces the concept of gaming and illustrates the concept with several simple management games, which can be both entertaining and useful. When used in the context of traditional business courses, gaming cements theory and practice. Principles are seen in the light of practical decision making.

The popular management games used by business schools are complex models. One of their goals is to promote teamwork among the members of the management team. Each period of play involves many decisions concerning several product lines. Budgets and forecasts are required. Each

member of the team oversees one functional area of the firm. Teams compete in the same market place.

GAMES USING A SINGLE DECISION VARIABLE

All management games do not have to be complex. Simple games illustrate specific principles. The games in this chapter are simple in nature with few decision variables.

Newspaper Vendor

The simple game in Program 8-1 involves one or more newspaper vendors choosing the quantity of papers to sell. Figure 8-1 shows the results.

The Newsvendor program is not a competitive game since the decision of one player does not interact with that of the others. Even so, two or more players facing the same demand at the same time will develop a competitive spirit while searching for the optimum order quantity.

Hotdog Sales

The demand for hotdogs at a ballgame is influ-

Program 8-1

```
100 REM *******************************
102 REM *     8-1                       *
104 REM *******************************
106 REM    AUTHOR
108 REM        COPYRIGHT 1982
110 REM        BY LAWRENCE MCNITT.
112 REM    PURPOSE
114 REM        FORECASTING DEMAND
116 REM        FOR NEWSPAPER SALES.
118 REM    SYSTEM
120 REM        UNIVERSAL SUBSET
122 REM        OF BASIC.
200 REM *******************************
202 REM *     ORGANIZATION              *
204 REM *******************************
206 REM    900   MAIN ROUTINE
208 REM        1000    INITIAL MESSAGE
210 REM        1100    INITIALIZE
212 REM        1200    PLAY
214 REM                2000    GET ORDER QUANTITIES
216 REM                2100    EVALUATE RESULTS
218 REM        1300    SUMMARY
220 REM        1400    FINAL MESSAGE
300 REM *******************************
302 REM *     VARIABLES                 *
304 REM *******************************
306 REM    T(9)   UP TO NINE PLAYERS
307 REM    Q(9)   ORDER QUANTITIES
308 REM    U$    USER RESPONSE
310 REM    N     NUMBER OF PERIODS
312 REM    I     CURRENT PERIOD
314 REM    M     NUMBER OF PLAYERS
316 REM    J     CURRENT PLAYER
318 REM    D     DEMAND FOR PERIOD
320 REM    P     PROFIT
322 REM    C1    WHOLESALE COST PER PAPER
324 REM    C2    RETAIL COST PER PAPER
326 REM    S     PAPERS SOLD
900 REM *******************************
902 REM *     MAIN ROUTINE              *
904 REM *******************************
906 RANDOM
908 REM INITIAL MESSAGE
910 GOSUB 1006
```

```
914 REM INITIALIZE
916 GOSUB 1106
918 REM PLAY
920 GOSUB 1206
922 REM SUMMARY
924 GOSUB 1306
926 REM FINAL MESSAGE
928 GOSUB 1406
930 IF U$ = "Y" THEN 916
932 PRINT
934 PRINT "END OF PROGRAM"
999 STOP
1000 REM ****************************
1002 REM *    INITIAL MESSAGE      *
1004 REM ****************************
1006 PRINT
1008 PRINT
1010 PRINT
1012 PRINT "PROGRAM 8-1"
1014 PRINT
1016 PRINT "ONE OR MORE NEWSPAPER VENDORS"
1018 PRINT "CHOOSE THE NUMBER OF PAPERS TO"
1020 PRINT "MEET THEIR DAILY DEMAND FOR"
1022 PRINT "PAPERS. THE DEMAND VARIES FROM"
1024 PRINT "DAY TO DAY.  EACH VENDOR FACES"
1026 PRINT "THE SAME DEMAND."
1099 RETURN
1100 REM ****************************
1102 REM *    INITIALIZE            *
1104 REM ****************************
1106 LET C1 = .23
1108 LET C2 = .35
1110 PRINT
1112 PRINT "WHOLESALE COST PER PAPER";C1
1114 PRINT "RETAIL PRICE PER PAPER";C2
1116 PRINT "DAILY DEMAND VARIES BETWEEN"
1118 PRINT "100 AND 150. EACH ROUND OF"
1120 PRINT "PLAY COVERS FIVE DAYS."
1122 PRINT
1124 PRINT "HOW MANY ARE PLAYING";
1126 INPUT M
1128 IF M < 10 THEN 1134
1130 PRINT "CANNOT EXCEED 9"
1132 GOTO 1122
1134 FOR J = 1 TO M
1136    LET T(J) = 0
```

```
1138 NEXT J
1140 LET N = 5
1199 RETURN
1200 REM *******************************
1202 REM *    PLAY                     *
1204 REM *******************************
1206 FOR I = 1 TO N
1208    LET D = 100 + INT(51 * RND(0))
1210    PRINT
1212    PRINT "PERIOD",I
1214    REM GET ORDER QUANTITIES
1216    GOSUB 2006
1217    PRINT
1218    PRINT "DEMAND",D
1220    PRINT
1222    PRINT "PLAY/ORDERED","REVENUE","COST","PROFIT"
1224    REM EVALUATE RESULTS
1226    GOSUB 2106
1228 NEXT I
1299 RETURN
1300 REM *******************************
1302 REM *    SUMMARY                  *
1304 REM *******************************
1306 PRINT
1308 PRINT "SUMMARY FOR FIVE DAYS"
1310 PRINT
1312 PRINT "PLAYER","TOTAL PROFIT","AVERAGE PROFIT"
1314 FOR J = 1 TO M
1316    PRINT J,T(J),T(J)/N
1318 NEXT J
1399 RETURN
1400 REM *******************************
1402 REM *    FINAL MESSAGE            *
1404 REM *******************************
1406 PRINT
1408 PRINT "TRY ANOTHER ROUND (Y/N)";
1410 INPUT U$
1412 IF U$ = "Y" THEN 1499
1414 IF U$ = "N" THEN 1499
1416 PRINT
1418 PRINT "INVALID RESPONSE"
1420 GOTO 1406
1499 RETURN
2000 REM *******************************
2002 REM *    GET ORDER QUANTITIES     *
2004 REM *******************************
```

```
2006 PRINT
2008 PRINT "NUMBER OF PAPERS ORDERED BY"
2010 FOR J = 1 TO M
2012    PRINT "PLAYER";J;
2014    INPUT Q(J)
2016 NEXT J
2099 RETURN
2100 REM ******************************
2102 REM *    EVALUATE RESULTS        *
2104 REM ******************************
2106 FOR J = 1 TO M
2108    LET S = Q(J)
2110    IF D >= S THEN 2114
2112    LET S = D
2114    LET P = C2 * S - C1 * Q(J)
2116    LET T(J) = T(J) + P
2118    PRINT J;Q(J),C2*S,C1*Q(J),P
2120 NEXT J
2199 RETURN
9999 END
```

```
PROGRAM 8-1

ONE OR MORE NEWSPAPER VENDORS
CHOOSE THE NUMBER OF PAPERS TO
MEET THEIR DAILY DEMAND FOR
PAPERS. THE DEMAND VARIES FROM
DAY TO DAY. EACH VENDOR FACES
THE SAME DEMAND.

WHOLESALE COST PER PAPER .23
RETAIL PRICE PER PAPER .35
DAILY DEMAND VARIES BETWEEN
100 AND 150. EACH ROUND OF
PLAY COVERS FIVE DAYS.

HOW MANY ARE PLAYING? 2

PERIOD             1

NUMBER OF PAPERS ORDERED BY
PLAYER 1 ? 110
PLAYER 2 ? 130

DEMAND             147
```

PLAY/ORDERED	REVENUE	COST	PROFIT
1 110	38.5	25.3	13.2
2 130	45.5	29.9	15.6

PERIOD   2

NUMBER OF PAPERS ORDERED BY
PLAYER 1 ? 120
PLAYER 2 ? 140

DEMAND   130

PLAY/ORDERED	REVENUE	COST	PROFIT
1 120	42	27.6	14.4
2 140	45.5	32.2	13.3

PERIOD   3

NUMBER OF PAPERS ORDERED BY
PLAYER 1 ? 120
PLAYER 2 ? 130

DEMAND   122

PLAY/ORDERED	REVENUE	COST	PROFIT
1 120	42	27.6	14.4
2 130	42.7	29.9	12.8

PERIOD   4

NUMBER OF PAPERS ORDERED BY
PLAYER 1 ? 120
PLAYER 2 ? 120

DEMAND   118

PLAY/ORDERED	REVENUE	COST	PROFIT
1 120	41.3	27.6	13.7
2 120	41.3	27.6	13.7

PERIOD   5

NUMBER OF PAPERS ORDERED BY
PLAYER 1 ? 110
PLAYER 2 ? 120

```
DEMAND                114

PLAY/ORDERED      REVENUE          COST            PROFIT
  1   110           38.5           25.3            13.2
  2   120           39.9           27.6            12.3

SUMMARY FOR FIVE DAYS

PLAYER              TOTAL PROFIT    AVERAGE PROFIT
  1                    68.9           13.78
  2                    67.7           13.54

TRY ANOTHER ROUND (Y/N)? N

END OF PROGRAM
```

Fig. 8-1. Sample results from Program 8-1.

enced by the weather. The weather service makes probabilistic forecasts. There is an optimum order quantity for fair weather and another optimum order quantity for rainy weather. The probabilistic weather forecast adds enough unpredictability to the model to assure that the optimum order will vary from day to day according to the weather forecast.

Program 8-3 includes the probabilistic weather forecast. Figure 8-2 shows the results.

Program 8-2

```
100 REM ********************************
102 REM *    8-2                       *
104 REM ********************************
106 REM   AUTHOR
108 REM        COPYRIGHT 1982
110 REM        BY LAWRENCE MCNITT.
112 REM   PURPOSE
114 REM        WEATHER FORECAST
116 REM        AND HOTDOG SALES.
118 REM   SYSTEM
120 REM        UNIVERSAL SUBSET
122 REM        OF BASIC.
200 REM ********************************
202 REM *    ORGANIZATION              *
204 REM ********************************
206 REM   900   MAIN ROUTINE
208 REM         1000   INITIAL MESSAGE
210 REM         1100   INITIALIZE
212 REM         1200   PLAY
214 REM              2000   GET ORDER QUANTITIES
```

```
216 REM                 2100    EVALUATE RESULTS
218 REM            1300    SUMMARY
220 REM            1400    FINAL MESSAGE
300 REM **********************************
302 REM *    VARIABLES                    *
304 REM **********************************
306 REM   T(9)   UP TO NINE PLAYERS
307 REM   Q(9)   ORDER QUANTITIES
308 REM   U$   USER RESPONSE
310 REM   N    NUMBER OF PERIODS
312 REM   I    CURRENT PERIOD
314 REM   M    NUMBER OF PLAYERS
316 REM   J    CURRENT PLAYER
318 REM   D    DEMAND FOR PERIOD
320 REM   P    PROFIT
322 REM   C1   WHOLESALE COST PER HOTDOG
324 REM   C2   RETAIL COST PER HOTDOG
326 REM   C3   REFUND PRICE FOR RETURNED HOTDOGS
328 REM   C4   DAILY CONCESSION COST
330 REM   W    PROBABILITY OF RAIN
332 REM   S    HOTDOGS SOLD
334 REM   R    REVENUE
336 REM   C    TOTAL COST
900 REM **********************************
902 REM *    MAIN ROUTINE                 *
904 REM **********************************
906 RANDOM
908 REM INITIAL MESSAGE
910 GOSUB 1006
914 REM INITIALIZE
916 GOSUB 1106
918 REM PLAY
920 GOSUB 1206
922 REM SUMMARY
924 GOSUB 1306
926 REM FINAL MESSAGE
928 GOSUB 1406
930 IF U$ = "Y" THEN 916
932 PRINT
934 PRINT "END OF PROGRAM"
999 STOP
1000 REM **********************************
1002 REM *    INITIAL MESSAGE              *
1004 REM **********************************
1006 PRINT
1008 PRINT
```

```
1010 PRINT
1012 PRINT "PROGRAM 8 - 2"
1014 PRINT
1016 PRINT "ONE OR MORE HOTDOG VENDORS"
1018 PRINT "CHOOSE THE NUMBER OF HOTDOGS TO"
1020 PRINT "MEET THEIR DEMAND. DEMAND IS"
1022 PRINT "STRONGLY AFFECTED BY BAD WEATHER."
1024 PRINT "THE WEATHER FORECAST IS GIVEN"
1026 PRINT "BEFORE ORDERING FOR THE NEXT DAY."
1028 PRINT
1030 PRINT "TYPE THE VALUE 1 TO CONTINUE";
1032 INPUT U$
1099 RETURN
1100 REM ******************************
1102 REM *    INITIALIZE              *
1104 REM ******************************
1106 LET C1 = .35
1108 LET C2 = .75
1110 LET C3 = .15
1112 LET C4 = 40
1114 PRINT
1116 PRINT "ON RAINY DAYS DEMAND VARIES BETWEEN"
1118 PRINT "100 AND 200 HOTDOGS. OTHERWISE IT"
1120 PRINT "VARIES BETWEEN 175 AND 275 HOTDOGS."
1122 PRINT
1124 PRINT "COST FIGURES"
1126 PRINT "DAILY COST OF CONCESSION",C4
1128 PRINT "WHOLESALE COST PER HOTDOG",C1
1130 PRINT "RETAIL PRICE PER HOTDOG",C2
1132 PRINT "REFUND FOR EACH DOG RETURNED",C3
1134 PRINT
1136 PRINT "EACH ROUND OF PLAY COVERS 5 DAYS"
1138 PRINT
1140 PRINT "HOW MANY ARE PLAYING";
1142 INPUT M
1144 IF M < 10 THEN 1150
1146 PRINT "CANNOT EXCEED 9"
1148 GOTO 1138
1150 FOR J = 1 TO M
1152    LET T(J) = 0
1154 NEXT J
1156 LET N = 5
1199 RETURN
1200 REM ******************************
1202 REM *    PLAY                    *
1204 REM ******************************
```

```
1206 FOR I = 1 TO N
1208    LET W = .1 * INT(10 * RND(0))
1210    PRINT
1212    PRINT "PERIOD",I
1214    PRINT "PROBABILITY OF RAIN IS";100*W;"PER CENT"
1216    REM GET ORDER QUANTITIES
1217    PRINT
1218    GOSUB 2006
1222    PRINT
1224    IF RND(0) < W THEN 1232
1226    PRINT "WEATHER IS GOOD"
1228    LET D = 175 + INT(100 * RND(0))
1230    GOTO 1236
1232    PRINT "WEATHER IS RAINY"
1234    LET D = 100 + INT(100 * RND(0))
1236    PRINT "DEMAND IS";D;"HOTDOGS PER VENDOR"
1238    PRINT
1240    PRINT "PLAYER/ORDER","REVENUE","COST","PROFIT"
1242    REM EVALUATE RESULTS
1244    GOSUB 2106
1246 NEXT I
1299 RETURN
1300 REM *****************************
1302 REM *    SUMMARY                *
1304 REM *****************************
1306 PRINT
1308 PRINT "SUMMARY FOR FIVE DAYS"
1310 PRINT
1312 PRINT "PLAYER","TOTAL PROFIT","AVERAGE PROFIT"
1314 FOR J = 1 TO M
1316    PRINT J,T(J),T(J)/N
1318 NEXT J
1399 RETURN
1400 REM *****************************
1402 REM *    FINAL MESSAGE          *
1404 REM *****************************
1406 PRINT
1408 PRINT "TRY ANOTHER ROUND (Y/N)";
1410 INPUT U$
1412 IF U$ = "Y" THEN 1499
1414 IF U$ = "N" THEN 1499
1416 PRINT
1418 PRINT "INVALID RESPONSE"
1420 GOTO 1406
1499 RETURN
2000 REM *****************************
```

```
2002 REM *    GET ORDER QUANTITIES    *
2004 REM *******************************
2006 PRINT
2008 PRINT "NUMBER OF HOTDOGS ORDERED BY"
2010 FOR J = 1 TO M
2012    PRINT "PLAYER";J;
2014    INPUT Q(J)
2016 NEXT J
2099 RETURN
2100 REM *******************************
2102 REM *    EVALUATE RESULTS         *
2104 REM *******************************
2106 FOR J = 1 TO M
2108    LET S = Q(J)
2110    IF D >= S THEN 2114
2112    LET S = D
2114    LET R = C2 * S
2116    LET C = C4 + C1 * Q(J)
2118    IF D >= Q(J) THEN 2122
2120    LET C = C - C3 * (Q(J) - D)
2122    LET P = R - C
2124    LET T(J) = T(J) + P
2126    PRINT J;Q(J),R,C,P
2128 NEXT J
2199 RETURN
9999 END
```

PROGRAM 8-2

ONE OR MORE HOTDOG VENDORS
CHOOSE THE NUMBER OF HOTDOGS TO
MEET THEIR DEMAND. DEMAND IS
STRONGLY AFFECTED BY BAD WEATHER.
THE WEATHER FORECAST IS GIVEN
BEFORE ORDERING FOR THE NEXT DAY.

TYPE THE VALUE 1 TO CONTINUE? 1

ON RAINY DAYS DEMAND VARIES BETWEEN
100 AND 200 HOTDOGS. OTHERWISE IT
VARIES BETWEEN 175 AND 275 HOTDOGS.

COST FIGURES
DAILY COST OF CONCESSION   40
WHOLESALE COST PER HOTDOG   .35

```
RETAIL PRICE PER HOTDOG          .75
REFUND FOR EACH DOG RETURNED      .15

EACH ROUND OF PLAY COVERS FIVE DAYS

HOW MANY ARE PLAYING? 2

PERIOD               1
PROBABILITY OF RAIN IS 30 PER CENT

NUMBER OF HOTDOGS ORDERED BY
PLAYER 1 ? 180
PLAYER 2 ? 230

WEATHER IS GOOD
DEMAND IS 221 HOTDOGS PER VENDOR

PLAYER/ORDER      REVENUE           COST            PROFIT
  1    180         135              103             32
  2    230         165.75           119.15          46.6
  .
  .
  .
PERIOD               5
PROBABILITY OF RAIN IS 80 PER CENT

NUMBER OF HOTDOGS ORDERED BY
PLAYER 1 ? 150
PLAYER 2 ? 170

WEATHER IS RAINY
DEMAND IS 177 HOTDOGS PER VENDOR
PLAYER/ORDER      REVENUE           COST            PROFIT
  1    150         112.5            92.5            20
  2    170         127.5            99.5            28

SUMMARY FOR FIVE DAYS

PLAYER            TOTAL PROFIT    AVERAGE PROFIT
  1                119.2           23.84
  2                135.8           27.16
TRY ANOTHER ROUND (Y/N)? N

END OF PROGRAM
```

Fig. 8-2. Sample results fro Program 8-2.

Exercise 8-1

1. Design a management game similar to the ones in this section having only one decision variable. They can involve decisions other than the order quantity.

GAMES USING MULTIPLE DECISION VARIABLES

The simplest games involve one decision variable. Adding decision variables increases the complexity of the game. If the decision variables are highly interactive, careful analysis is necessary.

Interactive games involve one or more players playing the game at the computer in an interactive manner. They typically simulate several periods in one session. Although interaction is desirable when possible, this rapid interaction is not possible with the more complex games having many decision variables.

Many retailers set prices for their products as well as order quantity. Price and quantity are highly interrelated for most products. Higher prices result in lower demand for the product. Lower prices tend to increase demand. If the demand function remains stable, the decision problem becomes one of finding the best combination of order quantity and price.

Doughnut Sales

Program 8-3 is a management game program that has the two decision variables price and quantity. Figure 8-3 shows the results.

Program 8-3

```
100 REM ******************************
102 REM *    8-3                      *
104 REM ******************************
106 REM   AUTHOR
108 REM       COPYRIGHT 1982
110 REM       BY LAWRENCE MCNITT.
112 REM   PURPOSE
114 REM       SET ORDER QUANTITY AND PRICE
116 REM       FOR DOUGHNUT SALES.
118 REM   SYSTEM
120 REM       UNIVERSAL SUBSET
122 REM       OF BASIC.
200 REM ******************************
202 REM *    ORGANIZATION             *
204 REM ******************************
206 REM   900   MAIN ROUTINE
208 REM         1000   INITIAL MESSAGE
210 REM         1100   INITIALIZE
212 REM         1200   PLAY
214 REM               2000   QUANTITIES AND PRICES
216 REM               2100   EVALUATE RESULTS
218 REM         1300   SUMMARY
220 REM         1400   FINAL MESSAGE
300 REM ******************************
302 REM *    VARIABLES                *
304 REM ******************************
305 REM   P(9)   PRICES
306 REM   Q(9)   ORDER QUANTITIES
```

```
307 REM   T(9)   TOTAL PROFITS
308 REM   U$    USER RESPONSE
310 REM   N     NUMBER OF PERIODS
312 REM   I     CURRENT PERIOD
314 REM   M     NUMBER OF PLAYERS
316 REM   J     CURRENT PLAYER
318 REM   D     DEMAND FOR PERIOD
320 REM   G     GROSS PROFIT
322 REM   R     REVENUES
324 REM   E     TOTAL COST
326 REM   S     DOUGHNUTS SOLD
328 REM   C1    WHOLESALE COST PER FRESH DOUGHNUT
330 REM   C2    BUY BACK PRICE OF UNSOLD DOUGHNUTS
900 REM *******************************
902 REM *    MAIN ROUTINE             *
904 REM *******************************
906 RANDOM
908 REM INITIAL MESSAGE
910 GOSUB 1006
914 REM INITIALIZE
916 GOSUB 1106
918 REM PLAY
920 GOSUB 1206
922 REM SUMMARY
924 GOSUB 1306
926 REM FINAL MESSAGE
928 GOSUB 1406
930 IF U$ = "Y" THEN 916
932 PRINT
934 PRINT "END OF PROGRAM"
999 STOP
1000 REM *******************************
1002 REM *    INITIAL MESSAGE          *
1004 REM *******************************
1006 PRINT
1008 PRINT
1010 PRINT
1012 PRINT "PROGRAM 8-3"
1014 PRINT
1016 PRINT "ONE OR MORE DOUGHNUT VENDORS"
1018 PRINT "SET RETAIL PRICES AND ORDER"
1020 PRINT "QUANTITIES FOR THEIR DOUGHNUTS."
1022 PRINT "THE DEMAND VARIES RANDOMLY, BUT IS"
1024 PRINT "STRONGLY AFFECTED BY PRICE. WHAT"
1026 PRINT "ORDER QUANTITY AND PRICE IS BEST?"
1028 PRINT
```

```
1030 PRINT "TYPE THE VALUE 1 TO CONTINUE";
1032 INPUT U$
1099 RETURN
1100 REM ******************************
1102 REM *    INITIALIZE              *
1104 REM ******************************
1106 LET C1 = .05
1108 LET C2 = .02
1110 PRINT
1112 PRINT "YOU ARE A VENDOR SELLING DOUGHNUTS."
1114 PRINT "EACH PERIOD YOU MUST SELECT A SELLING PRICE"
1116 PRINT "DOUGHNUTS COST $.05 EACH AND UNSOLD"
1118 PRINT "DOUGHNUTS ARE RETURNED FOR $.02 EACH.   DEMAND"
1120 PRINT "WILL AVERAGE 1,000 DOUGHNUTS AT A SELLING
PRICE"
1122 PRINT "OF $.20. A SUMMARY IS GIVEN AFTER 5 PERIODS."
1124 PRINT
1126 PRINT "HOW MANY ARE PLAYING";
1128 INPUT M
1130 IF M < 10 THEN 1136
1132 PRINT "CANNOT EXCEED 9"
1134 GOTO 1124
1136 FOR J = 1 TO M
1138    LET T(J) = 0
1140 NEXT J
1142 LET N = 5
1199 RETURN
1200 REM ******************************
1202 REM *    PLAY                    *
1204 REM ******************************
1206 FOR I = 1 TO N
1208    REM QUANTITIES AND PRICES
1210    GOSUB 2006
1212    PRINT
1214    PRINT "PLAYER/SOLD","REVENUE","COST","PROFIT"
1216    REM EVALUATE RESULTS
1217    PRINT
1218    GOSUB 2106
1220 NEXT I
1299 RETURN
1300 REM ******************************
1302 REM *    SUMMARY                 *
1304 REM ******************************
1306 PRINT
1308 PRINT "SUMMARY FOR FIVE DAYS"
1310 PRINT
```

```
1312 PRINT "PLAYER","TOTAL PROFIT","AVERAGE PROFIT"
1314 FOR J = 1 TO M
1316     PRINT J,T(J),T(J)/N
1318 NEXT J
1399 RETURN
1400 REM *****************************
1402 REM *    FINAL MESSAGE           *
1404 REM *****************************
1406 PRINT
1408 PRINT "TRY ANOTHER ROUND (Y/N)";
1410 INPUT U$
1412 IF U$ = "Y" THEN 1499
1414 IF U$ = "N" THEN 1499
1416 PRINT
1418 PRINT "INVALID RESPONSE"
1420 GOTO 1406
1499 RETURN
2000 REM *****************************
2002 REM *    QUANTITIES AND PRICES   *
2004 REM *****************************
2006 PRINT
2008 PRINT "PERIOD",I
2010 FOR J = 1 TO M
2012     PRINT
2014     PRINT "PLAYER";J
2016     PRINT "SELLING PRICE";
2018     INPUT P(J)
2020     PRINT "ORDER QUANTITY";
2022     INPUT Q(J)
2024 NEXT J
2099 RETURN
2100 REM *****************************
2102 REM *    EVALUATE RESULTS        *
2104 REM *****************************
2106 FOR J = 1 TO M
2108     IF P(J) < 1 THEN 2114
2110     LET D = 0
2112     GOTO 2120
2114     LET D = 1000 / (5 * P(J)) [ 2
2116     LET D = D * (.9 + .2 * RND(0))
2118     LET D = INT(D)
2120     LET S = D
2122     IF D <= Q(J) THEN 2126
2124     LET S = Q(J)
2126     LET R = P(J) * S
2128     IF S >= Q(J) THEN 2132
```

```
2130    LET R = R + (Q(J) - S) * C2
2132    LET E = C1 * Q(J)
2134    LET G = R - E
2136    PRINT J;S,R,E,G
2138    LET T(J) = T(J) + G
2140 NEXT J
2199 RETURN
9999 END
```

```
PROGRAM 8-3

ONE OR MORE DOUGHNUT VENDORS
SET RETAIL PRICES AND ORDER
QUANTITIES FOR THEIR DOUGHNUTS.
THE DEMAND VARIES RANDOMLY, BUT IS
STRONGLY AFFECTED BY PRICE. WHAT
ORDER QUANTITY AND PRICE IS BEST?

TYPE THE VALUE 1 TO CONTINUE? 1

YOU ARE A VENDOR SELLING DOUGHNUTS.

EACH PERIOD YOU MUST SELECT A SELLING PRICE.
DOUGHNUTS COST $.05 EACH AND UNSOLD
DOUGHNUTS ARE RETURNED FOR $.02 EACH. DEMAND
WILL AVERAGE 1,000 DOUGHNUTS AT A SELLING PRICE
OF $.20. A SUMMARY IS GIVEN AFTER FIVE PERIODS.

HOW MANY ARE PLAYING? 2

PERIOD               1

PLAYER 1
SELLING PRICE? .18
ORDER QUANTITY? 1300

PLAYER 2
SELLING PRICE? .21
ORDER QUANTITY? 1000

PLAYER/SOLD        REVENUE        COST         PROFIT
   1  1265          228.4          65           163.4
   2   857          182.83         50           132.83
```

```
    .
    .
    .

PERIOD              5

PLAYER 1
SELLING PRICE? .15
ORDER QUANTITY? 2000

PLAYER 2
SELLING PRICE? .18
ORDER QUANTITY? 1400

PLAYER/SOLD        REVENUE        COST           PROFIT
  1   1884         284.92         100            184.92
  2   1138         210.08          70            140.08

SUMMARY FOR FIVE DAYS

PLAYER             TOTAL PROFIT   AVERAGE PROFIT
  1                828.16         165.632
  2                676.57         135.314

TRY ANOTHER ROUND (Y/N)? N

END OF PROGRAM
```

Fig. 8-3. Sample results from Program 8-3.

Pie Shop

Including a third decision variable adds even more to the complexity of the game. Consider a retailer selling pies. The price influences the quantity demanded. The quantity is also related to advertising. Increasing the level of advertising will tend to increase demand. Demand is thus related to both price and advertising. The problem now becomes one of finding the best combination among the three decision variables of price, advertising, and quantity.

Program 8-4 employs the three decision variables. Figure 8-4 shows the results.

Exercise 8-2

1. Design a simple game having two or three decision variables.

COMPETITIVE GAMES

Competition is an effective motivator since many people possess a competitive spirit. The previous games involved no direct interaction among the players because the decisions made by one player had no direct effect on the outcomes experienced by the others. All players faced the same problem situation and experienced the same probabilistic outcomes.

Even though there was no direct interaction among the outcomes experienced by the players, those playing the games will compare their respective performances. Competition among the players will naturally arise.

Simulated enterprises may be in competition for the same market. A lower price by one player

Program 8-4

```
100 REM **********************************
102 REM *     8-4                        *
104 REM **********************************
106 REM    AUTHOR
108 REM        COPYRIGHT 1982
110 REM        BY LAWRENCE MCNITT.
112 REM    PURPOSE
114 REM        SET ORDER QUANTITY, PRICE, AND
116 REM        ADVERTISING FOR PIE SHOP.
118 REM    SYSTEM
120 REM        UNIVERSAL SUBSET
122 REM        OF BASIC.
200 REM **********************************
202 REM *    ORGANIZATION                *
204 REM **********************************
206 REM    900   MAIN ROUTINE
208 REM         1000    INITIAL MESSAGE
210 REM         1100    INITIALIZE
212 REM         1200    PLAY
214 REM                 2000   GET DECISIONS
216 REM                 2100   EVALUATE RESULTS
218 REM         1300    SUMMARY
220 REM         1400    FINAL MESSAGE
300 REM **********************************
302 REM *    VARIABLES                   *
304 REM **********************************
306 REM    P(9)   PRICES
308 REM    Q(9)   ORDER QUANTITIES
310 REM    A(9)   ADVERTISING
312 REM    T(9)   TOTAL PROFITS
314 REM    U$     USER RESPONSE
316 REM    N      NUMBER OF PERIODS
318 REM    I      CURRENT PERIOD
320 REM    M      NUMBER OF PLAYERS
322 REM    J      CURRENT PLAYER
324 REM    D      DEMAND FOR PERIOD
326 REM    R      REVENUE
328 REM    C      COST
330 REM    G      GROSS PROFIT
332 REM    S      UNITS SOLD
334 REM    C1     WHOLESALE COST PER PIE
336 REM    C2     RETURN PRICE PER PIE UNSOLD
338 REM    C3     OVERHEAD COST PER DAY
900 REM **********************************
```

```
902 REM *    MAIN ROUTINE              *
904 REM ******************************
906 RANDOM
908 REM INITIAL MESSAGE
910 GOSUB 1006
914 REM INITIALIZE
916 GOSUB 1106
918 REM PLAY
920 GOSUB 1206
922 REM SUMMARY
924 GOSUB 1306
926 REM FINAL MESSAGE
928 GOSUB 1406
930 IF U$ = "Y" THEN 916
932 PRINT
934 PRINT "END OF PROGRAM"
999 STOP
1000 REM ******************************
1002 REM *    INITIAL MESSAGE         *
1004 REM ******************************
1006 PRINT
1008 PRINT
1010 PRINT
1012 PRINT "PROGRAM 8-4"
1014 PRINT
1016 PRINT "ONE OR MORE PIE SHOPS SET REAIL PRICES,"
1018 PRINT "ADVERTISING, AND ORDER QUANTITIES."
1020 PRINT "THE DEMAND VARIES BUT IS AFFECTED BY"
1022 PRINT "ADVERTISING AND PRICE PER PIE."
1024 PRINT "TRY TO FIND THE BEST COMBINATION OF"
1026 PRINT "QUANTITY, PRICE, AND ADVERTISING."
1028 PRINT
1030 PRINT "TYPE THE VALUE 1 TO CONTINUE";
1032 INPUT U$
1099 RETURN
1100 REM ******************************
1102 REM *    INITIALIZE              *
1104 REM ******************************
1106 LET C1 = 1.75
1108 LET C2 = .75
1110 LET C3 = 100
1112 PRINT
1114 PRINT "YOU ARE MANAGING A PIE SHOP.  EACH PERIOD"
1116 PRINT "YOU MUST SELECT AN ADVERTISING LEVEL,"
1118 PRINT "A SELLING PRICE, AND AN ORDER QUANTITY."
1120 PRINT "DEMAND AVERAGES 150 PIES PER DAY AT"
```

```
1122 PRINT "A SELLING PRICE OF $3.00 PER PIE AND"
1124 PRINT "NO ADVERTISING."
1126 PRINT
1128 PRINT "PRODUCTION COST PER PIE",C1
1130 PRINT "REVENUE FROM DAY-OLD PIE",C2
1132 PRINT "OPERATING COST PER DAY",C3
1134 PRINT
1136 PRINT "EACH ROUND CONSISTS OF FIVE DAYS"
1138 PRINT
1140 PRINT "HOW MANY ARE PLAYING";
1142 INPUT M
1144 IF M < 10 THEN 1150
1146 PRINT "CANNOT EXCEED 9"
1148 GOTO 1138
1150 FOR J = 1 TO M
1152    LET T(J) = 0
1154 NEXT J
1156 LET N = 5
1199 RETURN
1200 REM ****************************
1202 REM *    PLAY                  *
1204 REM ****************************
1206 FOR I = 1 TO N
1208    REM GET DECISIONS
1210    GOSUB 2006
1212    PRINT
1214    PRINT "PLAYER/SOLD","REVENUE","COST","PROFIT"
1216    REM EVALUATE RESULTS
1217    PRINT
1218    GOSUB 2106
1220 NEXT I
1299 RETURN
1300 REM ****************************
1302 REM *    SUMMARY               *
1304 REM ****************************
1306 PRINT
1308 PRINT "SUMMARY FOR FIVE DAYS"
1310 PRINT
1312 PRINT "PLAYER","TOTAL PROFIT","AVERAGE PROFIT"
1314 FOR J = 1 TO M
1316    PRINT J,T(J),T(J)/N
1318 NEXT J
1399 RETURN
1400 REM ****************************
1402 REM *    FINAL MESSAGE         *
1404 REM ****************************
```

```
1406 PRINT
1408 PRINT "TRY ANOTHER ROUND (Y/N)";
1410 INPUT U$
1412 IF U$ = "Y" THEN 1499
1414 IF U$ = "N" THEN 1499
1416 PRINT
1418 PRINT "INVALID RESPONSE"
1420 GOTO 1406
1499 RETURN
2000 REM *****************************
2002 REM *    GET DECISIONS           *
2004 REM *****************************
2006 PRINT
2008 PRINT "PERIOD",I
2010 FOR J = 1 TO M
2012    PRINT
2014    PRINT "PLAYER";J
2016    PRINT "SELLING PRICE";
2018    INPUT P(J)
2020    PRINT "ORDER QUANTITY";
2022    INPUT Q(J)
2024    PRINT "ADVERTISING";
2026    INPUT A(J)
2028 NEXT J
2099 RETURN
2100 REM *****************************
2102 REM *    EVALUATE RESULTS        *
2104 REM *****************************
2106 FOR J = 1 TO M
2108    IF P(J) < 20 THEN 2114
2110    LET D = 0
2112    GOTO 2120
2114    LET D = 150 * (1 + A(J)) [ .2 / (P(J) / 3) [ 2
2116    LET D = D * (.9 + .2 * RND(0))
2118    LET D = INT(D)
2120    LET S = D
2122    IF D <= Q(J) THEN 2126
2124    LET S = Q(J)
2126    LET R = P(J) * S
2128    IF S >= Q(J) THEN 2132
2130    LET R = R + (Q(J) - S) * C2
2132    LET C = C3 + A(J) + C1 * Q(J)
2134    LET G = R - C
2136    PRINT J;S,R,C,G
2138    LET T(J) = T(J) + G
```

```
2140 NEXT J
2199 RETURN
9999 END
```

PROGRAM 8-4

ONE OR MORE PIE SHOPS SET RETAIL PRICES,
ADVERTISING, AND ORDER QUANTITIES.
THE DEMAND VARIES BUT IS AFFECTED BY
ADVERTISING AND PRICE PER PIE.
TRY TO FIND THE BEST COMBINATION OF
QUANTITY, PRICE, AND ADVERTISING.

TYPE THE VALUE 1 TO CONTINUE? 1

YOU ARE MANAGING A PIE SHOP. EACH PERIOD
YOU MUST SELECT AN ADVERTISING LEVEL,
A SELLING PRICE, AND AN ORDER QUANTITY.
DEMAND AVERAGES 150 PIES PER DAY AT
A SELLING PRICE OF $3.00 PER PIE AND
NO ADVERTISING.

PRODUCTION COST PER PIE   1.75
REVENUE FROM DAY-OLD PIE   .75
OPERATING COST PER DAY   100

EACH ROUND CONSISTS OF FIVE DAYS

HOW MANY ARE PLAYING? 2

PERIOD   1

PLAYER 1
SELLING PRICE? 3
ORDER QUANTITY? 350
ADVERTSING? 50

PLAYER 2
SELLING PRICE? 5
ORDER QUANTITY? 150
ADVERTISING? 100

PLAYER/SOLD	REVENUE	COST	PROFIT
1 342	1032	762.5	269.5
2 147	737.25	462.5	274.75

```
             .
             .
             .
SUMMARY FOR FIVE DAYS

PLAYER            TOTAL PROFIT    AVERAGE PROFIT
  1                  917.5           183.5
  2                 1000.5           200.1

TRY ANOTHER ROUND (Y/N)? N

END OF PROGRAM
```

Fig. 8-4. Sample results from Program 8-4.

will attract customers away from the other players. Total industry demand will vary according to the average industry price. Price wars can break out resulting in less than optimum profit levels for all players concerned.

Some years ago filling stations within a small geographic region would become embroiled in price wars. In some cases the price per gallon of gas would drop below the wholesale cost per gallon. The game of this section is taken from the context of the price wars among filling stations.

Gas Price Wars

Program 8-5 illustrates a competitive game using the price wars of the gasoline industry. Figure 8-5 shows the results.

Program 8-5

```
100 REM ********************************
102 REM *    8-5                       *
104 REM ********************************
106 REM   AUTHOR
108 REM       COPYRIGHT 1982
110 REM       BY LAWRENCE MCNITT.
112 REM   PURPOSE
114 REM       GASOLINE SALES
116 REM       COMPETITIVE GAME.
118 REM   SYSTEM
120 REM       UNIVERSAL SUBSET
122 REM       OF BASIC.
200 REM ********************************
202 REM *    ORGANIZATION              *
204 REM ********************************
206 REM   900   MAIN ROUTINE
208 REM         1000   INITIAL MESSAGE
210 REM         1100   INITIALIZE
212 REM         1200   PLAY
```

```
214 REM                 2000    SET PRICES
216 REM                 2100    ALLOCATE DEMAND
218 REM                 2200    EVALUATE RESULTS
220 REM         1300    SUMMARY
222 REM         1400    FINAL MESSAGE
300 REM *****************************
302 REM *    VARIABLES                 *
304 REM *****************************
306 REM  F(9)   REMAINING FUEL
308 REM  P(9)   SELLING PRICE PER GALLON
310 REM  D(9)   DEMAND FOR DAY IN GALLONS
312 REM  S(9)   SALES FOR DAY IN GALLONS
314 REM  T(9)   TOTAL PROFIT
315 REM  W(9)   WEIGHTS FOR ALLOCATING DEMAND
316 REM  N     NUMBER OF PERIODS IN ROUND
318 REM  I     CURRENT PERIOD
320 REM  M     NUMBER OF STATIONS
322 REM  J     CURRENT STATION
324 REM  F1    MAXIMUM FUEL TANK SIZE TO LAST FOR ROUND
326 REM  D1    BASE DEMAND PER DAY AT TYPICAL RETAIL PRICE
328 REM  P1    TYPICAL RETAIL SELLING PRICE PER GALLON
330 REM  P2    WHOLESALE PRICE PER GALLON
332 REM  C1    OVERHEAD COST PER DAY IF CLOSED
334 REM  C2    ADDITIONAL OPERATING COST IF OPEN
336 REM  R     REVENUE FOR THE DAY
338 REM  E     TOTAL EXPENSES FOR THE DAY
340 REM  A     AVERAGE RETAIL PRICE FOR THE PERIOD
342 REM  Z1    TOTAL DEMAND TO ALLOCATE
344 REM  Z2    SUM OF WEIGHTS FOR ALLOCATION
346 REM  U$    USER RESPONSE
900 REM *****************************
902 REM *    MAIN ROUTINE              *
904 REM *****************************
906 RANDOM
908 REM INITIAL MESSAGE
910 GOSUB 1006
914 REM INITIALIZE
916 GOSUB 1106
918 REM PLAY
920 GOSUB 1206
922 REM SUMMARY
924 GOSUB 1306
926 REM FINAL MESSAGE
928 GOSUB 1406
930 IF U$ = "Y" THEN 916
932 PRINT
```

```
934 PRINT "END OF PROGRAM"
999 STOP
1000 REM *****************************
1002 REM *     INITIAL MESSAGE       *
1004 REM *****************************
1006 PRINT
1008 PRINT
1010 PRINT
1012 PRINT "PROGRAM 8-5"
1014 PRINT
1016 PRINT "TWO OR MORE GAS STATIONS COMPETE"
1018 PRINT "FOR GASOLINE SALES IN A HIGHLY"
1020 PRINT "COMPETITIVE AREA IN WHICH CUSTOMERS"
1022 PRINT "ARE VERY SENSITIVE TO RELATIVE"
1024 PRINT "PRICE. FOR EACH DAY YOU CHOOSE WHETHER"
1026 PRINT "TO STAY OPEN AND SET THE PRICE PER"
1028 PRINT "GALLON IF OPEN."
1030 PRINT
1032 PRINT "TYPE THE VALUE 1 TO CONTINUE";
1034 INPUT U$
1099 RETURN
1100 REM ******************************
1102 REM *     INITIALIZE              *
1104 REM ******************************
1106 LET P1 = 1.35
1108 LET P2 = 1.09
1110 LET N = 5
1112 LET C1 = 50
1114 LET C2 = 150
1116 LET F1 = 7500
1118 LET D1 = 1200
1119 PRINT
1120 PRINT "EACH DAY YOU MAY DECIDE WHETHER TO"
1122 PRINT "OPEN FOR BUSINESS. TOTAL DAILY"
1124 PRINT "DEMAND DEPENDS ON AVERAGE PRICE."
1126 PRINT "AVERAGE DAILY DEMAND PER STATION IF"
1128 PRINT "ALL STATIONS CHARGE";P1;"PER GALLON     ";D1
1130 PRINT "WHOLESALE COST PER GALLON OF GAS            ";P2
1132 PRINT "OVERHEAD COST PER DAY EVEN IF CLOSED    ";C1
1134 PRINT "ADDITIONAL COST PER DAY IF OPEN         ";C2
1136 PRINT "FUEL TANK CAPACITY IN GALLONS           ";F1
1138 PRINT
1140 PRINT "NUMBER OF STATIONS";
1142 INPUT M
1144 FOR J = 1 TO M
1146     LET T(J) = 0
```

```
1148    LET F(J) = F1
1150 NEXT J
1199 RETURN
1200 REM ****************************
1202 REM *    PLAY                  *
1204 REM ****************************
1206 FOR I = 1 TO N
1208    REM SET PRICES
1210    GOSUB 2006
1216    REM ALLOCATE DEMAND
1217    PRINT
1218    GOSUB 2106
1220    REM EVALUATE RESULTS
1222    GOSUB 2206
1224 NEXT I
1299 RETURN
1300 REM ****************************
1302 REM *    SUMMARY               *
1304 REM ****************************
1306 PRINT
1308 PRINT "SUMMARY FOR FIVE DAYS"
1310 PRINT
1312 PRINT "STATION","TOTAL PROFIT","AVERAGE PROFIT"
1314 FOR J = 1 TO M
1316    PRINT J,T(J),T(J)/N
1318 NEXT J
1399 RETURN
1400 REM ****************************
1402 REM *    FINAL MESSAGE         *
1404 REM ****************************
1406 PRINT
1408 PRINT "TRY ANOTHER ROUND (Y/N)";
1410 INPUT U$
1412 IF U$ = "Y" THEN 1499
1414 IF U$ = "N" THEN 1499
1416 PRINT
1418 PRINT "INVALID RESPONSE"
1420 GOTO 1406
1499 RETURN
2000 REM ****************************
2002 REM *    SET PRICES           *
2004 REM ****************************
2006 PRINT
2008 PRINT "PERIOD",I
2010 PRINT
2012 PRINT "USE A SELLING PRICE OF 0 IF"
```

```
2014 PRINT "YOU WANT TO REMAIN CLOSED"
2016 PRINT
2018 PRINT "SELLING PRICE FOR"
2020 FOR J = 1 TO M
2022     PRINT "STATION";J;
2024     INPUT P(J)
2026 NEXT J
2028 LET A = 0
2030 FOR J = 1 TO M
2032     LET A = A + P(J)
2034     IF P(J) <> 0 THEN 2038
2036     LET A = A + P1
2038 NEXT J
2040 LET A = A / M
2099 RETURN
2100 REM *****************************
2102 REM *     ALLOCATE DEMAND        *
2104 REM *****************************
2106 LET Z2 = 0
2108 FOR J = 1 TO M
2110     LET W(J) = 0
2112     IF P(J) = 0 THEN 2118
2114     LET W(J) = (A / P(J)) [ 5
2116     LET Z2 = Z2 + W(J)
2118 NEXT J
2120 FOR J = 1 TO M
2121     IF Z2 = 0 THEN 2124
2122     LET W(J) = W(J) / Z2
2124 NEXT J
2126 LET Z1 = M * D1 * (P1 / A) [ 3
2128 LET Z1 = Z1 * (.95 + .1 * RND(0))
2130 FOR J = 1 TO M
2132     LET D(J) = INT(Z1 * W(J))
2134 NEXT J
2199 RETURN
2200 REM *****************************
2202 REM *     EVALUATE RESULTS       *
2204 REM *****************************
2206 FOR J = 1 TO M
2208     LET S(J) = D(J)
2210     IF S(J) <= F(J) THEN 2214
2212     LET S(J) = F(J)
2214 NEXT J
2216 PRINT
2218 PRINT "STATION/GALS","REVENUE","EXPENSES","PROFIT"
2220 FOR J = 1 TO M
```

```
2222      LET R = P(J) * S(J)
2224      LET E = C1
2226      IF P(J) = 0 THEN 2230
2228      LET E = E + C2 + P2 * S(J)
2230      LET G = R - E
2232      LET T(J) = T(J) + G
2234      PRINT J;S(J),R,E,G
2236 NEXT J
2299 RETURN
9999 END
```

PROGRAM 8-5

TWO OR MORE GAS STATIONS COMPETE
FOR GASOLINE SALES IN A HIGHLY
COMPETITIVE AREA IN WHICH CUSTOMERS
ARE VERY SENSITIVE TO RELATIVE
PRICE. FOR EACH DAY YOU CHOOSE WHETHER
TO STAY OPEN AND SET PRICE PER
GALLON IF OPEN.

TYPE THE VALUE 1 TO CONTINUE? <u>1</u>

EACH DAY YOU MAY DECIDE WHETHER TO
OPEN FOR BUSINESS. TOTAL DAILY
DEMAND DEPENDS ON AVERAGE PRICE.
AVERAGE DAILY DEMAND PER STATION OF

ALL STATIONS THAT CHARGE 1.35 PER GALLON	1200
WHOLESALE COST PER GALLON OF GAS	1.09
OVERHEAD COST PER DAY EVEN IF CLOSED	50
ADDITIONAL COST PER DAY IF OPEN	150
FUEL TANK CAPACITY IN GALLONS	7500

NUMBER OF STATIONS? <u>2</u>

PERIOD   1

USE A SELLING PRICE OF 0 IF
YOU WANT TO REMAIN CLOSED

SELLING PRICE FOR
STATION 1 ? <u>1.30</u>
STATION 2 ? <u>1.40</u>

```
STATION/GALS      REVENUE           EXPENSES          PROFIT
  1   1412          1835.6           1739.08           96.5202
  2   975           1365             1262.75           102.25

  .
  .
  .

SUMMARY FOR FIVE DAYS

STATION             TOTAL PROFIT     AVERAGE PROFIT
  1                   557.671          111.534
  2                   569.741          113.948

TRY ANOTHER ROUND (Y/N)? N

END OF PROGRAM
```

Fig. 8-5. Sample results from Program 8-5.

Exercise 8-3

1. Design a competitive game involving interaction among simulated enterprises.

COMPLEX GAMES

Games and gaming come from the war games used for officer training. In these games, troop and other placements are illustrated on a map, and opposing officers send orders to their forces. A referee evaluates the orders and arranges the board for the next play of the game.

Management games became popular in education in the 1960's. The largest games model the total enterprise including marketing, financial, and production functions. A team operates each hypothetical firm. The summary for each period includes an income statement and a balance sheet for each firm as well as an industry summary.

Included with the games are quarterly and annual reports together with board meetings and reviews of management performance. Some games are so complex that only one play per week is possible. Several hours of labor are required before making the decision for the next period. These games are the complex extensions of the simple games of this chapter.

There are also games emphasizing a particular area such as marketing, finance, or production. These games are more complex than the simple games of this chapter, but they are not as complex as the largest games incorporating all functional areas. Games having even further specialization are available. There are games featuring quality control systems, job scheduling, and inventory control.

Most large management games and simulation models use the FORTRAN language. They consist of several large computer programs and one or more data files. They typically operate in batch mode in which the large numbers of decisions are placed in a file for use by the programs. The status of the company at the end of the last period is also saved in a file. The simulation run for the current period applies the decisions to the status information from the last run to create the income statement, balance sheet, and other summary information, as well as the updated status file for use by the next run.

Because complex management games will have twenty or more decision values for each of several teams, there will be one hundred or more values saved from one period to the next reflecting the status of the firms and the economy. The computer will save these values in disk files for use in the following period.

As with many large programming projects, the debugging of the large management game is a continuous process. Some of the ratios involved will eventually develop pathologies, such as division by zero, that the programmer overlooked. Unusual combinations of circumstances will result in outcomes that are nonsensical such as negative values where only positive values are possible. Designing complex games, installing them on a computer, and overcoming the inevitable bugs is a major undertaking.

Exercise 8-4

1. Find a program listing of a moderately complex management game. Put it in a form suitable for interactive analysis. This may require a special program to create the file of decision values. Install the game on the computer.

Chapter 9
Simulation Languages

There are several simulation languages. Some are adept at handling waiting line problems. Others are designed for the simulation of continuous flow processes. Some are good in terms of feedback and control with lagged variables. General purpose programming languages are also commonly used.

The earlier chapters introduced the concepts of simulation modeling in the context of the BASIC language and microcomputers. The widespread availability of inexpensive personal computers makes the use of computer simulations practical. This chapter gives a brief survey of computer simulation as implemented on larger computers. Some of the specialized simulation languages will be implemented on the inexpensive computers of the future.

GENERAL PURPOSE LANGUAGES

General purpose programming languages provide the most flexibility. The analyst and programmer can design any model and save measurements for any variable. The model does not have to fit into the confines of a specialized language.

Unfortunately, flexibility entails cost. The specialized simulation languages perform the housekeeping operations that consume so much of the programming effort when general purpose languages are used. Models that fit within the framework of the specialized language are much easier to implement with that language.

Algebraic Languages

Among the general purpose languages, the algebraic ones are preferred for simulation. One feature that is useful is the closed subroutine from the external subroutine library. Sophisticated simulation packages can be formed from specialized subroutine libraries. File handling capability is desirable for simulation modeling. Facilities allowing good human interaction with the model at run time are also a definite plus.

FORTRAN is the primary general purpose language for simulation. It is widely available on large computers, but it is not as widely used on the least expensive microcomputers. FORTRAN programs run more efficiently than those for most other higher-level languages. The ability to incorporate subroutines from subroutine libraries is one of the best features of the language. On the negative side, the versions of FORTRAN implemented on many computer systems are archaic and harder to use than the modern versions of the language.

BASIC is similar to FORTRAN. In many respects BASIC is a simple subset of FORTRAN. BASIC introduces the powerful concept of interactive analysis and makes writing interactive programs easy. This is not true for all computer programming languages. Some languages are not designed for interactive programs.

BASIC programs for many systems run much more slowly than FORTRAN programs. This occurs because the BASIC translator is an interpreter rather than a compiler. Interpretation increases the flexibility of the BASIC system, but it reduces the speed of the running program. Since simulation programs place an enormous drain on the raw computing speed of the computer, this can be a problem.

The forte of BASIC is its ease of use and its availability on virtually any computer regardless of size. BASIC compilers, which speed up the program significantly are available. BASIC does suffer from a relatively clumsy subroutine mechanism. Because of this, BASIC will not prove a good choice for the largest simulation models, but the fact that BASIC is the language available for microcomputers ensures its increasing importance for simulation modeling.

APL is an interactive algebraic language that is promising for simulation modeling. It's an extremely powerful language with good subroutine capability. APL is superb in its handling of vectors and matrices. It includes a comprehensive set of very powerful operators defined by special symbols.

APL requires a unique keyboard for its special symbols. APL translators are interpreters and suffer from some of the same efficiency problems as BASIC interpreters. Because of the inherent power of the language, however, well-designed APL programs can be quite efficient.

PASCAL is relatively new. In many ways it is superior to the older languages. Its subroutine

mechanism is good. Interaction may be weak on some systems, however. It is not as easy to learn as some languages, especially BASIC. PASCAL is an excellent choice and will gain in acceptance as good translators become more widely available.

Other languages are also reasonable choices. PL/I is widely used by some installations, but is ignored by most. It is one of the better languages for simulation, but FORTRAN preceded it. The C programming language is ideal for systems programming and should, in theory, provide more efficient running programs than the other higher-level languages.

The choice of the programming language is largely a matter of personal preference and experience. It will be made on the basis of the availability of languages and on the ease of converting simulation models to run on future computers. Previous experience with a language is one of the primary factors governing the choice of the simulation programming language. The availability of the language on the computer used for the simulation runs is another factor influencing the choice of a language.

SPECIALIZED LANGUAGES

Financial analysis relies heavily on modeling concepts. A primary need is the ability to make minor adjustments in a financial model predicting future financial transactions and observe the effect on the financial position of the firm. The financial analyst needs a system to use in answering the "what if" questions that arise.

One approach to financial modeling is to develop a subroutine library for an existing language such as FORTRAN or APL. The resulting financial modeling schemes are as powerful and as flexible as the parent language. The financial analyst is handicapped if his knowledge of the parent language is limited. He does not want or need a technical FORTRAN specialist to modify the model for every little change.

Financial Analysis Languages

Another approach to financial modeling is to develop a specialized language for financial analysis that is easier for the financial analyst to use. A preprocessor may generate a program representing the specific financial model. This approach often appeals to the financial analysts who wants to interact directly with the language without working through a computer programmer.

A recent innovation that has had great impact on financial analysis is the proliferation of spread sheet languages. VISICALC by VISICORP is the best known language of this type. The computer's memory is visualized as a large matrix having many columns and rows. Each cell can contain messages for identification, values set by the user, or values calculated as the result of operations on other values of the matrix.

Simple commands provide column totals and many other common operations. After changing one of the user assigned values, the model will recalculate the values of all locations dependent on that change. Spread sheet languages are a natural for answering "what if" questions. Many of the financial models use the matrix format that spread sheet languages process so easily.

Simulation Languages

GPSS (General Purpose System Simulation) is the best known simulation language. Its purpose is to aid in the analysis of waiting line problems. GPSS reduces the need for programming assistance since the analyst works entirely in the GPSS environment using terms defined in queuing theory.

SIMSCRIPT is another simulation language. The focus is on events. The analyst writes event routines describing how the system changes as a result of the events. These event routines are similar to FORTRAN so that knowledge of FORTRAN is highly desirable. SIMSCRIPT, however, does assume the burden of much of the housekeeping that would otherwise be necessary.

GASP consists of a set of subroutines in FORTRAN. These subroutines perform functions needed in the creation of simulation models. Of the three simulation languages that have been discussed, GASP is the most flexible, but requires the most programming ability on the part of the analyst. SIMSCRIPT is very flexible in its definition of

events but requires technical programming ability. GPSS is the easiest to use but is the most restricted in its application.

Industrial Dynamics Languages

Industrial dynamics emphasizes information feedbacks and delays in the system and their impact on system behavior. The purpose is to study the response of the system to shocks represented by changes to the values of parameters.

Industrial dynamics views the individual firm or the industry much as an aircraft engineer views an aircraft flying on automatic pilot. The goal of the engineer is to develop a set of policies that will control the aircraft under turbulence and shifting wind conditions.

World dynamics extends the concepts of industrial dynamics to the world and its natural resources. In industrial dynamics, the system is constantly dusting rates of change to reflect levels observed one or more periods before. Policies control the magnitude and direction of adjustments in the rates of change.

DYNAMO is a special language for developing industrial dynamics models. DYNAMO uses a discrete approximation to the continuous flow model idealized in industrial dynamics. Dynamo contains sophisticated graphics capabilities to use in plotting values over time intervals. These graphs help the analyst identify the magnitude and duration of responses caused by shocks to the system.

Continuous Simulation Languages

Digital computers represent quantities as discrete symbols. Analog computers represent quantities using a continuous measure such as voltage or current. Digital computers are inherently more accurate, but analog computers are closer in nature to continuous systems that are being modeled.

Many models from physics and engineering involve complex continuous systems. The aircraft flying on automatic pilot is one such system. The models involve integrals, derivatives, and differential equations with continuous functions.

The analog computer is a natural for many of these models. Changing settings of input variables gives immediate feedback about the response of the model. The digital computer can approximate the continuous function using many fine discrete estimates, but the massive number of calculations needed may delay the response of the model when the discrete approximations required by the digital computer are used.

The field of analog computation is, by its nature, simulation oriented. The analog computer is viewed by the engineer as a simulator. It becomes the simulation model. Analog computers have limited memory and their precision is only four or five significant digits. They are not as flexible as digital computer for general purpose calculation.

Several simulation languages for digital computers provide discrete approximations to models described in terms of continuous functions. Like industrial dynamics, these models include rates of change and functions defining levels. These languages allow the digital computer to simulate an analog computer.

Appendix

Answers to Selected Exercises

The following are suggested answers for some of the exercises found throughout the book. They are not the only possible responses.

Exercise 1-1, Number 1

```
100 REM ******************************
102 REM *    E1-1                    *
104 REM ******************************
106 REM   AUTHOR
108 REM      COPYRIGHT 1983
110 REM      BY LAWRENCE MCNITT.
112 REM   PURPOSE
114 REM      FUTURE VALUE OF
116 REM      AN INVESTMENT.
118 REM   SYSTEM
120 REM      UNIVERSAL SUBSET
122 REM      OF BASIC.
200 REM ******************************
202 REM *    ORGANIZATION            *
204 REM ******************************
206 REM   900   MAIN ROUTINE
208 REM         1000   INITIAL MESSAGE
210 REM         1100   GET DATA
```

```
212 REM          1200  PROCESS
214 REM          1300  FINAL MESSAGE
300 REM **********************************
302 REM *   VARIABLES                    *
304 REM **********************************
306 REM    U$  USER RESPONSE
308 REM    P   INITIAL INVESTMENT
310 REM    N   NUMBER OF YEARS
312 REM    Q   COMPOUNDING PERIODS PER YEAR
314 REM    R   INTEREST RATE (FRACTION)
316 REM    Y   CURRENT YEAR
318 REM    F   FUTURE VALUE
900 REM **********************************
902 REM *   MAIN ROUTINE                 *
904 REM **********************************
906 REM INITIAL MESSAGE
908 GOSUB 1006
910 REM GET DATA
912 GOSUB 1106
914 REM PROCESS
916 GOSUB 1206
918 REM FINAL MESSAGE
920 GOSUB 1306
922 IF U$ = "Y" THEN 912
924 PRINT
926 PRINT "END OF PROGRAM"
999 STOP
1000 REM **********************************
1002 REM *    INITIAL MESSAGE             *
1004 REM **********************************
1006 PRINT
1008 PRINT
1010 PRINT
1012 PRINT "FUTURE VALUE OF AN INVESTMENT"
1014 PRINT
1016 PRINT "COMPUTE THE FUTURE VALUE OF AN INITIAL"
1018 PRINT "INVESTMENT AT THE END OF EACH OF THE"
1020 PRINT "FIRST FEW YEARS ASSUMING INTEREST"
1022 PRINT "COMPOUNDING."
1099 RETURN
1100 REM **********************************
1102 REM *    GET DATA                    *
1104 REM **********************************
1106 PRINT
1108 PRINT "INITIAL INVESTMENT";
1110 INPUT P
```

```
1112 PRINT
1114 PRINT "INTEREST RATE (PER CENT)";
1116 INPUT R
1118 PRINT
1120 PRINT "NUMBER OF YEARS";
1122 INPUT N
1124 PRINT
1126 PRINT "COMPOUNDING PERIODS PER YEAR";
1128 INPUT Q
1199 RETURN
1200 REM *******************************
1202 REM *     PROCESS                 *
1204 REM *******************************
1206 LET R = R / 100
1208 PRINT
1210 PRINT "YEAR","FUTURE VALUE"
1212 FOR Y = 1 TO N
1214    LET F = P * (1 + R / Q) [ (Y * Q)
1216    LET F = .01 * INT[.5 + 100 * F)
1218    PRINT Y,F
1220 NEXT Y
1299 RETURN
1300 REM *******************************
1302 REM *     FINAL MESSAGE           *
1304 REM *******************************
1306 PRINT
1308 PRINT "TRY ANOTHER SET OF DATA (Y/N)";
1310 INPUT U$
1312 IF U$ = "Y" THEN 1399
1314 IF U$ = "N" THEN 1399
1316 PRINT
1318 PRINT "INVALID RESPONSE"
1320 GOTO 1306
1399 RETURN
9999 END

RUN


FUTURE VALUE OF AN INVESTMENT

COMPUTE THE FUTURE VALUE OF AN INITIAL
INVESTMENT AT THE END OF EACH OF THE
FIRST FEW YEARS ASSUMING INTEREST
COMPOUNDING.
```

```
INITIAL INVESTMENT? 12500

INTEREST RATE (PER CENT)? 13.75

NUMBER OF YEARS? 5

COMPOUNDING PERIODS PER YEAR? 4

YEAR                FUTURE VALUE
  1                   14309.4
  2                   16380.8
  3                   18751.9
  4                   21466.3
  5                   24573.6

TRY ANOTHER SET OF DATA (Y/N)? N

END OF PROGRAM
```

Exercise 1-1, Number 2

```
LIST
100 REM *****************************
102 REM *    E1-2                   *
104 REM *****************************
106 REM   AUTHOR
108 REM        COPYRIGHT 1983
110 REM        BY LAWRENCE MCNITT.
112 REM   PURPOSE
114 REM        RANGE OF
116 REM        ARTILLERY PIECE.
118 REM   SYSTEM
120 REM        UNIVERSAL SUBSET
122 REM        OF BASIC.
200 REM *****************************
202 REM *    ORGANIZATION           *
204 REM *****************************
206 REM   900   MAIN ROUTINE
208 REM         1000   INITIAL MESSAGE
210 REM         1100   GET DATA
212 REM         1200   PROCESS
214 REM         1300   FINAL MESSAGE
300 REM *****************************
302 REM *    VARIABLES              *
304 REM *****************************
306 REM    U$  USER RESPONSE
```

```
308 REM    A    ANGLE OF ELEVATION (DEGREES)
310 REM    A1   LOWER LIMIT FOR ANGLE
312 REM    A2   UPPER LIMIT FOR ANGLE
314 REM    A3   STEP SIZE OF ANGLE
316 REM    V    VERTICAL VELOCITY
318 REM    H    HORIZONTAL VELOCITY
320 REM    T    TIME IN THE AIR
322 REM    D    DISTANCE TO THE POINT OF IMPACT
324 REM    M    MUZZLE VELOCITY
326 REM    R    ANGLE IN RADIANS
900 REM ******************************
902 REM *    MAIN ROUTINE            *
904 REM ******************************
906 REM INITIAL MESSAGE
908 GOSUB 1006
910 REM GET DATA
912 GOSUB 1106
914 REM PROCESS
916 GOSUB 1206
918 REM FINAL MESSAGE
920 GOSUB 1306
922 IF U$ = "Y" THEN 912
924 PRINT
926 PRINT "END OF PROGRAM"
999 STOP
1000 REM ******************************
1002 REM *    INITIAL MESSAGE          *
1004 REM ******************************
1006 PRINT
1008 PRINT
1010 PRINT
1012 PRINT "ARTILLERY RANGE"
1014 PRINT
1016 PRINT "DISTANCE TO THE POINT OF IMPACT"
1018 PRINT "FOR AN ARTILLERY SHELL HAVING"
1020 PRINT "GIVEN MUZZLE VELOCITY AND ANGLES"
1022 PRINT "OF ELEVATION."
1099 RETURN
1100 REM ******************************
1102 REM *    GET DATA                 *
1104 REM ******************************
1106 PRINT
1108 PRINT "MUZZLE VELOCITY (FEET/SEC)";
1110 INPUT M
1112 PRINT
1114 PRINT "ANGLES IN DEGREES"
```

```
1116 PRINT
1118 PRINT "LOWER LIMIT";
1120 INPUT A1
1122 PRINT
1124 PRINT "UPPER LIMIT";
1126 INPUT A2
1128 PRINT
1130 PRINT "STEP SIZE";
1132 INPUT A3
1199 RETURN
1200 REM ********************************
1202 REM *     PROCESS                  *
1204 REM ********************************
1206 PRINT
1208 PRINT "ANGLE","DISTANCE (FEET)"
1210 FOR A = A1 TO A2 STEP A3
1212    LET R = A / 57.2958
1214    LET V = M * SIN(R)
1216    LET H = M * COS(R)
1218    LET T = 2 * V / 32.2
1220    LET D = H * T
1222    PRINT A,D
1224 NEXT A
1299 RETURN
1300 REM ********************************
1302 REM *     FINAL MESSAGE            *
1304 REM ********************************
1306 PRINT
1308 PRINT "TRY ANOTHER SET OF DATA (Y/N)";
1310 INPUT U$
1312 IF U$ = "Y" THEN 1399
1314 IF U$ = "N" THEN 1399
1316 PRINT
1318 PRINT "INVALID RESPONSE"
1320 GOTO 1306
1399 RETURN
9999 END

RUN

ARTILLERY RANGE

DISTANCE TO THE POINT OF IMPACT
FOR AN ARTILLERY SHELL HAVING
GIVEN MUZZLE VELOCITY AND ANGLES
OF ELEVATION.
```

```
MUZZLE VELOCITY (FEET/SEC)? 460

ANGLES IN DEGREES

LOWER LIMIT? 20

UPPER LIMIT? 60

STEP SIZE? 2

ANGLE           DISTANCE (FEET)
 20               4224.03
 22               4564.9
 24               4883.52
 26               5178.53
 28               5447.96
 30               5691.02
 32               5906.36
 34               6092.92
 36               6249.8
 38               6376.23
 40               6471.59
 42               6535.43
 44               6567.43
 46               6567.42
 48               6535.43
 50               6471.59
 52               6376.23
 54               6249.8
 56               6092.92
 58               5906.36
 60               5691.03

TRY ANOTHER SET OF DATA (Y/N)? N

END OF PROGRAM
```

Exercise 1-3, Number 1

```
100 REM **********************************
102 REM *    E1-3                        *
104 REM **********************************
106 REM   AUTHOR
108 REM       COPYRIGHT 1983
110 REM       BY LAWRENCE MCNITT.
```

```
112 REM   PURPOSE
114 REM      TRIAL AND ERROR ESTIMATE FOR
116 REM        INTERNAL RATE OF RETURN.
118 REM   SYSTEM
120 REM       UNIVERSAL SUBSET
122 REM        OF BASIC.
200 REM  ******************************
202 REM  *    ORGANIZATION             *
204 REM  ******************************
206 REM   900   MAIN ROUTINE
208 REM         1000   INITIAL MESSAGE
210 REM         1100   GET DATA
212 REM         1200   PROCESS
214 REM         1300   FINAL MESSAGE
300 REM  ******************************
302 REM  *    VARIABLES                *
304 REM  ******************************
306 REM    X(50)    ANNUAL NET CASH FLOWS
308 REM    U$   USER RESPONSE
310 REM    N    NUMBER OF PERIODS
312 REM    Y    CURRENT YEAR
314 REM    R    INTEREST RATE
316 REM    P    PRESENT VALUE
900 REM  ******************************
902 REM  *    MAIN ROUTINE             *
904 REM  ******************************
905 DIM X(50)
906 REM INITIAL MESSAGE
908 GOSUB 1006
910 REM GET DATA
912 GOSUB 1106
914 REM PROCESS
916 GOSUB 1206
918 REM FINAL MESSAGE
920 GOSUB 1306
922 IF U$ = "Y" THEN 912
924 PRINT
926 PRINT "END OF PROGRAM"
999 STOP
1000 REM ******************************
1002 REM *    INITIAL MESSAGE         *
1004 REM ******************************
1006 PRINT
1008 PRINT
1010 PRINT
1012 PRINT "INTERNAL RATE OF RETURN"
```

```
1014 PRINT
1016 PRINT "COMPUTE THE NET PRESENT VALUE"
1018 PRINT "FOR A SERIES OF ANNUAL NET CASH"
1020 PRINT "FLOWS USING ONE OR MORE DISCOUNT"
1022 PRINT "RATES."
1099 RETURN
1100 REM *****************************
1102 REM *    GET DATA                *
1104 REM *****************************
1106 PRINT
1108 PRINT "NUMBER OF PERIODS";
1110 INPUT N
1112 PRINT
1114 PRINT "NET CASH FLOW FOR"
1116 FOR Y = 1 TO N
1118    PRINT "YEAR";Y;
1120    INPUT X(Y)
1122 NEXT Y
1199 RETURN
1200 REM *****************************
1202 REM *    PROCESS                 *
1204 REM *****************************
1206 PRINT
1208 PRINT "DISCOUNT RATE (PER CENT)";
1210 INPUT R
1212 LET R = R / 100
1214 LET P = X(1)
1216 FOR Y = 2 TO N
1218    LET P = P + X(Y) / (1 + R) [ (Y - 1)
1220 NEXT Y
1222 PRINT
1224 PRINT "PRESENT VALUE",P
1226 PRINT
1228 PRINT "TRY ANOTHER DISCOUNT RATE (Y/N)";
1230 INPUT U$
1232 IF U$ = "Y" THEN 1206
1299 RETURN
1300 REM *****************************
1302 REM *    FINAL MESSAGE           *
1304 REM *****************************
1306 PRINT
1308 PRINT "TRY ANOTHER SET OF DATA (Y/N)";
1310 INPUT U$
1312 IF U$ = "Y" THEN 1399
1314 IF U$ = "N" THEN 1399
1316 PRINT
```

```
1318 PRINT "INVALID RESPONSE"
1320 GOTO 1306
1399 RETURN
9999 END

RUN


INTERNAL RATE OF RETURN

COMPUTE THE NET PRESENT VALUE
FOR A SERIES OF ANNUAL NET CASH
FLOWS USING ONE OR MORE DISCOUNT
RATES.

NUMBER OF PERIODS? 4

NET CASH FLOW FOR
YEAR 1 ? -25000
YEAR 2 ? 15000
YEAR 3 ? 15000
YEAR 4 ? 10000

DISCOUNT RATE (PER CENT)? 10

PRESENT VALUE     8546.21

TRY ANOTHER DISCOUNT RATE (Y/N)? Y

DISCOUNT RATE (PER CENT)? 40

PRESENT VALUE     -2988.33

TRY ANOTHER DISCOUNT RATE (Y/N)? Y

DISCOUNT RATE (PER CENT)? 30

PRESENT VALUE     -34.1362

TRY ANOTHER DISCOUNT RATE (Y/N)? Y

DISCOUNT RATE (PER CENT)? 29

PRESENT VALUE     300.118

TRY ANOTHER DISCOUNT RATE (Y/N)? Y
```

```
DISCOUNT RATE (PER CENT) 29.9

PRESENT VALUE    -1.07227

TRY ANOTHER DISCOUNT RATE (Y/N)? N

TRY ANOTHER SET OF DATA (Y/N)? N

END OF PROGRAM
```

Exercise 1-5, Number 1

```
1212 LET D = 1500 * (20 / P) ! 2

RUN


PROGRAM 1-12

ANALYZE THE EFFECT OF PRICING
ON DEMAND AND ECONOMIES OF
SCALE ON PROFITABILITY.

LIMITS FOR PRICES
LOWER LIMIT? 10
UPPER LIMIT? 50
STEP SIZE  ? 10

PRICE           QUANTITY        COST            PROFIT
  10              6000          36976.1         23023.9
  20              1500          16094.8         13905.9
  30              666.667        9894.08        10105.9
  40              375            7005.66         7994.34
  50              240            5359.9          6640.1

TRY ANOTHER PROBLEM (Y/N)? Y

LIMITS FOR PRICES
LOWER LIMIT? 2
UPPER LIMIT? 10
STEP SIZE  ? 2

PRICE           QUANTITY        COST            PROFIT
   2            150000          255085          44915.1
   4             37500          111032          38967.9
   6             16666.7         68255.8         31744.2
```

```
   8               9375            48329.6         26670.5
  10               6000            36976.1         23023.9

TRY ANOTHER PROBLEM (Y/N)? Y

LIMITS FOR PRICES
LOWER LIMIT? 1
UPPER LIMIT? 2
STEP SIZE  ? .2

PRICE           QUANTITY        COST            PROFIT
 1               600000          586031          13969.1
 1.2             416667          470873          29127.3
 1.4             306122          391352          37219.6
 1.6             234375          333409          41591.5
 1.8             185185          289464          43869.7
 2               150000          255085          44915.2
 2.2             123967          227517          45210.5
 2.4             104167          204959          45040.8
 2.6             88757.4         186189          44580.8
 2.8             76530.6         170346          43940

TRY ANOTHER PROBLEM (Y/N)? N

END OF PROGRAM
```

Exercise 1-5, Number 2

```
1214 LET C = 100 * D ! .8

RUN


PROGRAM 1-12

ANALYZE THE EFFECT OF PRICING
ON DEMAND AND ECONOMIES OF
SCALE ON PROFITABILITY.

LIMITS FOR PRICES
LOWER LIMIT? 20
UPPER LIMIT? 100
STEP SIZE  ? 20

PRICE           QUANTITY        COST            PROFIT
 20              300             9587.32         -3587.31
 40              75              3162.64         -162.635
```

```
60              33.3333         1653.12         346.885
80              18.75           1043.28         456.719
100             12              730.037         469.247
TRY ANOTHER PROBLEM (Y/N)? Y

LIMITS FOR PRICES
LOWER LIMIT? 90
UPPER LIMIT? 110
STEP SIZE  ? 4

PRICE           QUANTITY        COST            PROFIT
 90             14.8148         864.086         469.247
 94             13.5808         806.01          470.586
 98             12.4948         754.021         470.469
 102            11.534          707.269         469.202
 106            10.68           665.062         467.024
 110            9.91736         626.783         464.127


TRY ANOTHER PROBLEM (Y/N)? N

END OF PROGRAM
```

Exercise 2-5

Determine the price that maximizes profit and   revenue.

```
RUN


PROGRAM 2-5

FOR EACH SET OF PRICES,
ESTIMATE DEMAND, REVENUE,
COST, AND PROFIT. BOTH DEMAND
AND COST FUNCTIONS ARE LINEAR.

DEMAND FUNCTION
Y-INTERCEPT? 70000
SLOPE       ? -40000

COST FUNCTION
Y-INTERCEPT? 10000
SLOPE       ? .50

TOTAL INDUSTRY DEMAND? 200000

LIMITS FOR PRICES
```

```
LOWER LIMIT? .8
UPPER LIMIT? 1.0
STEP SIZE   ? .02

PRICE           REVENUE         PROFIT          MARKET SHARE
 .8             30400           1400             .19
 .82            30504           1904             .186
 .84            30576           2376             .182
 .86            30616           2816             .178
 .88            30624           3224             .174
 .9             30600           3600             .17
 .92            30544           3944             .166
 .94            30456           4256             .162
 .96            30336           4536             .158
 .98            30184           4784             .154
1               30000           5000             .15

TRY ANOTHER SET OF PRICES (Y/N)? Y

LIMITS FOR PRICES
LOWER LIMIT? 1
UPPER LIMIT? 1.2
STEP SIZE   ? .02

PRICE           REVENUE         PROFIT          MARKET SHARE
1               30000           5000             .15
1.02            29784           5184             .146
1.04            29536           5336             .142
1.06            29236           5456             .138
1.08            28944           5544             .134
1.1             28600           5600             .13
1.12            28224           5624             .126
1.14            27816           5616             .122
1.16            27376           5576             .118
1.18            26904           5504             .114
1.2             26400           5400             .11

TRY ANOTHER SET OF PRICES (Y/N)? N

END OF PROGRAM
```

A price of .88 maximizes revenue at 30624. A price of 1.12 maximizes profit at 5624.

Exercise 2-6, Number 2

Because of the effect of relative prices on demand, the solution involves selling product 2 at a loss with a high price and little or no advertising budget, and selling product 1 at a low price with a high advertising budget resulting in a very high sales rate and overall profitability. The results are nonsensical unless constraints are placed on the amount by which the prices of the two products can differ.

Make the following changes in Program 3-1.

```
1209 LET T = O
1229 LET T = T + 12.75*(D-L) - 2.3*V - 8.4*L
1232 PRINT
1234 PRINT "TOTAL PROFIT",T
RUN


PROGRAM 3-1

EVALUATE INVENTORY ORDERING POLICY
THAT SELECTS THE ORDER QUANTITY
NEEDED TO RAISE THE INVENTORY LEVEL
TO A STATED FRACTION ABOVE THE DEMAND
FOR THE PREVIOUS PERIOD.

MULTIPLIER GIVING THE INVENTORY
LEVEL NEEDED FOR THE FOLLOWING
PERIOD FROM THE CURRENT DEMAND? 1.05

BEGINNING      DEMAND          LOST         ORDER
INVENTORY                      SALES        QUANTITY
 120           100             0            85
 105           100             0            100
 105           120             15           126
 126           120             0            120
 126           120             0            120
 126           100             0            79
 105           100             0            100
 105           100             0            100
 105           120             15           126
 126           120             0            120

TOTAL PROFIT    10734

TRY ANOTHER MULTIPLIER (Y/N)? Y

MULTIPLIER GIVING THE INVENTORY
LEVEL NEEDED FOR THE FOLLOWING
PERIOD FROM THE CURRENT DEMAND? 1.1
```

BEGINNING INVENTORY	DEMAND	LOST SALES	ORDER QUANTITY
120	100	0	90
110	100	0	100
110	120	10	132
132	120	0	120
132	120	0	120
132	100	0	78
110	100	0	100
110	100	0	100
110	120	10	132
132	120	0	120

TOTAL PROFIT   10819

TRY ANOTHER MULTIPLIER (Y/N)? <u>Y</u>

MULTIPLIER GIVING THE INVENTORY
LEVEL NEEDED FOR THE FOLLOWING
PERIOD FROM THE CURRENT DEMAND? <u>1.15</u>

BEGINNING INVENTORY	DEMAND	LOST SALES	ORDER QUANTITY
120	100	0	95
115	100	0	100
115	120	5	138
138	120	0	120
138	120	0	120
138	100	0	77
115	100	0	100
115	100	0	100
115	120	5	138
138	120	5	120

TOTAL PROFIT   10904

TRY ANOTHER MULTIPLIER (Y/N)? <u>Y</u>

MULTIPLIER GIVING THE INVENTORY
LEVEL NEEDED FOR THE FOLLOWING
PERIOD FROM THE CURRENT DEMAND? <u>1.2</u>

BEGINNING INVENTORY	DEMAND	LOST SALES	ORDER QUANTITY
120	100	0	100
120	100	0	100
120	120	0	144

```
     144            120            0            120
     144            120            0            120
     144            100            0            76
     120            100            0            100
     120            100            0            100
     120            120            0            144
     144            120            0            120

TOTAL PROFIT    10989

TRY ANOTHER MULTIPLIER (Y/N)? Y

MULTIPLIER GIVING THE INVENTORY
LEVEL NEEDED FOR THE FOLLOWING
PERIOD FROM THE CURRENT DEMAND? 1.25

BEGINNING       DEMAND         LOST         ORDER
INVENTORY                      SALES        QUANTITY
    120            100            0            105
    125            100            0            100
    125            120            0            145
    150            120            0            120
    150            120            0            120
    150            100            0            75
    125            100            0            100
    125            100            0            100
    125            120            0            145
    150            120            0            120

TOTAL PROFIT    10862.6

TRY ANOTHER MULTIPLIER (Y/N)? N

END OF PROGRAM
```

The multiplier of 1.2 maximizes profit for this de-   **Exercise 3-3, Number 1**
mand pattern.

```
RUN

PROGRAM 3-4


TEST OF UNIFORM RANDOM NUMBERS
USING THE CHI SQUARE GOODNESS
OF FIT TEST FOR EQUAL FREQUENCIES.
```

```
NUMBER OF RANDOM NUMBERS? 100

NUMBER OF CATEGORIES? 4

CHI SQUARE      1.84
DEG OF FR        3

DISPLAY FREQUENCIES (Y/N)? Y

CATEGORY        FREQUENCY
  1                20
  2                27
  3                29
  4                24

TRY ANOTHER TEST (Y/N)? Y

NUMBER OF RANDOM NUMBERS? 1000

NUMBER OF CATEGORIES? 4

CHI SQUARE      2.704
DEG OF FR        3

DISPLAY FREQUENCIES (Y/N)? Y

CATEGORY        FREQUENCY
  1               239
  2               255
  3               269
  4               237

TRY ANOTHER TEST (Y/N)? Y

NUMBER OF RANDOM NUMBERS? 1000

NUMBER OF CATEGORIES? 10

CHI SQUARE      6
DEG OF FR       9

DISPLAY FREQUENCIES (Y/N)? Y

CATEGORY        FREQUENCY
  1                98
  2               100
```

```
    3               89
    4               92
    5               97
    6               100
    7               106
    8               114
    9               111
    10              93

TRY ANOTHER TEST (Y/N)? Y

NUMBER OF RANDOM NUMBERS? 10000

NUMBER OF CATEGORIES? 10

CHI SQUARE      10.352
DEG OF FR       9

DISPLAY FREQUENCIES (Y/N)? Y

CATEGORY        FREQUENCY
    1               1056
    2               971
    3               1015
    4               963
    5               981
    6               980
    7               990
    8               968
    9               1036
    10              1040

TRY ANOTHER TEST (Y/N)? Y

NUMBER OF RANDOM NUMBERS? 10000

NUMBER OF CATEGORIES? 100

CHI SQUARE      92.08
DEG OF FR       99

DISPLAY FREQUENCIES (Y/N)? N

TRY ANOTHER TEST (Y/N)? N
```

The expected value of the chi square distribution is equal to the number of degrees of freedom. In none of the above cases is there a significant deviation from equal frequencies for each category.

Exercise 3-3, Number 2

```
RUN


PROGRAM 3-5

TEST OF UNIFORM RANDOM NUMBERS
USING THE RUNS TESTS OF VARIOUS
LENGTHS AND THE CHI SQUARE TEST
OF FREQUENCIES.

NUMBER OF RANDOM NUMBERS? 100

EXPECTED NUMBER OF RUNS        66.3333
OBSERVED NUMBER OF RUNS        69

SIZE OF RUN      OBSERVED        EXPECTED
  1                47            41.75
  2                17            18.1
  3                 4            5.14722
OVER 3             1            1.33611

CHI SQUARE      .984429
DEG OF FR       4

TRY ANOTHER TEST (Y/N)? Y

NUMBER OF RANDOM NUMBERS? 100

EXPECTED NUMBER OF RUNS        66.3333
OBSERVED NUMBER OF RUNS        63

SIZE OF RUN      OBSERVED        EXPECTED
  1                35            41.75
  2                21            18.1
  3                 7            5.14722
OVER 3             0            1.33611

CHI SQUARE      2.24979
DEG OF FR       4

TRY ANOTHER TEST (Y/N)? Y
```

```
NUMBER OF RANDOM NUMBERS? 100

EXPECTED NUMBER OF RUNS        66.3333
OBSERVED NUMBER OF RUNS        71

SIZE OF RUN      OBSERVED        EXPECTED
  1                50            41.75
  2                16            18.1
  3                4             5.14722
OVER 3             1             1.33611

CHI SQUARE       2.13128
DEG OF FR        4

TRY ANOTHER TEST (Y/N)? Y

NUMBER OF RANDOM NUMBERS? 1000

EXPECTED NUMBER OF RUNS        666.333
OBSERVED NUMBER OF RUNS        680

SIZE OF RUN      OBSERVED        EXPECTED
  1                438           416.75
  2                178           183.1
  3                54            52.6472
  4                8             11.4667
  5                2             2.02426
OVER 5             0             .345154

CHI SQUARE       2.30888
DEG OF FR        6

TRY ANOTHER TEST (Y/N)? Y

NUMBER OF RANDOM NUMBERS? 10000

EXPECTED NUMBER OF RUNS        6666.33
OBSERVED NUMBER OF RUNS        6677

SIZE OF RUN      OBSERVED        EXPECTED
  1                4149          4166.75
  2                1872          1833.1
  3                539           527.647
  4                98            1·15.038
  5                19            20.3278
  6                0             3.02957
```

```
OVER 6             0                .44043

CHI SQUARE       6.78519
DEG OF FR        7

TRY ANOTHER TEST (Y/N)? N

END OF PROGRAM
```

Exercise 3-6, Number 1

Make the following changes to Program 3-10.

```
1020 PRINT "POPULATION USING THE UNIFORM"
1222 LET X = RND(0)
RUN

PROGRAM 3-10

ESTIMATE THE TAIL AREA FOR T DIST
FOR SAMPLES DRAWN FROM A NONNORMAL
POPULATION USING THE UNIFORM
DISTRIBUTION FOR THE POPULATION.

POPULATION
MEAN? .5

SAMPLE SIZE? 4

NUMBER OF SAMPLES? 1000

T SCORE FOR
.05 LEVEL? 2.353
.01 LEVEL? 4.541

T SCORE         ESTIMATED TAIL AREA
-2.353            .058
-4.541            .019
 2.353            .063
 4.541            .025

GENERATE ANOTHER SET OF VALUES (Y/N)? Y

POPULATION
MEAN? .5

SAMPLE SIZE? 10
```

```
NUMBER OF SAMPLES? 1000

T SCORE FOR
.05 LEVEL? 1.833
.01 LEVEL? 2.821

T SCORE          ESTIMATED TAIL AREA
-1.833               .053
-2.821               .013
 1.833               .046
 2.821               .015

GENERATE ANOTHER SET OF VALUES (Y/N)? Y

POPULATION
MEAN? .5

SAMPLE SIZE? 30

NUMBER OF SAMPLES? 1000

T SCORE FOR
.05 LEVEL? 1.69
.01 LEVEL? 2.45

T SCORE          ESTIMATED TAIL AREA
-1.69                .06
-2.45                .01
 1.69                .047
 2.45              7E-03

GENERATE ANOTHER SET OF VALUES (Y/N)? N

END OF PROGRAM
```

Exercise 4-1, Number 3

The following is a summary of the results for several replications using Program 4-3 with the same probabilities used by the test run in the text:

REPLICATION	LOCATION		DISTANCE
1	16 NORTH	16 WEST	22.6274
2	27 NORTH	5 WEST	27.4591
3	29 NORTH	9 WEST	30.3645
4	38 NORTH	4 EAST	38.21
5	28 NORTH	16 WEST	32.249
6	35 NORTH	21 WEST	40.8167

Exercise 4-2, Number 1

```
RUN

PROGRAM 4-4

SIMULATE OUTPUT FROM BERNOULLI
(BINOMIAL) PROCESS WITH PARAMETER
UNDERGOING RANDOM WALK.

LOT SIZE? 100

NUMBER OF LOTS? 10

PROBABILITY DISTRIBUTION FOR
RANDOM WALK OF PARAMETER

NUMBER OF STATES? 3

ADJUSTMENT, PROBABILITY FOR
STATE 1 ? 0,.4
STATE 2 ? .01,.5
STATE 3 ? .05,.1

INITIAL FRACTION DEFECTIVE? .05

LOT             BERNOULLI      NUMBER
                PARAMETER      OBSERVED
 1                .06            8
 2                .11            7
 3                .12           11
 4                .13           18
 5                .13           12
 6                .14           13
 7                .15            5
 8                .15           17
 9                .16           17
10                .16           14

TRY ANOTHER SIMULATION RUN (Y/N)? Y

LOT SIZE? 100

NUMBER OF LOTS? 10

PROBABILITY DISTRIBUTION FOR
RANDOM WALK OF PARAMETER
```

```
NUMBER OF STATES? 3

ADJUSTMENT, PROBABILITY FOR
STATE 1 ? .4
STATE 2 ? .5
STATE 3 ? .1

INITIAL FRACTION DEFECTIVE? .05

LOT             BERNOULLI       NUMBER
                PARAMETER       OBSERVED
  1               .05             6
  2               .05             5
  3               .05            10
  4               .05             3
  5               .06             7
  6               .06             4
  7               .07             5
  8               .08            10
  9               .13            11
 10               .13             8

TRY ANOTHER SIMULATION RUN (Y/N)? Y

LOT SIZE? 100

NUMBER OF LOTS? 10

PROBABILITY DISTRIBUTION FOR
RANDOM WALK OF PARAMETER

NUMBER OF STATES? 3

ADJUSTMENT, PROBABILITY FOR
STATE 1 ? 0,.4
STATE 2 ? .01,.5
STATE 3 ? .05,.1

INITIAL FRACTION DEFECTIVE? .05

LOT             BERNOULLI       NUMBER
                PARAMETER       OBSERVED
  1               .06             6
  2               .07             8
  3               .08            10
  4               .09             6
```

```
5              .09         12
6              .1          7
7              .15         15
8              .15         16
9              .16         19
10             .21         22

TRY ANOTHER SIMULATION RUN (Y/N)? N

END OF PROGRAM
```

Exercise 4-4, Number 1

Make the following change to Program 4-6.

```
2006 LET Y = .389 * 2.73 ! (-.5 * X * X)
RUN


PROGRAM 4-6

NUMERICAL INTEGRATION USING
MONTE CARLO SIMULATION.

NUMBER OF TRIALS? 1000

LIMITS OF X FOR INTEGRATION
LOWER LIMIT? 0
UPPER LIMIT? 1.5

ESTIMATED AREA    .422603

TRY ANOTHER SIMULATION RUN (Y/N)? N

END OF PROGRAM
```

Exercise 4-5, Number 2

Make the following changes to Program 4-8.

```
2011 LET X(I) = INT(1 + X(I))
DELETE 2014-2016
RUN


PROGRAM 4-8

MONTE CARLO OPTIMIZATION
```

313

```
OF A NONLINEAR OBJECTIVE
FUNCTION SUBJECT TO NONLINEAR
AND INTEGER CONSTRAINTS.

NUMBER OF ITERATIONS? 100

ITERATION        9

F(X) =           25111

VARIABLE         VALUE
  1               67
  2               28
  3               5
  4               70
  5               21

CONTINUE SIMULATION (Y/N)? Y

NUMBER OF ITERATIONS? 100

ITERATION        50

F(X) =           45941

VARIABLE         VALUE
  1               18
  2               98
  3               4
  4               95
  5               13

CONTINUE SIMULATION (Y/N)? N

END OF PROGRAM
```

Exercise 4-5, Number 3
First use the original limits for the decision variables X1, X2, X3, X4, and X5 in Program 4-8.

```
PROGRAM 4-8

MONTE CARLO OPTIMIZATION
OF A NONLINEAR OBJECTIVE
FUNCTION SUBJECT TO NONLINEAR
AND INTEGER CONSTRAINTS.
```

```
NUMBER OF ITERATIONS? 100

ITERATION          3

F(X) =             17538.5

VARIABLE        VALUE
  1              28
  2              62.3543
  3              4.22032
  4              55.6552
  5              21

ITERATION          17

F(X) =             31361.7

VARIABLE        VALUE
  1              14
  2              78.1986
  3              11.6299
  4              78.1255
  5              18

ITERATION          24
F(X) =             37630.9

VARIABLE        VALUE
  1              60
  2              45.4612
  3              2.12171
  4              89.9972
  5              11

ITERATION          36

F(X) =             43392.1

VARIABLE        VALUE
  1              20
  2              92.3952
  3              9.33722
  4              94.8277
  5              15

CONTINUE SIMULATION (Y/N)? N
```

```
END OF PROGRAM

LIST 9000-9999
9000 DATA 5
9001 DATA 0,99
9002 DATA 0,99
9003 DATA 0,50
9004 DATA 50,99
9005 DATA 10,40
9999 END

Change in limits for decision variables
9001 DATA 20,40
9002 DATA 60,80
9003 DATA 0,20
9004 DATA 90,99
9005 DATA 10,20
RUN


PROGRAM 4-8

MONTE CARLO OPTIMIZATION
OF A NONLINEAR OBJECTIVE
FUNCTION SUBJECT TO NONLINEAR
AND INTEGER CONSTRAINTS.

NUMBER OF ITERATIONS? 100

ITERATION         3

F(X) =            44450.5

VARIABLE        VALUE
  1               38
  2               72.3663
  3               7.9821
  4               97.258
  5               13

ITERATION         4

F(X) =            45113

VARIABLE        VALUE
  1               39
```

```
2               74.948
3               5.78822
4               97.3485
5               17

ITERATION       24

F(X) =          46195.8

VARIABLE        VALUE
1               32
2               78.571
3               6.10815
4               98.4026
5               19

ITERATION       55

F(X) =          46606.9

VARIABLE        VALUE
1               33
2               79.0846
3               .30538
4               98.8701
5               19

CONTINUE SIMULATION (Y/N)? N

END OF PROGRAM
```

 Change the limits for the decision variables so   that they are closer to the best values found so far.

```
9001 DATA 30,40
9002 DATA 75,85
9003 DATA 0,5
9004 DATA 97,99
9005 DATA 13,23

RUN

PROGRAM  4-8

MONTE CARLO OPTIMIZATION
OF A NONLINEAR OBJECTIVE

FUNCTION SUBJECT TO NONLINEAR
AND INTEGER CONSTRAINTS.
```

```
NUMBER OF ITERATIONS? 1000

ITERATION          1

F(X) =             46625.3

VARIABLE         VALUE
  1                37
  2                84.8928
  3                3.46541
  4                97.6054
  5                16

ITERATION          7

F(X) =             47261.1

VARIABLE         VALUE
  1                38
  2                82.2111
  3                3.26137
  4                98.8175
  5                17

ITERATION          56

F(X) =             47548.1

VARIABLE         VALUE
  1                40
  2                82.839
  3                4.75745
  4                98.9151
  5                16

ITERATION          343

F(X) =             47857.2

VARIABLE         VALUE
  1                37
  2                84.7537
  3                1.43861
  4                98.9743
  5                19

CONTINUE SIMULATION (Y/N)? N

END OF PROGRAM
```

Exercise 5-4

The following table summarizes the results using Listing 5-3 with the order quantities of 370, 380, and 430 as well as those given in the example in the text.

Order quantity	Average profit	Order quantity	Average profit	Order quantity	Average profit
370	55.38	390	57.468	420	59.040
370	55.33	400	58.034	420	59.094
380	56.65	400	58.248	430	58.342
380	56.716	410	58.540	430	59.108
390	57.244	410	58.036		

The results of using Listing 5-4 with this information is shown below.

```
PROGRAM 5 - 4

SIMPLE LINEAR REGRESSION

ANALYSIS GIVING Y-INTERCEPT,
SLOPE, CORRELATION, AND
STANDARD ERROR OF ESTIMATE.

NUMBER OF OBSERVATIONS? 14

VALUES Y,X FOR
OBS 1 ? 55.38,370
OBS 2 ? 55.33,370
OBS 3 ? 56.65,380
OBS 4 ? 56.716,380
OBS 5 ? 57.244,390
OBS 6 ? 57.468,390
OBS 7 ? 58.034,400
OBS 8 ? 58.248,400
OBS 9 ? 58.540,410
OBS 10 ? 58.036,410
OBS 11 ? 59.04,420
OBS 12 ? 59.094,420
OBS 13 ? 58.342,430
OBS 14 ? 59.108,430

Y-INTERCEPT      35.07
SLOPE            .0564732

STD ERROR        .484963
CORRELATION      .929143
F RATIO          75.7872

TRY ANOTHER SET OF DATA
  (Y/N)? N
END OF PROGRAM
```

Exercise 5-5

Price and order quantity are highly interrelated. A price of .11 with an order quantity of 1300 gives an average profit of about $77.

Exercise 6-1, Number 1

```
PROGRAM 6-1

USE EXPONENTIAL SMOOTHING
TO ESTIMATE THE MEAN AND
STANDARD DEVIATION OF A
SERIES OF RANDOM VALUES.

GENERATE NORMALLY DISTRIBUTED VALUES
```

```
POPULATION
MEAN    ? 100
STD DEV? 20

NUMBER OF VALUES? 25

SMOOTHING CONSTANT? .2

INITIAL ESTIMATE FOR
MEAN    ? 100
STD DEV? 20

VALUE           MEAN            STD DEV
 87.6453        97.5291          18.4265
 81.5965        94.3426          17.4391
124.814        100.437           19.0301
 68.7471        94.0988          20.4514
 90.0813        93.2953          18.3486
131.985        101.033           21.4696
125.362        105.899           21.0836
110.1          106.739           18.9176
116.321        108.656           17.2641
 85.6311       104.051           17.5014
112.371        105.715           15.9342
124.867        109.545           15.8136
 66.6769       100.972           20.8634
 97.8416       100.972           18.6942
 76.1524        95.5077          18.8283
 98.3585        96.0778          16.8714
 81.4616        93.1546          15.9706
103.943         95.3123          14.7968
 87.0186        93.6535          13.5632
 95.8885        94.1005          12.1577
100.987         95.4779          11.1498
 99.2342        96.2292          10.0628
115.282        100.04            11.2905
102.769        100.586           10.1456
105.567        101.582            9.24784

TRY ANOTHER SET OF DATA (Y/N)? Y

GENERATE NORMALLY DISTRIBUTED VALUES

POPULATION
MEAN    ? 100
STD DEV? 20
```

```
NUMBER OF VALUES? 25

SMOOTHING CONSTANT? .05

INITIAL ESTIMATE FOR
MEAN    ? 100
STD DEV? 20

VALUE           MEAN            STD DEV
 106.506         100.325         19.5425
 158.999         103.259         22.7632
 105.378         103.365         22.1914
 110.06          103.7           21.6762
 85.1998         102.775         21.4898
 91.9347         102.233         21.0718
 81.6391         101.203         20.9991
 97.1627         101.001         20.4854
 94.1031         100.656         20.0204
 82.0331         99.7249         19.9104
 145.762         102.027         21.7312
 86.5848         101.255         21.4334
 103.529         101.368         20.8963
 74.607          100.03          21.1457
 98.0665         99.9321         20.6145
 93.6387         99.6174         20.1369
 103.789         99.826          19.6471
 114.969         100.583         19.4179
 78.8618         99.4971         19.4806
 113.637         100.204         19.2234
 145.198         102.454         21.0337
 108.432         102.753         20.5404
 128.461         104.038         20.7517
 101.892         103.931         20.2314
 118.066         104.638         19.9465

TRY ANOTHER SET OF VALUES (Y/N)? N

END OF PROGRAM
```

Exercise 6-4, Number 1

```
PROGRAM 6-4

SINGLE CHANNEL SINGLE STATION
QUEUE ANALYSIS WITH POISSON
ARRIVAL AND SERVICE RATES
```

```
(EXPONENTIAL ARRIVAL AND
SERVICE TIMES).

ARRIVAL RATE? 6
SERVICE RATE? 8

COST PER UNIT OF TIME FOR
CUSTOMER WAITING? 9
SERVICE FACILITY? 15

UTILIZATION RATE                  .75
IDLE TIME RATE                    .25

EXPECTED NUMBER IN THE SYSTEM 3
EXPECTED NUMBER IN THE QUEUE  2.25

EXPECTED TIME IN THE SYSTEM  .5
EXPECTED TIME IN THE QUEUE   .375

SYSTEM COSTS PER UNIT OF TIME
CUSTOMER WAITING                  27
SERVICE FACILITY                  15
TOTAL                             42

DISPLAY PROBABILITY DISTRIBUTION (Y/N)? N

TRY ANOTHER SET OF DATA (Y/N)? Y

ARRIVAL RATE? 6
SERVICE RATE? 10

COST PER UNIT OF TIME FOR
CUSTOMER WAITING? 9
SERVICE FACILITY? 25

UTILIZATION RATE                  .6
IDLE TIME RATE                    .4

EXPECTED NUMBER IN THE SYSTEM 1.5
EXPECTED NUMBER IN THE QUEUE  .9

EXPECTED TIME IN THE SYSTEM  .25
EXPECTED TIME IN THE QUEUE   .15

SYSTEM COSTS PER UNIT OF TIME
CUSTOMER WAITING                  13.5
```

```
SERVICE FACILITY              25
TOTAL                         38.5

DISPLAY PROBABILITY DISTRIBUTION (Y/N)? N

TRY ANOTHER SET OF DATA (Y/N)? Y

ARRIVAL RATE? 6
SERVICE RATE? 14

COST PER UNIT OF TIME FOR
CUSTOMER WAITING? 9
SERVICE FACILITY? 35

UTILIZATION RATE             .428571
IDLE TIME RATE               .571429

EXPECTED NUMBER IN THE SYSTEM .75
EXPECTED NUMBER IN THE QUEUE  .321429

EXPECTED TIME IN THE SYSTEM   .125
EXPECTED TIME IN THE QUEUE    .0535714

SYSTEM COSTS PER UNIT OF TIME
CUSTOMER WAITING              6.75
SERVICE FACILITY             35
TOTAL                        41.75

DISPLAY PROBABILITY DISTRIBUTION (Y/N)? N

TRY ANOTHER SET OF DATA (Y/N)? N

END OF PROGRAM
```

Exercise 6-4, Number 2

```
PROGRAM 6-5

MULTIPLE STATION SINGLE CHANNEL
QUEUE ANALYSIS WITH POISSON
ARRIVAL AND SERVICE RATES.

ARRIVAL RATE              ? 50
SERVICE RATE PER STATION  ? 8
NUMBER OF STATIONS        ? 7
```

```
COST PER UNIT OF TIME FOR
CUSTOMER WAITING      ? 9
ONE SERVICE STATION   ? 15

EXPECTED NUMBER IN THE SYSTEM    12.0973
EXPECTED NUMBER IN THE QUEUE     5.84728

EXPECTED TIME IN THE SYSTEM      .241946
EXPECTED TIME IN THE QUEUE       .116946

SYSTEM COSTS PER UNIT OF TIME
CUSTOMER WAITING                 108.876
SERVICE FACILITY                 105
TOTAL                            213.876

DISPLAY PROBABILITY DISTRIBUTION (Y/N)? N

TRY ANOTHER SET OF DATA (Y/N)? Y

ARRIVAL RATE              ? 50
SERVICE RATE PER STATION ? 8
NUMBER OF STATIONS       ? 8

COST PER UNIT OF TIME FOR
CUSTOMER WAITING      ? 9
ONE SERVICE STATION   ? 15

EXPECTED NUMBER THE SYSTEM       7.74364
EXPECTED NUMBER THE QUEUE        1.49364

EXPECTED TIME IN THE SYSTEM      .154873
EXPECTED TIME IN THE QUEUE       .0298728

SYSTEM COSTS PER UNIT OF TIME
CUSTOMER WAITING                 69.6927
SERVICE FACILITY                 120
TOTAL                            189.693

DISPLAY PROBABILITY DISTRIBUTION (Y/N)? N
TRY ANOTHER SET OF DATA (Y/N)? Y

ARRIVAL RATE              ? 50
SERVICE RATE PER STATION ? 8
NUMBER OF STATIONS       ? 9

COST PER UNIT OF TIME FOR
```

```
CUSTOMER WAITING       ? 9
ONE SERVICE STATION    ? 15

EXPECTED NUMBER IN THE SYSTEM     6.78626
EXPECTED NUMBER IN THE QUEUE      .536263

EXPECTED TIME IN THE SYSTEM       .135725
EXPECTED TIME IN THE QUEUE        .0107253

SYSTEM COSTS PER UNIT OF TIME
CUSTOMER WAITING                  61.0764
SERVICE FACILITY                  135
TOTAL                             196.076

DISPLAY PROBABILITY DISTRIBUTION (Y/N)? N

TRY ANOTHER SET OF DATA (Y/N)? N

END OF PROGRAM
```

Exercise 7-1

```
INVENTORY ANALYSIS TO DETERMINE
THE ECONOMIC ORDER QUANTITY
ASSUMING CONSTANT DEMAND AND
NO LEAD TIME.

COST PER ORDER PLACED         ? 50
ANNUAL PER-UNIT HOLDING COST  ? 15
UNITS DEMANDED PER YEAR       ? 4000

ORDER         ANNUAL INVENTORY COSTS
QUANTITY      ORDERING      HOLDING        TOTAL
  162         1234.57       1215           2449.57
  163         1226.99       1222.5         2449.49
  164         1219.51       1230           2449.51

TRY ANOTHER SET OF DATA (Y/N)? N

END OF PROGRAM

LOAD "P7102"
RUN


PROGRAM 7-2
```

```
COMPARE A SET OF INVENTORY ORDER
QUANTITIES GIVING THE ANNUAL
ORDERING COSTS, HOLDING COSTS,
AND TOTAL INVENTORY COSTS.

COST PER ORDER PLACED          ? 50
ANNUAL PER-UNIT HOLDING COST   ? 15
UNITS DEMANDED PER YEAR        ? 4000

ORDER QUANTITIES TO COMPARE

SMALLEST QUANTITY              ? 140
LARGEST QUANTITY               ? 180
STEP SIZE BETWEEN QUANTITIES   ? 10

ORDER           ANNUAL INVENTORY COSTS
QUANTITY        ORDERING      HOLDING          TOTAL
  140           1428.57       1050             2478.57
  150           1333.33       1125             2458.33
  160           1250          1200             2450
  170           1176.47       1275             2451.47
  180           1111.11       1350             2461.11

TRY ANOTHER SET OF DATA (Y/N)? N

END OF PROGRAM
```

Exercise 7-2

The following table summarizes the results for simulation runs of 100 periods with many combinations of reorder points and order quantities:

Reorder point	order quantity	Estimated inventory costs per period			
		Ordering	Holding	Stockout	Total
5	20	10.2	1.5855	16.35	28.1355
10	20	12.6	1.8945	10.25	24.7445
10	50	5.4	4.2465	4.6	14.2465
10	70	3.9	5.6175	3.85	13.3675
11	70	3.9	5.8755	1.9	11.6755
12	70	3.9	5.8785	2.7	12.4785
13	70	4.2	5.8755	1.8	11.8755
13	70	3.6	6.492	2.65	12.742
13	80	3.6	6.684	1.45	11.734
13	90	3.3	7.7265	.6	11.6265
13	90	3.3	7.446	1.1	11.846
13	100	2.4	9.4995	.2	12.0995

The following used simulation runs of 200 periods:

14	60	4.8	5.25825	2	12.0583
14	70	4.2	6.3225	.825	11.3475
14	80	3.6	6.79425	1.075	11.4693
13	80	3.6	6.8205	1.075	11.4955
14	90	3.15	7.51575	1.575	12.2407

Exercise 7-3

The following table summarizes the costs for various combinations of reorder points and order quantities:

Reorder point	Order quantity	Annual inventory costs Ordering	Holding	Stockout	Total
12	50	340.08	233.24	503.319	1076.64
12	60	283.4	283.24	419.432	986.072
12	70	242.914	333.24	359.513	935.668
12	80	212.55	383.24	314.574	910.364
10	80	212.55	363.24	481.213	1057
12	80	212.55	383.24	314.574	910.364
14	80	212.55	403.24	249.959	865.749
16	80	212.55	423.24	185.344	821.134
18	80	212.55	443.24	120.728	776.518
20	80	212.55	463.24	56.1132	731.903
22	80	212.55	483.24	6.8016	702.592
24	80	212.55	503.24	0.0	715.79
22	50	340.08	333.24	10.8826	684.203
22	60	283.4	383.24	'9.0688	675.709
22	70	242.914	433.24	7.77326	683.928
22	80	212.55	483.24	6.8016	702.592

Exercise 7-4

From the standpoint of the user, Program 7-5 operates in the same way as Program 7-4. The difference is that this program uses simulation methods. The expected costs will differ slightly from those of Program 7-4 which uses probability tree methods to compute exact probabilities.

Glossary

Alternative hypothesis—The hypothesis that receives the burden of proof.

Amplification—The process through which small variations in input result in increased variations in output.

Analysis of variance—The process of testing hypotheses about the equality of population means using the F test.

Analytic solution—Mathematical solution of equations. This is in contrast to trial-and-error solutions.

Arrival time—The length of time between arrivals in a waiting line problem.

Assembly line balancing—The assignment of tasks to work stations on an assembly line so as to balance the workloads.

Backorder—An order for an item that is needed by a customer but is not in inventory. The customer agrees to wait until it is received.

BASIC—The Beginners All-purpose Symbolic Instruction Code is a computer programming language that is widely available on computers of all sizes.

Bisection—The method of searching for the value of X for which the function f(X) satisfies a specified property by successively dividing the interval being searched in half.

Central limit theorem—A theorem that states that the sum of a set of n independent random values will approach the normal distribution as n increases. More specifically, it indicates that the distribution consisting of all possible sample means for samples of size n will be about normally distributed for large n's.

Chi square test—A method of testing the significance of the difference between a set of observed frequencies and corresponding set of expected frequencies.

Classical statistics—The branch of statistics involving tests of hypothesis, regression analysis, and simple data description.

Competitive games—Games involving competition between players with the computer acting as referee.

Constrained optimization—Maximization or minimization of one function subject to one or more constraints specified by equations or inequalities.

Constraints—The individual equations that place restrictions on the feasible solutions.

Continuous distribution—A distribution whose possible values form an interval without gaps or interruptions.

Controllable factors—Decision variables under the control of the decision maker.

Correlation—An interdependence between two variables.

Critical limits—The boundary value for the sample result that determines whether the null hypothesis or the alternative hypothesis will be accepted.

Curse of dimensionality—The difficulty caused by problems that have a large number of decision variables and become increasingly difficult to solve. Each decision variable constitutes one dimension.

Dampening—The process through which the variation in the input variable is decreased when transformed to the output variable of the system.

Decision variable—The variable for which the decision maker can choose the value.

Degrees of freedom—The number of values in the sample that are free to vary. This concept is usually used in calculating the sample variance.

Dependent variable—The variable to be predicted. For the equation $Y = f(X)$ the variable Y is the dependent variable.

Deterministic model—A model that is not subject to uncertainty. There is only one outcome for any one set of values for the decision variables.

Discrete distribution—A distribution in which the possible values of the random variable do not form continuous intervals.

Dynamic system—A system that changes states over time without changes in decision variables.

Econometrics—The application of mathematics, statistics, and quantitative methods in the field of economics.

Economies of scale—The tendency for an increased volume of production to result in a lower per unit cost of production.

Environment—The external factors affecting the behavior of a system.

EOQ—Economic order quantity. The number of units to order at a time that minimizes the relevant total inventory costs.

Evolutionary operation—An iterative method of making small changes to two or three variables at a time and using the methods of analysis of variance to evaluate the results.

Exponential distribution—The probability distribution for the interval between successes (arrivals or service completions) if the successes are assumed to be randomly distributed throughout the period.

Exponential smoothing—A method of calculating a running average by computing the new mean as a weighted average of the old mean and the new value.

External variable—A variable that is not under the control of the decision maker.

Extrapolation—The process of extending the solution results to ranges of values of the internal and external variables not included in the solution process.

Factor—A variable that is tested for its effect on the response variable in analysis of variance.

Factor levels—The possible settings (values) of the variables (factors) that are being tested for their effect on the response variable in the analysis of variance.

Feedback—The output of a system feeds back into the system as input. This is an important concept in the design of systems that are adaptive and goal seeking.

F ratio—The measure used to test the equality of two population variances. The F ratio normally consists of the ratio of two sample variances.

F test—The statistical test used to test the equality of population variances. It is used in both regression analysis and analysis of variance.

Game of life—Visual simulation involving births and deaths. Starting with an initial population pattern, the distribution changes according to strict rules relating to the number of occupied neighboring cells.

Gaming—The use of games for instructional purposes or as an aid in decision making.

Global optimum—The overall maximum or minimum, in contrast to a local optimum.

Hierarchical program organization—A method of constructing a computer program using subroutines so that a main routine calls subroutines that call lower-level subroutines.

Hypothesis—A statement about a population which is open to doubt.

Idle time—The amount of time that a service facility or work station is idle.

Independent variable—The variable used in the prediction of the dependent variable. In the equation $Y=f(X)$ the variable X is the independent variable.

Index of pressure—A measure of the pressure on a manager resulting from the deviation of observed performance from the desired goal.

Infinite queue—The line that will result, in theory, if the expected demand exceeds the service capacity.

Integer programming—A constrained optimization procedure for which the values of the decision variables must be integers. This is usually an extension of linear programming.

Integral calculus—A branch of mathematics applied to finding areas under continuous functions.

Interaction effect—An effect occurring in the analysis of variance in which two factors interact with each other in such a way that they obscure their true impact on the response variable.

Interactive game—A game that involves repeated interaction between the computer and player during the course of the game.

Interpolation—The estimation of the value of a function for a point between two known points.

Job-shop—A manufacturing facility containing numerous general purpose machines. Jobs are routed among the machines in various sequences depending on the requirements of the job.

Job-shop scheduling—The scheduling of jobs and assigning of jobs to machines on a period-by-period basis.

Lagged variable—The value of a variable from a previous period used in the calculations of the model for a later period.

Lead time—The time between the placement of the order and its arrival.

Level of significance—The probability of rejecting the null hypothesis if it is true.

Linear programming—A method of solving a constrained optimization problem involving a linear objective function and one or more linear constraints.

Linear regression—The process of estimating the dependent variable Y as a linear function of one or more independent variables.

Local optimum—The relative maximum point or relative minimum point in a small neighborhood. It corresponds to a local mountain top, for example.

Main effects—In analysis of variance, those effects attributable to the factor alone without respect to other factors and interaction effects.

Management games—Games used in management education to illustrate the decision making process.

Mathematical model—A model stated in terms of mathematical equations and relationships.

Mean—The average of a set of data obtained by dividing the total by the number of items.

Mode—The most likely (most frequent) value from a set of values.

Model—A representation of a system.

Modular program—A computer program that has been divided into sections (modules).

Monte Carlo method—An estimation procedure involving random sampling. It may involve searching for the optimum or estimating other properties such as area or volume.

Monte Carlo optimization—The process of estimating the optimum value of a function using random sampling procedures.

Multiple objectives—Many potentially conflicting objectives involved in a problem situation.

Multiple station queue—A queue situation involving more than one service facility. The stations may be in series forming a single channel, in parallel, or in an interconnected network.

Network—A set of nodes interconnected by branches. The nodes are the termination points for the branches.

Nonlinear programming—A method of solving a constrained optimization problem in which either the objective function or the contraints can consist of nonlinear equations and inequalities.

Normal distribution—The familiar bell-shaped distribution that is common to many natural phenomena and is frequently used in statistics.

Null hypothesis—The statement about the population that is given the benefit of the doubt.

Numerical analysis—The branch of mathematics concerned with the proper use of numerical calculation.

Numerical integration—The process that provides numerical solutions for the problems of integral calculus.

Objective function—The function used to calculate the measure of performance for a set of values for the decision variables.

Optimization—The maximization or minimization of the value of function.

Overcontrol—The condition resulting from the use of a decision rule that is designed to bring a system to its desired state but instead causes the system to overshoot its intended goal requiring even larger corrections. The amplification of actions and reactions results in an inherently unstable system.

Performance objective—The measure used to judge the effectiveness of a decision policy.

Poisson distribution—The probability distribution giving the probability for the number of successes in a given interval when the expected number of successes is known and the successes occur randomly throughout the interval.

Population—The set of all possible objects of interest for a problem situation.

Predator-prey models—Models representing the population levels of life forms in a food chain in which some animals depend on others for food.

Primitive program—A one-shot program that is not written with readability or understandability as objectives.

Process control—The act of maintaining the quality level of an ongoing process through the use of computer control procedures.

Program—A set of instructions for a computer or machine to follow.

Pseudorandom number—A value generated by a mathematical procedure that exhibits the properties of randomness.

Quality control—The process of maintaining the quality level of a production process including incoming or outgoing shipments.

Random walk—A problem involving random steps, the analysis of position, and the distance from the origin after a certain number of steps.

Replications—Repeated evaluations of the model using the same decision rule or variable values.

Resolution—The refinement of a solution using

additional terms or smaller subintervals in the calculations.

Runs test—A procedure used to test for patterns in the values of a variable.

Safety stock—The inventory level needed to provide an acceptable risk of stockout until the next order arrives.

Sample—A set of objects taken from a population.

Sampling error—The unavoidable variability in samples.

Simulation—The model of a process itself or the method for analyzing the model.

Smoothing—The process of removing the variability of a stream of values.

Standard deviation—The measure of variability for a set of values or for a probability distribution.

Standard score—The number of standard deviation units between a given value and the mean (average).

Static model—A model that does not change over time.

Steady state—The condition of a dynamic model that eventually settles down to a fixed state.

Stimulus—A shock to a system that may cause the system to require corrective measures.

Stochastic—Probabilistic.

Stockout—The condition of having insufficient inventory on hand to meet the demand.

Subroutine—A subprogram within a computer program called from another part of the program.

System—A collection of entities having a common goal or purpose.

Systems analysis—The analysis of a system for the purpose of improving performance.

Tail area—The probability distribution that gives the probability of rejecting the null hypothesis when it is true.

t distribution—A probability distribution for testing hypotheses about population means.

Tests of hypotheses—The process of stating null and alternative hypotheses and drawing conclusions about them.

Transient shocks—Random shocks to a system.

Transient states—The states through which a system moves before it settles into an equilibrium or steady state.

Uncontrollable factors—Factors that affect the performance of the system but that cannot be controlled by the decision maker.

Undercontrol—The condition resulting from the use of a decision rule that provides insufficient control resulting in an unstable system or one that does not attain desired performance objectives.

Uniform random numbers—Values within a specified range, usually 0 to 1, that have equal probabilities of occurring.

Utilization rate—The fraction of the total time that a service facility is used.

Validation—The process of testing the closeness of the behavior of the model to that of the system it represents.

Variance—The measure of variability giving the average squared deviation of the values around the mean.

White space—Blank lines used to make computer output more readable.

Index

Index

BASIC Computer Simulation

If you are intrigued with the possibilities of the programs included in *BASIC Computer Simulation* (TAB book no. 1585), you should definitely consider having the ready-to-run disk containing the software applications. This software is guaranteed free of manufacturer's defects. (If you have any problems, return the disk within 30 days, and we'll send you a new one.) Not only will you save the time and effort of typing the programs, the disk eliminates the possibility of errors that can prevent the programs from functioning. Interested?

Available on disk for the TRS-80 Model III, 32K at $29.95 for each disk plus $1.00 each shipping and handling.